AMERICAN LITERATURE, ENGLISH LITERATURE, AND WORLD LITERATURES IN ENGLISH: AN INFORMATION GUIDE SERIES

Series Editor: Theodore Grieder, Curator, Division of Special Collections, Fales Library, New York University, New York, New York

Associate Editor: Duane DeVries, Associate Professor, Polytechnic Institute of New York, Brooklyn, New York

Other books on world literatures in this series:

SCOTTISH LITERATURE IN ENGLISH—*Edited by William Aitken**

INDIAN LITERATURE IN ENGLISH, 1825-1976—*Edited by Amritjit Singh and Rajiva Verma**

MODERN AUSTRALIAN POETRY—*Edited by Herbert C. Jaffa**

MODERN AUSTRALIAN PROSE—*Edited by A. Grove Day**

NEW ZEALAND LITERATURE TO 1975—*Edited by J.E.P. Thomson**

IRISH LITERATURE, 1800-1875—*Edited by Brian McKenna*

IRISH LITERATURE, 1876-1950—*Edited by Brian McKenna**

ASIAN LITERATURE IN ENGLISH—*Edited by George Anderson**

ENGLISH-CANADIAN LITERATURE TO 1900—*Edited by R.G. Moyles*

MODERN ENGLISH-CANADIAN PROSE—*Edited by Peter Stevens**

AUSTRALIAN LITERATURE TO 1900—*Edited by Barry Andrews and W.H. Wilde**

WEST INDIAN LITERATURE IN ENGLISH—*Edited by Priscilla Tyler**

AFRICAN LITERATURE IN ENGLISH—*Edited by Bernth Lindfors**

*in preparation

The above series is part of the
GALE INFORMATION GUIDE LIBRARY

The Library consists of a number of separate series of guides covering major areas in the social sciences, humanities, and current affairs.

General Editor: Paul Wasserman, Professor and former Dean, School of Library and Information Services, University of Maryland

Managing Editor: Denise Allard Adzigian, Gale Research Company

Modern English-Canadian Poetry

A GUIDE TO INFORMATION SOURCES

*Volume 15 in the American Literature, English
Literature, and World Literatures in English
Information Guide Series*

Peter Stevens

*Professor of English
University of Windsor
Windsor, Ontario*

Gale Research Company
Book Tower, Detroit, Michigan 48226

Library of Congress Cataloging in Publication Data

Stevens, Peter, 1927-
    Modern English-Canadian poetry.

    (American literature, English literature, and world literatures
in English information guide series; v.15) (Gale information guide
library)
    Includes indexes.
    1. Canadian poetry—20th century—History and criticism—
Bibliography. 2. Canadian poetry—20th century—Bibliography.
I. Title.
Z1377.P7S79   [PR9184.3]   016.811'5   73-16994
ISBN 0-8103-1244-1

VITA

Peter Stevens has published widely in magazines and anthologies (including BEST POEMS OF 1969 and BEST POEMS OF 1973) in Canada, the United States, Australia, the United Kingdom, and India, and has published six books of poetry: NOTHING BUT SPOONS (1969), A FEW MYTHS (1971), BREADCRUSTS AND GLASS (1972), FAMILY FEELINGS AND OTHER POEMS (1974), MOMENTARY STAY (1974), and AND THE DYING SKY LIKE BLOOD (1974). From 1968 to 1973 Stevens was poetry editor of CANADIAN FORUM. Until 1974 he was the Ontario (excluding Metro Toronto) representative of the League of Canadian Poets.

Stevens has published critical and review articles in a wide variety of journals and newspapers in Canada, and was one of the authors of the new SUPPLEMENT TO THE OXFORD COMPANION TO CANADIAN HISTORY AND LITERATURE. His essay on Canadian literature appears in WORLD LITERATURES IN ENGLISH (1974). He is the editor of two books, THE McGILL MOVEMENT (1969) and, with J.L. Granatstein, FORUM (1972), and has prepared a selection of the prose of Canadian writer Raymond Knister, published in the University of Toronto Press series, The Literature of Canada. He is a founding director of Sesame Press in Windsor, a new publishing venture in the field of Canadian poetry. At present Stevens is professor of English at the University of Windsor, Ontario.

CONTENTS

Contents

Contents

ACKNOWLEDGMENTS

As I mention in my opening chapter, any bibliographer of Canadian literature is in debt to the work of R.E. Watters. I have also been assisted in my work by some other books, particularly William Toye, ed., SUPPLEMENT TO THE OXFORD COMPANION TO CANADIAN HISTORY AND LITERATURE (Toronto: Oxford University Press, 1973), and Frank Davey, FROM THERE TO HERE (Erin, Ont.: Press Porcepic, 1974).

The staff members, particularly Pat Murray, of the University of Windsor library, have helped in my researches. Ann Marie George was especially adept at converting my scribblings into typescript.

Chapter I

INTRODUCTION

Canadian literature, and the study of it, are in an amorphously expanding state. Most of the authors esteemed in the twentieth century are still living and producing poetry, so that the selections of authors for a bibliography devoted to Canadian poetry written in English in this century will of necessity be made on a personal basis, as Canadian criticism is only just now beginning to keep pace with contemporary writing and with the work of the recent past. Thus, it is not possible to select authors for inclusion purely on the basis of critical estimation.

This bibliography, then, is really only tentative, as any bibliography of contemporary literature and living authors will be. But the attempt is worth making at this moment, for Canadian literature has produced a considerable amount of interesting writing capable of standing on its own merits in the world of literature. This is no time for the meticulous focus of the professional bibliographer who often seems too timid to fix something that will by its very nature have changed by the time his listings are in print. For some bibliographers the very word "selective" is meaningless in relation to bibliographies; but if a literature is living, any bibliography of it will be selective, and when a literature is most thoroughly alive and developing, selectiveness will be a specific element to be accepted. Canadian literature is now in that expansionist state; and although there may be omissions and shortcuts that some professional bibliographers may question, the necessity for this working bibliography of Canadian literature in English is increasingly apparent.

The state of Canadian bibliography is hardly flourishing: the first national conference devoted to bibliography was held only in 1974. Yet there have been significant breakthroughs. Anyone attempting a bibliography in Canadian literature will owe an enormous debt to R.E. Watters and his CHECKLIST OF CANADIAN LITERATURE 1628-1960. The National Library's CANADIANA is doing a sterling job at keeping a continuous bibliographic record; and in its first years, the journal CANADIAN LITERATURE published yearly checklists, a service which has now been taken over by the JOURNAL OF CANADIAN FICTION. But apart from Michael Gnarowski's CONCISE BIBLIOGRAPHY OF ENGLISH-CANADIAN LITERATURE, a bibliography compiled within even more rigorous structures than this present one, no single volume has gathered the significant bibliographic information together with some descriptive matter. This volume, it is hoped, will fill that gap.

The approach decided upon to provide a workable bibliographic scheme for English-Canadian poetry of the twentieth century is one of division into three distinct periods, even though some poets cross over these divisions. The first period is covered in chapter VI, "The Beginnings: 1900-1940," and includes the early decades of this century when the first stirrings of modernism were being felt in Canadian poetry, although the work of some modernist poets, most notably W.W.E. Ross and Raymond Knister, was not published in bulk until much later. Other poets who began their careers by publishing work in small magazines in the 1920's and 1930's often did not publish a volume until the 1940's--such poets as F.R. Scott, A.M. Klein, and A.J.M. Smith being examples of this lag in publication. Others who became established poets did manage to publish some volumes at the same time that their work was appearing in the magazines--for example, E.J. Pratt and Dorothy Livesay, although Livesay has gone through two significant transformations since the publication of her first two volumes and has suffered the publication lapse of the other poets as a result of her first major change of direction. Although these poets are probably the most significant figures of those beginnings, it is interesting to note that three of them are still living and that Livesay and Scott are still producing poetry, in Livesay's case, a particularly contemporary poetry.

At the same time that this burgeoning of modernist principles was making itself felt in Canadian poetry, other voices were trying to hang on to the rather colonialist notions of traditional poetry based on English diction and sentiment. Often these poets were trapped in a never-never land of traditionalism, or they tried to merge their conservatism with sprinklings of imagism and free verse. As these poets tended to be the ones chosen for book publication, some of them have been included in this section of the bibliography.

The development of poetry in English Canada gathered momentum in the 1940's with the emergence of new magazines: CONTEMPORARY VERSE on the west coast, and FIRST STATEMENT and PREVIEW (later to be merged as NORTHERN REVIEW) in Montreal. These magazines and others developed later were a direct result of a new movement which is covered in chapter VII, "Poetic Renaissance: The 1940's and Beyond." The different magazines propounded different views of poetry and gave rise to some healthy feuding, out of which came some terms which have become standard in Canadian criticism, particularly the division into native and cosmopolitan schools. From these groupings came significant poets: Earle Birney (though he tended to be outside these developments as he was out of the country for some time), Irving Layton, Raymond Souster, and P.K. Page, among others. Another school was added in the 1950's under the influence of Northrop Frye, a so-called mythopoeic school which included such poets as Jay MacPherson and James Reaney.

Since these schools were never clearly defined, the groupings tended to break down. Certain poets moved their poetic positions; and the contemporary period of the 1960's to the present has seen a considerable flux. Outside influences such as the Black Mountain orientation from Charles Olson and others had a profound effect on the younger poets on the west coast in the early 1960's. During this period Canadian concrete and sound poetry found its two most energetic voices, b p nichol and Bill Bissett. Together with these developments over the last fifteen years and with new poets coming to the fore, older poets have worked out their own distinctive voices, coming to terms with new methods while retaining their own individuality. Dorothy Livesay and Earle Birney have already been mentioned; other poets in this category are Milton Acorn, Al Purdy, and Eli Mandel, even though their writing careers began in the previous decades.

Another significant factor has been the establishment of new magazines and small presses, particularly in Toronto, a development that corresponds to some extent to the same process in Montreal in the 1940's. Out of this has emerged the important poet Margaret Atwood. All of these developments of the 1960's and 1970's are covered in chapter VIII, "Contemporary Poetry: The 1960's and '70's."

The works and criticism of individual authors are listed in chapters VI, VII, and VIII, representing the three major divisions of Canadian poetry in this century. Entries give all publishing information, and not simply titles, since Canadian publication, particularly in the field of poetry, is often limited to short runs, soon putting many books out of print. Annotations have been added only to those titles which mark an advance in a poet's development, a change of direction, or a gathering of the poet's work. The prose works of poets have also been included where they have a bearing on the poetry--that is, auto-biographical writings, critical statements, and novels.

Canadian literary criticism is only just now establishing itself in volume, and as yet there is no significant number of critical books on individual authors. Thus, for many poets the entries under criticism list only periodical articles and significant lead reviews. Sometimes, journals have published special issues devoted to individual poets. In these instances the entire issue is cited, rather than a listing of the separate articles contained in the issue. Similarly, where articles have been reprinted in collections, those articles are not given a separate entry, but the collections themselves are annotated. The reader will be able to get the full bibliographic information as it is given in these collections. Occasionally exceptions are made to this guideline where certain articles and essays are of particular importance and the reader's attention needs to be drawn specifically to their significance.

From the time of the poetic outpouring of the 1940's and on, a great deal of ephemeral material has been produced in one form or another--mimeographed magazines and pamphlets, short-lived magazines, broadsides, posters, chapbooks from private presses. Many of these are difficult to trace and have in general been omitted from this bibliography when the material has been included in later publications by an author. Some of this flimsy and often privately distributed work, however, has become of immense importance in the development of English-Canadian poetry, for example: W.W.E. Ross's EXPERIMENT and some of the publications by the leading concrete poets in Canada, b p nichol and Bill Bissett. Every effort has been made to check this kind of material, but it has been impossible to trace every item. Where a publication, however ephemeral or badly printed, has been deemed significant, it has been included with full annotation. As it has not always been possible to check every single volume listed in this bibliography, some entries are not fully described. In such cases the number of pages has been omitted and sometimes the date of publication is approximate or has been left out altogether.

These working guidelines have been adopted in order to encompass as much ground as possible without excessive detail--Watters' work provides additional bibliographic detail should the reader wish to pursue his work in that direction. This bibliography is, then, selective. It is the hope of the compiler that the bibliography contains a listing of the most readily accessible sources of information about general and critical topics and about specific authors in the field of modern and contemporary Canadian poetry in English.

Chapter II
REFERENCE SOURCES

A. BIBLIOGRAPHIES

There are no bibliographies specifically devoted to modern Canadian poetry in English, but a full section appears in Watters, cited below, section A, and references to modern poetry titles occur in the works listed in this section. While limited bibliographies compiled as special projects by libraries and students in library schools have been omitted, these can be traced by reference to the works listed here, particularly to Lochhead's BIBLIOGRAPHY OF CANADIAN BIBLIOGRAPHIES. Some useful bibliographies occur in theses (see section D, below) and in some of the works cited in chapter III, as is indicated in the annotations there.

Amtmann, Bernard. CONTRIBUTIONS TO A SHORT TITLE CATALOGUE OF CANADIANA. Montreal: Author, 1971-- .

> Amtmann is a Montreal bookseller; this bibliography, which is a work in progress, is a compilation from his catalogs since 1950. It is useful in that it lists many literary items hard to locate, especially ephemeral pamphlets.

Bell, Inglis Freeman, and Rita Butterfield. CANADIAN LITERATURE 1959-1970: A CHECKLIST. Vancouver, B.C.: CANADIAN LITERATURE, 1959-70.

> This checklist appeared annually as a supplement in the periodical CANADIAN LITERATURE, and is a compilation of literary works published each year. It contains a separate section on Canadian poetry in English as well as a section listing criticism on individual poets. I.F. Bell compiled the checklists for 1959-63 and Rita Butterfield those for 1964-70. This annual checklist is now published in the JOURNAL OF CANADIAN FICTION (see Bruce Nesbitt, ed., below, this section).

Bell, Inglis Freeman, and Jennifer Gallup. A REFERENCE GUIDE TO ENGLISH, AMERICAN AND CANADIAN LITERATURE: AN ANNOTATED CHECKLIST OF

BIBLIOGRAPHICAL AND OTHER REFERENCE MATERIALS. Vancouver: University of British Columbia Press, 1971. xii, 139 p.

A very general checklist which attempts to cover three literatures. Useful entries.

Bell, Inglis Freeman, and Susan W. Port. CANADIAN LITERATURE/LITTERATURE CANADIENNE: A CHECKLIST OF CREATIVE AND CRITICAL WRITINGS/ BIBLIOGRAPHIE DE LA CRITIQUE ET DES OEUVRES D'IMAGINATION. Vancouver: Publications Centre, University of British Columbia, 1966. 140 p. Illustrated.

This is an amended cumulation of the annual checklists (including both English- and French-Canadian works) published originally in CANADIAN LITERATURE (see Bell and Butterfield, above, this section).

CANADIANA. Ottawa: The National Library, 1951-- .

Published monthly with annual cumulations, this is the most comprehensive continuing guide to Canadian publications. It is compiled as a catalog of all publications received by the National Library. It is divided into eight sections with a classified table of contents. Microforms and films are also listed.

CANADIAN BOOKS IN PRINT/CATALOGUE DES LIVRES CANADIENS EN LIBRARIE. Toronto: Canadian Books in Print Committee, 1967-- .

A catalog kept in progress by compiling titles from publishers' lists, it is arranged in three sections under author, title, and publisher.

CANADIAN CATALOGUE OF BOOKS PUBLISHED IN CANADA, ABOUT CANADA, AS WELL AS THOSE WRITTEN BY CANADIANS, WITH IMPRINT 1921-1949. Consolidated English language reprint edition with cumulated author index. Toronto: Toronto Public Libraries, 1967. Var. pag.

The work begun in the compilation of this catalog is now continued by CANADIANA (see above, this section).

CANADIAN NOTES AND QUERIE/QUESTIONS ET REPONSES CANADIENNES. Montreal: Amtmann et al., 1968-- .

This quarterly publication offers interesting questions on and answers to a wide range of topics within the field of both English- and French-Canadian publications.

CULTURE: REVUE TRIMESTRIELLE, SCIENCES RELIGIEUSES ET SCIENCES PROFANES AU CANADA. Vols. 1-31. Quebec City, Que.: 1940-70.

Each number of this periodical contains an annotated bibliographic index of studies in Canadian literature in both French and English.

DICTIONARY CATALOG OF THE HARRIS COLLECTION OF AMERICAN POETRY AND PLAYS. 13 vols. Boston: G.K. Hall, 1972.

This collection at Brown University contains more than 150,000 items by American, Canadian, and Mexican authors. It is particularly strong in Canadian poetry. See also under Brown University, in section F, below.

Gnarowski, Michael. A CONCISE BIBLIOGRAPHY OF ENGLISH-CANADIAN LITERATURE. Toronto: McClelland & Stewart, 1973. 127 p.

This listing, which is very selective because it deals with the whole of English-Canadian literature, is still useful, particularly for authors in the modern period. It gives details of book reviews as well as selected criticism, though there are some omissions in the listing of critical articles.

_____. "Contact Press; 1952-67, A Check List of Titles." CULTURE, 30 (September 1969), 227-32.

Contact Press arose out of the magazine CONTACT and was operated by three poets: Raymond Souster, Louis Dudek, and Peter Miller. It was responsible for publishing work of new poets in Canada who have since become established names.

_____. "A Reference and Bibliographical Guide to the Study of English-Canadian Literature." Ph.D. thesis, University of Ottawa, 1967.

Graham, Allen, ed. ISLAND PROSE AND POETRY: AN ANTHOLOGY. Charlottetown: The Literary Committee, Prince Edward Island 1973 Centennial Commission, 1972. viii, 226 p. Illustrated.

Issued for the centennial of Prince Edward Island's becoming a province of Canada, this anthology contains a useful bibliography of books written by authors from the island.

Harlowe, Dorothy. A CATALOGUE OF CANADIAN MANUSCRIPTS COLLECTED BY LORNE PIERCE AND PRESENTED TO QUEEN'S UNIVERSITY. Toronto: Ryerson, 1946. xii, 164 p.

Of special interest in the field of modern Canadian poetry in English are entries listing the holdings by such writers as Earle Birney, Arthur Bourinot, Carol Coates, Wilson MacDonald, Tom MacInnes, Anne Marriott, and Marjorie Pickthall.

Harvard University Library. CANADIAN HISTORY AND LITERATURE; CLASSI-

FICATION SCHEDULE, CLASSIFIED LISTING BY CALL NUMBER, ALPHABETI-
CAL LISTING BY AUTHOR OR TITLE, CHRONOLOGICAL LISTING. Widener
Library Shelflist, 20. Cambridge, Mass.: Harvard University Library, dis-
tributed by Harvard University Press, 1968. v, 411 p.

JOURNAL OF CANADIAN FICTION. Fredericton, N.B., and Montreal:
Journal of Canadian Fiction Association, 1972-- .

> Although this journal specializes in Canadian fiction, since 1973
> it has taken over the annual bibliography published by CANADIAN
> LITERATURE for the years 1959-70. See entries under Bell and
> Butterfield, above, this section, and Nesbitt, below, this section.

JOURNAL OF COMMONWEALTH LITERATURE. Leeds, Engl.: Heinemann
Educational Books, 1965-- .

> This journal has published a bibliography of Canadian books since
> 1964, but on occasions it has given only spotty coverage.

"The Last Five Years of Canadian Poetry, a List of What's Available." QUILL
& QUIRE, 33 (February/March 1967), 16-18.

THE LAWRENCE LANDE COLLECTION OF CANADIANA IN THE REDPATH
LIBRARY OF McGILL U; A BIBLIOGRAPHY. Collected, arranged, and anno-
tated with an introd. by Edgar Andrew Collard. Montreal: Lawrence Lande
Foundation for Canadian Historical Research, 1965. xxxv, 301 p. Illustrations,
maps.

> Divided into three parts: (1) Basic Canadiana, (2) Canadiana in
> the West and North, and (3) Cultural and Supplementary Cana-
> diana. The third part contains some items of interest in the field
> of modern poetry, but in general the entries are concerned with
> material published before the twentieth century. It has a full
> apparatus of subject and title indexes. See RARE & UNUSUAL CA-
> NADIANA, cited below, this section, for the supplement to this work.

Lochhead, Douglas. BIBLIOGRAPHY OF CANADIAN BIBLIOGRAPHIES. 2nd
ed., rev. and enl., with an index compiled by Peter E. Grieg. Toronto:
University of Toronto Press, in association with the Bibliographic Society of
Canada, 1972. xiv, 312 p.

> This indispensable volume is a continuation of the work begun in
> the first edition compiled under the direction of Raymond Tanghe
> (Toronto: University of Toronto Press, 1960. vii, 206 p.).
> Supplements to that edition were compiled by Madeleine Pellerin
> and issued for the years 1960-61, 1962-63, and 1964-65.

Modern Humanities Research Association (MHRA). ANNUAL BIBLIOGRAPHY
OF ENGLISH LANGUAGE AND LITERATURE. Cambridge: 1920-- .

This annual bibliography lists books and some periodical articles dealing with Canadian literature.

Modern Language Association (MLA). INTERNATIONAL BIBLIOGRAPHY OF BOOKS AND ARTICLES ON THE MODERN LANGUAGES AND LITERATURES. New York: 1921-- .

Issued annually, this bibliography contains a small section on Canadian literature in subsection 2.

Moyles, R.G., and Catherine Siemens. ENGLISH-CANADIAN LITERATURE: A STUDENT GUIDE AND ANNOTATED BIBLIOGRAPHY. Edmonton, Alta.: Athabascan Publishing Co., 1972. 44 p.

A useful summarizing guide to bibliographies and sources in the study of Canadian literature in English.

Nesbitt, Bruce, ed. "Canadian Literature/Literature Canadienne, 1972." JOURNAL OF CANADIAN FICTION. Spring, 1973-- .

This annotated bibliography is to be published annually as a continuation of the annual bibliographies published in CANADIAN LITERATURE 1959-1970: A CHECKLIST (see above, this section, under Bell and Butterfield). The editor states the purpose of this bibliography is an attempt "to record all books, articles, theses and reviews of books and theatrical productions published during 1972 and directly related to the study of Canadian literature." On the evidence of the first annual bibliography this series promises to be more extensive and informative than the annual bibliographies published in CANADIAN LITERATURE.

PAPERS OF THE BIBLIOGRAPHICAL SOCIETY OF CANADA/CAHIERS DE LA SOCIETE BIBLIOGRAPHIQUE DU CANADA. Toronto: The Society, 1962-- .

A continuing publication of articles concerned with all aspects of Canadian bibliography.

Peel, Bruce Braden. A BIBLIOGRAPHY OF THE PRAIRIE PROVINCES TO 1953 WITH BIOGRAPHICAL INDEX. 2nd ed., rev. and enl. Toronto: University of Toronto Press, 1973. 780 p.

The first edition of this work was published in 1956 by the same press in cooperation with the Saskatchewan Golden Jubilee Committee and the University of Saskatchewan. A supplement to it was published in 1963. It contains a list of poetry books by prairie authors, although the compiler has suggested that R.E. Watters' CHECKLIST OF CANADIAN LITERATURE (see below, this section) has superseded his own listing of prairie literary works.

RARE & UNUSUAL CANADIANA; FIRST SUPPLEMENT TO THE LANDE BIBLIOG-
RAPHY. Lawrence Lande Foundation for Canadian Historical Research, no. 6.
Montreal: McGill University, 1971. xxi, 779 p.

> This supplement to the Lawrence Lande Collection (see above, this
> section) contains some items of interest, conveniently listed with a
> short note in a special subject index. The note suggests that "the
> material in question is so varied in quality and authors' intention that
> it would be described in more appropriate, if general terms as occa-
> sional or amateur verse."

Rome, David. JEWS IN CANADIAN LITERATURE; A BIBLIOGRAPHY. 2nd
rev. ed. 2 vols. Montreal: Canadian Jewish Congress and Jewish Public
Library, 1964. xiv, 252 p.

> See next item for supplement.

_____. RECENT CANADIAN JEWISH AUTHORS. A SUPPLEMENT TO JEWS
IN CANADIAN LITERATURE. Pref. Joseph Kage. Montreal: Jewish Public
Library, 1970.

> See next item for annotation.

_____. A SELECTED BIBLIOGRAPHY OF JEWISH CANADIANA. Montreal:
Canadian Jewish Congress and Jewish Public Library, 1959.

> These three books give bibliographic details about such important
> Jewish Canadian poets as Leonard Cohen, A.M. Klein, Irving
> Layton, Eli Mandel, and Miriam Waddington. The supplement
> deals with the period from 1964, and gives information about
> such poets as Joe Rosenblatt, Bill Bissett, Stanley Cooperman,
> and George Jonas.

Roy, George Ross. CANADIAN POETRY; A SUPPLEMENTARY BIBLIOGRAPHY
COMPILED BY G. ROSS ROY AND M. GNAROWSKI. Quebec: CULTURE,
1964. 13 p.

> This is a bibliography of items published before 1950. It supple-
> ments Watters' CHECKLIST OF CANADIAN LITERATURE. The
> items are located in the G.R. Roy Collection of Canadiana in
> the library of the University of Montreal and the library of Lake-
> head College of Arts, Science, and Technology, (now Lakehead
> University), Port Arthur (now Thunder Bay),Ontario. This supple-
> ment was first published in CULTURE, 25 (June 1964), 160-70.

Ryder, Dorothy E. CANADIAN REFERENCE SOURCES; A SELECTIVE GUIDE.
Ottawa: Canadian Library Association, 1973. x, 185 p.

> This useful guide covers many areas of Canadiana.

Thierman, Lois Mary. INDEX TO CANADIAN LITERATURE IN ENGLISH BY
VERNON BLAIR RHODENIZER. Edmonton, Alta.: La Survivance Printing Co.,
[1968]. ix, 469 p.

> Rhodenizer's book is a bio-bibliographic study published in 1965.
> It is listed under Rhodenizer in section B of this chapter.

Tod, Dorothea D., and Audrey Cordingley. A CHECK LIST OF CANADIAN
IMPRINTS 1900-1925/CATALOGUE D'OUVRAGES IMPRIMES AU CANADA.
Ottawa: Canadian Bibliographic Centre and Public Archives of Canada, 1950.
370 p.

> A title index for this work is being prepared, and it may be ex-
> tended to other checklists for the same period.

UNION LIST OF MANUSCRIPTS IN CANADIAN REPOSITORIES. Ottawa:
Canadian National Library, 1968.

> An alphabetical listing of manuscripts, although there are gaps in
> the area of literary papers. For a fuller listing of papers of
> twentieth-century Canadian poets, see section F of this chapter.

UNIVERSITY OF TORONTO QUARTERLY. LETTERS IN CANADA. Toronto,
1935-- .

> Since 1935 this periodical has included a critical survey by an
> established Canadian critic (in the past the poetry section has
> been written by such critics as Northrop Frye and Milton Wilson)
> of the Canadian literary works published in the previous year.

Wallace, William S. THE RYERSON IMPRINT; A CHECKLIST OF THE BOOKS
AND PAMPHLETS PUBLISHED BY THE RYERSON PRESS SINCE THE FOUNDA-
TION OF THE HOUSE IN 1829. Toronto: Ryerson, 1954. 141 p.

> The Ryerson Press has played an important part in the field of
> modern Canadian poetry in English. It published a series of
> poetry chapbooks starting in 1925. From the appointment of
> Lorne Pierce as editor in 1920, the press became a leading pub-
> lisher of Canadian literature. This checklist gives some informa-
> tion about these activities, although it is selective.

Watters, Reginald Eyre. A CHECKLIST OF CANADIAN LITERATURE AND
BACKGROUND MATERIALS, 1628-1960. IN TWO PARTS: FIRST, A COM-
PREHENSIVE LIST OF THE BOOKS WHICH CONSTITUTE CANADIAN LITERA-
TURE WRITTEN IN ENGLISH; AND SECOND, A SELECTIVE LIST OF OTHER
BOOKS BY CANADIAN AUTHORS WHICH REVEAL THE BACKGROUNDS OF
THAT LITERATURE. 2nd ed., rev. and enl. Toronto: University of Toronto
Press, 1972. xxiv, 1085 p.

> This is the major bibliography of Canadian literature. It lists

works of poetry, poetry and prose, fiction, drama, biography, essays and speeches, local history and description, religion and morality, social history, scholarship, and travel and description, in separate sections. It contains an index of anonymous titles as well as a general index.

Watters, Reginald Eyre, and Inglis Freeman Bell. ON CANADIAN LITERATURE 1806-1960. A CHECK LIST OF ARTICLES, BOOKS, AND THESES ON ENGLISH-CANADIAN LITERATURE, ITS AUTHORS, AND LANGUAGE. Rev. ed. Toronto: University of Toronto Press, 1973. xi, 165 p.

In a sense, this is a companion volume to Watters' CHECKLIST OF CANADIAN LITERATURE (above, this section), but it is more specifically related to literature. It consists of two parts: (1) listings under the headings of general bibliography; Canadian culture and background; Canadian English: language and linguistics; Canadian literature--general; drama and theatre; fiction; poetry; literary criticism; literary history; regionalism; songs; folksongs and folklore; journalism; publishing and periodicals; libraries and reading; censorship and copyright; and (2) a listing of works on and by individual authors.

B. BIOGRAPHICAL REFERENCES

The DICTIONARY OF CANADIAN BIOGRAPHY, now being compiled, will be the prime source of biographical information about Canadian writers; but as it now stands, only three volumes have been completed: volume 1: 1000-1700; volume II: 1701-1740; volume X: 1871-1880. Obviously the entries do not cover the period of this bibliography.

Some writers' biographies occur in other general biographical works, such as THE CANADIAN WHO'S WHO and WHO'S WHO IN CANADIAN JEWRY, but entries on poets do not loom large in these volumes. There are as well brief biographies of individual poets in some of the anthologies and critical surveys listed in chapter III of this bibliography. Entries on some Canadian poets appear in standard biographical works devoted to twentieth-century writers, such as Stanley Kunitz's TWENTIETH CENTURY AUTHORS, the series CONTEMPORARY WRITERS published by St. James Press in London (St. Martin's Press in New York), and the Gale Research Company's continuing CONTEMPORARY AUTHORS, which now comprises some forty volumes.

The biographical references listed below are the best works for information about Canadian poets of the twentieth century.

CANADIAN BIOGRAPHIES: ARTISTS, AUTHORS, MUSICIANS. Ottawa: Canadian Library Association, 1948. Unpaged.

A loose-leaf pamphlet concerned with artists working in the 1940's.

CREATIVE CANADA; A BIOGRAPHICAL DICTIONARY OF TWENTIETH CENTURY
CREATIVE AND PERFORMING ARTS. 2 vols. Toronto: University of Toronto
Press, 1971-72. xiv, 310 p.; xiv, 306 p.

> The biographies are written in note form, giving the essential
> facts of the life with a listing of the poet's work.

Daiches, David, ed. THE PENGUIN COMPANION TO LITERATURE IN
BRITAIN AND THE COMMONWEALTH. London: Penguin Books, 1971. 576 p.

> A gathering of information in short entries, but weak on Cana-
> dian literature.

ENCYCLOPAEDIA CANADIANA. 10 vols. Ottawa: Canadian Co., 1957-65.

> A general reference work which contains some biographies of poets.

MANITOBA AUTHORS/ECRIVAINS DE MANITOBA. Pref. Guy Sylvestre.
Ottawa: National Library, 1970. Unpaged. Photographs.

> Very brief biographies of the few poets who are Manitobans.

Pacey, Desmond. TEN CANADIAN POETS; A GROUP OF BIOGRAPHICAL
AND CRITICAL ESSAYS. Toronto: Ryerson, 1958. ix, 350 p.

> This book has separate bio-critical essays on some Canadian poets
> of the twentieth century: Earle Birney, A.M. Klein, E.J. Pratt,
> F.R. Scott, and A.J.M. Smith.

Percival, W.P., ed. LEADING CANADIAN POETS. Toronto: Ryerson, 1948.
x, 271 p.

> This collection of short bio-critical essays, uneven in quality,
> includes pieces on Earle Birney, Audrey Alexandra Brown, Dorothy
> Livesay, Wilson MacDonald, Tom MacInnes, Marjorie Pickthall,
> E.J. Pratt, and A.J.M. Smith, with some nineteenth-century poets
> and also some now forgotten poets.

Rhodenizer, Vernon Blair. CANADIAN LITERATURE IN ENGLISH. Montreal:
Quality Press, ca. 1965. 1,055 p.

> Very brief bio-bibliographical entries. An index is published
> separately, listed under Lois Mary Thierman in section A, above.

Shain, Merle. "Some of Our Best Poets Are Women." CHATELAINE, 45
(October 1972), 48-50, 103-7.

> An interesting article in a woman's magazine giving biographical
> sketches of Margaret Atwood, Margaret Avison, Phyllis Gotlieb,

Dorothy Livesay, Gwendolyn MacEwen, Susan Musgrave, P.K.
Page, Miriam Waddington, and Phyllis Webb.

Story, Norah. THE OXFORD COMPANION TO CANADIAN HISTORY AND
LITERATURE. Toronto: Oxford University Press, 1967. xx, 935 p. Maps.

This massive compendium includes not only biographical information
but also some surveys of literary genres and a list of the winners
of the major literary prize of Canada, the Governor-General's
Award.

Sylvestre, Guy; Brandon Conron; and Carl F. Klinck. CANADIAN WRITERS/
ECRIVAINS CANADIENS; A BIBLIOGRAPHICAL DICTIONARY. Rev. and enl.
Toronto: Ryerson, 1966. xviii, 186 p.

A slim volume that covers a sizeable area in Canadian literature,
both English and French. There are brief biographies, and a list
of individual works as well as some criticism.

Thomas, Clara. OUR NATURE--OUR VOICES; A GUIDEBOOK TO ENGLISH-
CANADIAN LITERATURE. Vol. 1. Toronto: New Press, 1972. ix, 175 p.
Photographs.

A selective annotation of certain writers in English-Canadian
literature, the book consists of short but instructive bio-critical
essays with useful bibliographies. There are also essays giving
general social and historical background to specific periods in
Canadian life. The modern poets included are Earle Birney,
Leonard Cohen, A.M. Klein, Irving Layton, E.J. Pratt, Al
Purdy, James Reaney, F.R. Scott, A.J.M. Smith, and Miriam
Waddington. Volume 2 of this book, to be edited by Frank
Davey, is intended to extend the coverage of twentieth-century
writers.

C. INDEXES TO SERIAL PUBLICATIONS

Indexes to serial publications in Canadian literature have been only scantily
annotated, but there are signs that progress is being made. The Canadian
Library Association is sponsoring an index to a selection of little magazines
published between 1920 and 1970, although this project is still in the very
early stages. Michael Gnarowski in the 1960's compiled some indexes of im-
portant little magazines of the 1940's and 1950's. Some magazines publish their
own indexes annually, but at times these are produced only haphazardly. Some
Canadian serials are recorded in a variety of small press indexes and in THE
INTERNATIONAL DIRECTORY OF LITTLE MAGAZINES AND SMALL PRESSES.
The following entries list the main indexes for these serials, though few of them
are devoted entirely to poetry.

Indexes to specific journals are listed alphabetically by title of journal, not by compiler or title of index. For listings of periodicals, see chapter V, below.

A BIBLIOGRAPHY OF CANADIAN CULTURAL PERIODICALS (ENGLISH AND FRENCH FROM COLONIAL TIMES TO 1950). Compiled by Emilio Goggio, Beatrice Corrigan, and Jack H. Parker. Toronto: Department of Italian, Spanish and Portuguese, University of Toronto, 1955. 47 p.

CANADIAN CULTURAL PUBLICATIONS. Vols. 1-13. Sponsored by the Canadian Foundation and the Canadian Council. Ottawa: Canadian Culture Information Centre, 1951?--1965?

> This annual publication gave a brief descriptive list of magazines related to the arts.

CANADIAN FORUM, A MONTHLY JOURNAL OF LITERATURE AND PUBLIC AFFAIRS. INDEX, VOLS. 1-9, 1920-29. Compiled by G.R. Adshead. Ottawa: Canadian Library Association, 1973. 84 p.

> The indexing of this journal is continued in WILSON'S READER'S GUIDE for the years 1930-37 and in CANADIAN PERIODICAL INDEX from January 1938 to date.

[CANADIAN LITERATURE]. AN INDEX TO THE CONTENTS OF CANADIAN LITERATURE. NUMBERS 1-50 WITH AN ADDENDUM FOR NUMBERS 51-4. Compiled by Glenn Clever with the assistance of Burris Devanney and George Martin. Ottawa: Golden Dog Press, 1973. 170 p.

> CANADIAN LITERATURE is the most important journal of criticism devoted to Canadian literature; this index is an essential documentation of its contents. See also the listing for CANADIAN LITERATURE in chapter V.

"CANADIAN LITERATURE: The First Three Years." CANADIAN LITERATURE, 13 (Summer 1962), 89-100.

> This is an index to numbers 1-12.

CANADIAN PERIODICAL INDEX/INDEX DE PERIODIQUES CANADIENS. Ottawa: Canadian Library Association, 1938-- .

> This index lists articles in periodicals, entered under author and subject. A section is devoted to reviews under the heading "Book Reviews," and these are listed under the author's not the reviewer's name. Since 1960 it has been a monthly publication with annual cumulations. From 1948 to 1963 its title was CANADIAN INDEX TO PERIODICALS AND DOCUMENTARY FILMS.

CANADIAN SERIALS DIRECTORY/REPERTOIRE DES PUBLICATIONS SERIEES

CANADIENNES. Toronto: University of Toronto Press, 1972. x, 961 p.

Entries are listed under separate sections by title, subject, and publisher.

[CIV/n]. INDEX TO CIV/n, A LITTLE MAGAZINE EDITED BY AILEEN COLLINS IN ASSOCIATION WITH JACKIE GALLAGHER, WANDA STANISZEWSKA, STAN ROSYNSKI IN 1953 AND 1954 FOR A TOTAL OF SEVEN ISSUES; AN AUTHOR/TITLE INDEX WITH SELECT SUBJECT HEADINGS. Ed. Michael Gnarowski. Introd. Louis Dudek. Montreal: Delta, 1965. First published in CULTURE, 26 (June 1965), 220–38.

[See also the entry for CIV/n in chapter V.]

CONTACT 1952-1954; BEING AN INDEX TO THE CONTENTS OF CONTACT, A LITTLE MAGAZINE EDITED BY RAYMOND SOUSTER, TOGETHER WITH NOTES ON THE HISTORY AND THE BACKGROUND OF THE PERIODICAL. Compiled by Michael Gnarowski. Some afterthoughts on CONTACT by Raymond Souster. Montreal: Delta, 1966. vii, 37 p.

[DIRECTION]. INDEX TO DIRECTION, A LITTLE MAGAZINE EDITED BY RAYMOND SOUSTER, WILLIAM GOLDBERG, DAVID MULLEN BETWEEN NOVEMBER, 1945 AND FEBRUARY, 1946, FOR A TOTAL OF TEN ISSUES; AN AUTHOR/TITLE INDEX WITH SELECT SUBJECT HEADINGS. Ed. Michael Gnarowski. Quebec: Delta, 1965. First published in CULTURE, 25 (December 1964), 405–16.

AN INDEX TO BOOK REVIEWS IN THE HUMANITIES. Detroit: P. Thomson, 1960-- .

This annual publication is arranged alphabetically by author and includes some entries for some of the major Canadian journals.

AN INDEX TO LITTLE MAGAZINES OF ONTARIO. Compiled by Clarke Leverette. London, Ont.: Killaly Press, 1972-- .

This index is published spasmodically and so far has covered in four separate volumes the years 1971, 1972, 1973, and 1967-70.

PERIODICALS IN THE SOCIAL SCIENCES AND HUMANITIES CURRENTLY RECEIVED BY CANADIAN LIBRARIES/INVENTAIRE DES PERIODIQUES DE SCIENCES SOCIALES ET D'HUMANITES QUE POSSEDENT LES BIBLIOTHEQUES CANADIENNES. 2 vols. Ottawa: National Library of Canada, 1968. xiii, 970 p.; ix, 860 p.

This work lists many titles up to the time of compilation (1965) and gives general information about the periodicals, such as place of publication and date of first issue.

READER'S GUIDE TO PERIODICAL LITERATURE. New York: H.W. Wilson Co., 1905--

> Published annually, this guide includes details of a few Canadian journals until the first annual publication of the CANADIAN PERIODICAL INDEX in 1938.

D. INDEXES TO THESES

Until recently the study of Canadian literature at the graduate level has been minimal, and only within the very recent past has there been a significant increase in theses completed at the Ph.D. level. Some theses on Canadian literature are noted in compilations such as DISSERTATION ABSTRACTS INTERNATIONAL; there have been some indexes published since 1950, as well as the mimeographed lists compiled by Carl Klinck during the years 1960-70. Between 1959 and 1971 the journal CANADIAN LITERATURE also included a list of theses in the English-Canadian section of its annual supplement devoted to a checklist of Canadian literary publications. This has been continued in the annual bibliography now included in the JOURNAL OF CANADIAN FICTION.

CANADIAN GRADUATE THESES IN THE HUMANITIES AND SOCIAL SCIENCES, 1921-46/THESES DES GRADUES CANADIENS DANS LES HUMANITES ET LES SCIENCES SOCIALES. Ottawa: Canadian Bibliographic Centre, 1948; rpt. Ottawa: King's Printer, 1951. 194 p.

> This index gives a short description of theses which are listed alphabetically by university and author. There is a section devoted to Canadian literature.

CANADIAN THESES; A LIST OF THESES ACCEPTED BY CANADIAN UNIVERSITIES/ THESES CANADIENNES; UNE LISTE DES THESES ACCEPTEES PAR LES UNIVERSITIES CANADIENNES. Ottawa: Queen's Printer, 1952-- .

> This is an annual compilation, but the 1952 issue is out of print. A new series started in 1961. Within the Canadian literature section the universities are listed alphabetically. There is also an alphabetical author list.

CANADIAN THESES/THESES CANADIENNES 1947-1960. 2 vols. Ottawa: National Library, 1973. xix, 791 p.

> This publication gives a short description of theses, beginning in 1947 where CANADIAN GRADUATE THESES . . . 1921-46 left off (see above, this section). The entries are listed by subject, university, and author. There is also an index of the writers dealt with in the theses.

Klinck, Carl F. "Canadian Literature: Theses In Preparation." London: University of Western Ontario, 1960-70. Mimeographed.

> This publication consists of annual lists of completed theses and theses in preparation for the period 1959-67. A useful compilation, though it lists some theses in preparation which were never completed. Some of these titles have found their way into Naaman's guide (see below, this section).

Mills, Judy, and Irene Dombra. UNIVERSITY OF TORONTO DOCTORAL THESES, 1897-1967. Toronto: University of Toronto Press, 1968. xi, 186 p.

> Because very few Ph.D. theses on Canadian literature were written prior to 1967, the closing date of this compilation, there are only a few such titles in this work.

Naaman, Antoine. GUIDE BIBLIOGRAPHIQUE DES THESES LITTERAIRES CANADIENNES DE 1921 A 1969. Montreal: Cosmos, 1970. 340 p.

> The most comprehensive compilation of theses in both English- and French-Canadian literature, this listing includes titles of theses in preparation taken from Klinck's annual index and, thus, contains some bibliographic ghosts. Otherwise, this is a good index.

E. INDEXES TO MICROMATERIALS

The field of twentieth-century Canadian poetry in English has comparatively little available in microforms. Occasional entries for such material may be found in such standard reference works as the NATIONAL REGISTER OF MICROFORM MASTERS, SERIALS IN MICROFORM, the GUIDE and SUBJECT GUIDE TO MICROFORMS IN PRINT, and BIBLIOGRAPHIC CONTROL OF MICROFORMS. A few catalogs and indexes devoted to Canadian materials exist, however, and those that include references relevant to this bibliography are listed below. CANADIANA also includes entries on microforms (see section A of this chapter).

CANADIAN THESES ON MICROFILM/THESES CANADIENNES SUR MICROFILM. Ottawa: National Library, 1969. 251 p.

> This catalog and price list, together with the annual supplements issued from 1969 on, includes theses submitted to Canadian universities and available on microfilm.

NEWSPAPERS, PERIODICALS, RARE BOOKS MARKETED IN MICROFORM. Calgary, Alta.: Commonwealth Microfilm Library, 1970. 24 p.

> This publisher's catalog contains a section titled "Canadian Collection" which lists newspapers and periodicals. The periodicals

are listed in alphabetical order.

UNION LIST OF MICROFORM SETS IN O.C.U.L. LIBRARIES. Ed. Anni Liebl and Jean S. Yoltan. Toronto: Ontario Council of University Libraries, 1971.

> Contains a page of entries about Canadian politics and literature which could be of interest to researchers in the field of twentieth-century Canadian poetry in English.

F. MANUSCRIPT COLLECTIONS AND SPECIAL COLLECTIONS

There has been a growing interest by university libraries in the collection of the papers of modern and contemporary Canadian writers. Some of the older and larger university libraries have extensive manuscript holdings. Many Canadian libraries are now collecting all Canadian publications; for instance, Metropolitan Toronto Central Library since 1968 has been buying all Canadian creative works in the English language, no matter what the source or quality. Many other public libraries in the major cities follow the same policy. In this way libraries across the country are becoming strong in the collection of material which reflects current publishing activity. In addition to acquiring modern Canadian literature, libraries are endeavoring to remedy retrospective shortcomings in their collections. The researcher can often find interesting collections in the public libraries, though the main manuscript and special collections are to be found in university libraries.

University of Alberta, Edmonton.

> The library holds the Dorothy Livesay papers, which consist of approximately 2,000 pages of manuscript and typescript poetry for the period 1919-74. This collection, which is continuing, also includes some correspondence.

University of British Columbia, Vancouver.

> Earle Birney's papers for the years 1949-52 are held here. They include the typescript and proof of TRIAL OF A CITY AND OTHER VERSE as well as manuscripts and proofs of his novel TURVEY.

> Birney was also chiefly responsible for the large collection of the papers of Malcolm Lowry, which includes manuscripts relating to his published and unpublished fiction and poetry as well as correspondence. The bibliography of Malcolm Lowry, compiled by Earle Birney and published in CANADIAN LITERATURE (Nos. 8 and 9, Spring 1961 and Summer 1961), contains descriptive entries devoted to this material.

> Of interest to students of Canadian bibliography are the original papers, 1955-59, of Reginald Watters, for these include manuscript

and research materials related to his B.C. CENTENNIAL AN-
THÓLOGY and CHECKLIST OF CANADIAN LITERATURE.

Brown University, Providence, R.I.

Since the 1880's the library has held the Harris Collection of
American Poetry and Plays. The collection has been continued
and now contains more than 150,000 printed books, pamphlets,
and plays by American, Canadian, and Mexican authors as well
as more than 25,000 pieces of broadside verse. An index to this
collection is available in the DICTIONARY CATALOG OF THE
HARRIS COLLECTION OF AMERICAN POETRY AND PLAYS (see
section A above, under title entry). A separate catalog of broad-
sides will be published, and supplements are planned.

Harvard University, Cambridge, Mass.

This collection of Canadiana is indexed in CANADIAN HISTORY
AND LITERATURE, Widener Library Shelflist, 20, cited under
Harvard University Library in section A of this chapter.

Lakehead University, Thunder Bay, Ont.

Raymond Souster and Al Purdy are the poets whose work is held
in this collection. The Souster material includes manuscript, type-
script, and proof material as well as correspondence. Al Purdy is
represented by some manuscripts of poems.

McGill University, Montreal.

This library has an extensive collection of manuscript material of
Canadian authors. Of interest in the field of twentieth-century
Canadian poetry in English are the papers of such poets as Patrick
Anderson, Margaret Avison, and Arthur Stringer. The typescript of
the collection of Canadian satirical verse, THE BLASTED PINE,
edited by A.J.M. Smith and F.R. Scott, is held in the Rare Book Room
Department of the library. In the archives collection, amonq the
papers of Frank Cyril James, a former vice-chancellor of McGill
University, is a recording of Leonard Cohen reading his own book
of poems, LET US COMPARE MYTHOLOGIES.

The largest holding devoted to a single modern author is the Mal-
colm Lowry collection. This has approximately 250 titles, in-
cluding books by or containing material about Lowry, books by
Margerie Bonner (Mrs. Lowry), books about Lowry, books men-
tioning or connected with Lowry, and pertinent serial issues.
There is also come manuscript material: correspondence between
Earle Birney and Thomas J. Jackson with reference to work on
the Lowry bibliography.

McMaster University, Hamilton, Ont.

The Mills Memorial Library here publishes LIBRARY RESEARCH
NEWS which periodically gives information about manuscript
material and special collections. Volume 2, number 2, for
instance, is a catalog of the modern Canadian poetry collection
as it stood in January 1973. The manuscript material of modern
Canadian poetry in English is strong in the work of such con-
temporary poets as Nelson Ball, John Robert Colombo, Doug
Fetherling, and Jane Shen.

University of New Brunswick, Fredericton.

The library's Rufus Hathaway Collection of Canadian Literature is
mainly devoted to nineteenth-century literature; but it also con-
tains first editions and signed copies of books by Pratt, MacInnes,
Pickthall, and Stringer, and holds some manuscripts of the poets
Raymond Souster, Dorothy Roberts, and Harry Howith.

Queen's University, Kingston, Ont.

The Douglas Library here houses the Lorne Pierce Collection of
Canadiana, for which a catalog exists (see section A above,
under Dorothy Harlowe). In addition to this, the library holds
letters and literary manuscripts of such poets as Arthur Bourinot,
A.A. Brown, and E.J. Pratt, as well as the original typescript
of John Sutherland's book on the poetry of E.J. Pratt.

The library has a significant collection of manuscript material in
literature and the arts; a listing of this material is currently being
prepared for publication.

University of Saskatchewan, Saskatoon.

The library has substantial collections of some major figures in
modern Canadian poetry in English. It holds a significant col-
lection of manuscript material of Ralph Gustafson. This includes
manuscripts and typescripts of the poet's own work as well as some
interesting correspondence with poets whom Gustafson contacted
when he was gathering poems for THE PELICAN BOOK OF CANA-
DIAN POETRY (1942).

The Al Purdy manuscript material covers much of his career up to
1963. It includes a good selection of his letters to Irving Layton,
whose manuscripts and typescripts form the basis of the Layton ma-
terial in the library. Other material includes a full collection of
material covering the career of Phyllis Webb up to 1967, and the
manuscripts, drafts, and correspondence of Peter Stevens for the
years 1964-69; Stevens was a lecturer and assistant professor at the
university during those years.

Simon Fraser University, Burnaby, B.C.

The manuscript material in this library consists of photocopies of poems by Frank Davey, photocopies of a critical essay by Lionel Kearns, and drafts and variant versions of a long poem by Fred Wah. These three poets were all associated with the new movement in Canadian poetry in the early 1960's which gave rise to the magazine TISH. Bill Bissett also participated in the west coast resurgence of interest in experimental poetry, and the library holds some of his original manuscripts and letters.

Two older poets represented in this collection are Milton Acorn and Irving Layton. The collection contains autographed manuscripts of poems by Acorn, and a few letters of Layton to a student.

Sir George Williams University, Montreal.

This library holds an almost complete manuscript collection of Irving Layton, apart from the material held in Saskatchewan and Toronto. The library has a catalog of the Layton manuscript holdings and a comprehensive Layton bibliography, both of which the library hopes to publish. The introductory section of the catalog explains some of the principles behind the collection. In addition to Layton's manuscripts, the collection includes "4000 letters and a comprehensive set of his published works." The library has been attempting "to acquire in original or copy all printed criticism of Layton, and . . . there are still nearly 400 items in the review section of this category alone." The collection also contains "recordings, photographs, and many hundreds of newspaper clippings." Layton has committed all his future work to this library.

Another collection assembled here is the manuscript material of John Sutherland. This includes correspondence, manuscripts of his prose and poetry, clippings, and submissions to the magazine NORTHERN REVIEW, together with some business papers connected with his editorship of this magazine.

University of Toronto, Toronto.

The Thomas Fisher Library buys as much published work as possible in modern Canadian poetry and has an extensive manuscript collection as well. The authors represented in this collection are as follows:

Margaret Atwood. Ca. 1958–69: correspondence; drafts of poems; notebooks; short stories; drafts of the novel THE EDIBLE WOMAN.

Earle Birney. Ca. 1915–69: correspondence; poems and prose by the poet himself and some other Canadian writers; transcripts; galley proofs of his novels TURVEY and DOWN THE LONG TABLE; teaching materials;

some Malcolm Lowry material; a collection of his books, chiefly presentation copies from other authors.

Leonard Cohen. Ca. 1955-67: correspondence; drafts and typescripts of poems, stories, plays, and novels.

Irving Layton. Ca. 1972-73: drafts and workbooks related to his book LOVERS AND LESSER MEN.

Gwendolyn MacEwen. Ca. 1960-72: correspondence; typescripts and proofs of poems, novels, plays.

John Newlove. Ca. 1950-68: correspondence; drafts; typescripts and proofs of GRAVE SIRS, MOVING IN ALONE, ELEPHANTS, MOTHERS AND OTHERS, and BLACK NIGHT WINDOW.

Al Purdy. 1959-69: correspondence; tapes; manuscripts of radio plays and a story; worksheets and typescripts of poems.

A.J.M. Smith. 1924-65: correspondence; drafts of poems; typescripts and proofs of books of poetry; drafts and typescripts of unpublished novels.

Anne Wilkinson. 1946-61: correspondence; typescripts of poems; autobiography; typescripts of THE HANGMAN TIES THE HOLLY, LIONS IN THE WAY, and SWANN AND DAPHNE.

University of Victoria, Victoria, B.C.

The chairman of the Department of Creative Writing at the University of Victoria is Robin Skelton, and the library there has manuscript material covering Skelton's career from his early life in Yorkshire, England, to his present literary activity in Canada.

York University, Downsview, Ont.

The library is collecting the work of Vancouver poet Bill Bissett. The collection includes his published work, proofs, manuscripts, correspondence, and art work. It also contains the publications from the poet's own Blew Ointment Press.

Chapter III

LITERARY HISTORIES, GENERAL AND CRITICAL STUDIES

Only a few studies devoted entirely to English-Canadian poetry of the twentieth century have been written. For the most part, poetry is included as a part of general studies of Canadian literature; such works have been included here with annotations to indicate how much apposite material occurs in each publication. Also included here are some collections of essays which elucidate the social and cultural context of Canadian literature, since the critical anthology seems to be a significant form in Canadian literature.

Ashcroft, Edith. "The Sonnet in Canadian Poetry." M.A. thesis, Queen's University, Kingston, Ont., 1932.

Atwood, Margaret [Eleanor]. SURVIVAL: A THEMATIC GUIDE TO CANADIAN LITERATURE. Toronto: Anansi, 1972. 287 p.

> A polemical book, endeavoring to place much Canadian literature, both English and French, within a schematic reading related to ideas of survival and victimization. Each chapter ends with a short bibliography, and the book concludes with "Resources," a listing enabling the reader "to acquire information about Canadian art, films, records, publishers and live speakers."

Beattie, A.M[unro]. "The Advent of Modernism in Canadian Poetry in English, 1912-1940." Ph.D. thesis, Columbia University, 1957.

> A useful survey which served as a basis for Beattie's articles in LITERARY HISTORY OF CANADA (see Klinck, below, this chapter).

Bradbrook, M.C. LITERATURE IN ACTION: STUDIES IN CONTINENTAL AND COMMONWEALTH SOCIETY. New York: Barnes & Noble, 1972. 200 p.

> Contains one chapter on Canadian literature, summarizing themes in a general way and concentrating more on novelists than poets, particularly Malcolm Lowry. Included is a very short reading list.

Brown, E.K. ON CANADIAN POETRY. Rev. ed. Toronto: Ryerson, 1944.
172 p.

A lively attempt to write "less an historical enquiry than a criti-
cal essay." Brown summarizes the questions his monograph tries
to answer as follows: "What are the peculiar difficulties which
have weighed upon the Canadian writer? . . . What Canadian
poetry remains alive and, in some degree at least, formative?
. . . How have the masters of our poetry achieved their success
and what are the kinds of success they have achieved?" The
book includes a brief history of the development of poetry in
Canada up to the 1940's, one chapter on the poetry of E.J.
Pratt, a bibliographic note, and a calendar of significant dates.

Careless, J.M.S., and R. Craig Brown, eds. THE CANADIANS 1867-1967.
Toronto: Macmillan, 1967. xix, 856 p. Photographs.

This book celebrating Canada's centennial in 1967 consists of two
parts: part I contains separate essays on the first ten decades of
Canadian history; part II contains essays on various aspects of
Canadian cultural, social, and political life. A useful book as
background for any literary study of these hundred years.

Collin, W.E. THE WHITE SAVANNAHS. Toronto: Macmillan, 1936. 288 p.

One of the first collections of critical essays on the new poets
in Canada in the 1920's and 1930's. A sympathetic treatment of,
among others, Marjorie Pickthall, E.J. Pratt, Dorothy Livesay,
F.R. Scott, A.M. Klein, A.J.M. Smith, and Leo Kennedy.

Deacon, W[illiam] A[rthur]. POTEEN: A POT-POURRI OF CANADIAN ESSAYS.
Ottawa: Graphic, 1926. 241 p.

The second half of this book is devoted to Canadian literature.
It contains charts to show the representation of poets in the
standard anthologies up to that time.

Djwa, Sandra Ann. "Metaphor, World View and the Continuity of Canadian
Poetry; A Study of the Major English-Canadian Poets with a Computer Con-
cordance to Metaphor." Ph.D. thesis, University of British Columbia, Van-
couver, 1968.

Dudek, Louis, and Michael Gnarowski, eds. THE MAKING OF MODERN
POETRY IN CANADA: ESSENTIAL ARTICLES ON CONTEMPORARY CANA-
DIAN POETRY IN ENGLISH. Toronto: Ryerson, 1967. ix, 303 p.

This work is a selection of most of the important statements and
debates occurring in the history of modern poetry in Canada. The
editors have written illuminating introductory matter to main sections
of the book, setting them in historical and cultural perspective.

Edwards, Mary Jane. "The Search for Unity; Modern Canadian Poetry and Its Critics." M.A. thesis, Queen's University, Kingston, Ont., 1963.

Farley, Thomas Ernest Hilary. "Love and Death in Canadian Poetry." M.A. thesis, Carleton University, Ottawa, 1963.

> D.G. Jones, whose BUTTERFLY ON ROCK (see below, this chapter) acknowledges this thesis as a starting point, summarizes the main argument thus: "English-Canadian poetry presents a world in which the past is to be preserved whereas the future is to be resisted. . . . Death alone is both triumphant and final. English-Canadian poetry is a poetry of exile, increasingly negative to the point of being neurotic."

Francis, Wynne. "Urban Images in Canadian Poetry." M.A. thesis, Sir George Williams University, Montreal, 1963.

Frye, Northrop. THE BUSH GARDEN: ESSAYS ON THE CANADIAN IMAGINATION. Toronto: Anansi, 1971. x, 251 p.

> In the preface the author defines his book as "a retrospective collection of some of my writings on Canadian culture, mainly literature, extending over a period of nearly thirty years." The volume thus includes some of his seminal thinking on patterns within Canadian culture as well as his important critical exegesis and comment on the volumes of poetry published in Canada during the years 1950-59. It closes with his general statement on English-Canadian literature, originally published as the conclusion to LITERARY HISTORY OF CANADA (see below, this chapter, under Klinck).

_____. ENGLISH CANADIAN LITERATURE 1929-1945. Toronto: Canadian Library Association, 1956.

> A very brief survey which concludes that the literature of this period has produced "a body of work which is partly a miscellany with no definite characteristics . . . and partly the expression of a recognizable type of English literature which is steadily growing in articulateness and power."

Fulford, Robert; David Godfrey; and Abraham Rotstein, eds. READ CANADIAN. Toronto: James Lewis & Samuel, 1972. xi, 275 p.

> The five main divisions of the book are under the headings history, economics and politics, society, literature and the arts, books and publishers. Each division is split into subsections, and the general editor, Robert Fulford, states that in each subsection "the writer has provided a description of the literature and bibliography." Dennis Lee is the author of the subsection on modern poetry (pp. 228-36).

Granatstein, J.L., and Peter Stevens, eds. FORUM: CANADIAN LIFE AND LETTERS 1920-70: SELECTIONS FROM THE CANADIAN FORUM. Toronto: University of Toronto Press, 1972. xv, 431 p. Illustrated.

> CANADIAN FORUM, Canada's leading review of politics and the arts, has published writings of many of the best poets and political commentators in the country. This anthology gives a clear picture of the social, political, and literary life of the country during the period 1920-70.

Harder, Helga Irene. "English-Canadian Poetry 1935-55, a Thematic Study." M.A. thesis, University of British Columbia, Vancouver, 1965.

Jones, D.G. BUTTERFLY ON ROCK; A STUDY OF THEMES AND IMAGES IN CANADIAN LITERATURE. Toronto: University of Toronto Press, 1970. x, 197 p.

> Working with Frye's ideas of the Canadian garrison mentality and Farley's notion of exile, Jones examines Canadian literature in terms of its images drawn from the Old Testament. Jones sees an emergence of a New Testament hope, with signs within contemporary poetry of the breaking down of barriers erected by a garrison culture.

Kilbourn, William, ed. CANADA: A GUIDE TO THE PEACEABLE KINGDOM. Toronto: Macmillan, 1970. xviii, 345 p.

> In the editor's words, the title was chosen "to suggest that it would serve as a travel companion for explorers of the Canadian spiritual landscape," and this volume presents a collection of cultural, political, and social views of Canada. The last section in the book, "Place des Arts," is devoted to general cultural questions and includes two essays on Canadian poetry.

Kilgallin, Anthony Raymond. "Toronto in Fiction, Poetry and Occasional Prose." Phil.M. thesis, University of Toronto, 1966.

King, Joanne. "Canadian Women Poets." Ph.D. thesis, University of Montreal, 1950.

Klinck, Carl F., et al., eds. LITERARY HISTORY OF CANADA; CANADIAN LITERATURE IN ENGLISH. Toronto: University of Toronto Press, 1965. xiv, 945 p.

> As the title implies, this is a compilation of chapters by individual scholars on the development of all aspects of Canadian literature in English. Parts III and IV are of specific interest to readers of the literature of the twentieth century with individual chapters on "Minor Poets (1880-1920)"; "Poetry (1920-1935)"; "Pratt"; "Poetry

(1935-1950)"; and "Poetry (1950-1960)." Includes a general bibliography, special bibliographies for each chapter, and a comprehensive index.

LITERARY HALF YEARLY (Mysore, India) 13 (July 1972), entire issue.

A number devoted to both creative and critical writing by Canadian authors. The guest editor, Hallvard Dahlie, suggests that the issue contains a "cross-section of critical opinion on . . . significant literary issues" with "a representative sampling of poetry and fiction."

Logan, J.D., and Donald G. French. HIGHWAYS OF CANADIAN LITERATURE: A SYNOPTIC INTRODUCTION TO THE LITERARY HISTORY OF CANADA (ENGLISH) FROM 1760 to 1924. Toronto: McClelland & Stewart, 1924. 418 p.

Contains some very general information about the early years of modern Canadian literature in English.

MacMechan, Archibald. HEADWATERS OF CANADIAN LITERATURE. 1924; rpt. Toronto: McClelland & Stewart, 1974. 247 p.

The editor of the reprint maintains that it is of "more than historical interest" because MacMechan was one of the first critics to try ot synthesize English- and French-Canadian elements. The book includes little discussion of twentieth-century Canadian poetry in English; it singles out Marjorie Pickthall for particular praise.

Mandel, Eli, ed. CONTEXTS OF CANADIAN CRITICISM. Chicago: University of Chicago Press, 1971. vii, 304 p.

A collection of critical essays with an introduction by the editor which attempts to map out the problems and patterns of the history of criticism in Canada. Included are some historical and philosophical essays, for Mandel believes that the "Canadian concern with historiography, social structure and esthetics can be viewed best as an expression of an almost paranoic self-consciousness or simply as part of an attempt to understand the importance of communication theories in a demanding physical setting." The contents are divided into three sections: "The Social and Historical Context," "The Theoretical Context," and "Patterns of Criticism." There is also a good bibliography of general studies of Canadian society and Canadian literature.

Mitchell, Beverley Jean. "A Critical Study of the Tish Group, 1961-1963." M.A. thesis, University of Calgary, Calgary, Alta., 1967.

The Tish group was comprised of young poets writing in Vancouver

in the early 1960's and effecting change in some aspects of con-
temporary Canadian poetry.

Murray, E.G.D., ed. STUDIA VARIA: ROYAL SOCIETY OF CANADA,
LITERARY AND SCIENTIFIC PAPERS. Toronto: University of Toronto Press,
1957. vii, 127 p.

    A collection of essays in French and English, including some
general writings on Canadian problems. Of particular value
on the subject of this bibliography are two essays: Desmond
Pacey's "The Canadian Writer and His Public, 1882-1952" and
Northrop Frye's "Preface to an Uncollected Anthology."

New, W.H. ARTICULATING WEST: ESSAYS ON PURPOSE AND FORM IN
MODERN CANADIAN LITERATURE. Toronto: New Press, 1972. xxvi, 282 p.

    This is a collection of various critical essays previously published
by New in journals, and held in a loose framework by a long
introduction which expresses a view of "the tension between order
and disorder, myth and reality, that underlies Canadian writing."
New concentrates on fiction, though there are five essays devoted
to modern English-Canadian poetry.

Pacey, Desmond. CREATIVE WRITING IN CANADA; A SHORT HISTORY OF
ENGLISH-CANADIAN LITERATURE. Rev. ed. Toronto: Ryerson, 1961. ix,
314 p.

    A straightforward account. The modern period looms large in the
book, and of particular interest are the last sections, "Modern
Canadian Poetry 1920-1950" (pp. 125-85) and "The Literature of
the Fifties" (pp. 230-67).

_____. ESSAYS IN CANADIAN CRITICISM 1938-1968. Toronto: Ryerson,
1969. x, 294 p.

    Pacey describes his book as bringing together "most of the articles
on Canadian literature which I have written over the past thirty
years." Some essays are of a general nature, but a number of
articles on modern poets and poetry are included, most notably on
the work of Dorothy Livesay and Leonard Cohen.

_____. TEN CANADIAN POETS; A GROUP OF BIOGRAPHICAL AND CRITI-
CAL ESSAYS. Toronto: Ryerson, 1958. ix, 350 p.

    Five of the poets discussed in these essays are writers of the modern
period: E.J. Pratt, A.J.M. Smith, F.R. Scott, A.M. Klein, and
Earle Birney. There is also a useful bibliography.

Park, Julian, ed. THE CULTURE OF CONTEMPORARY CANADA. Ithaca,
N.Y.: Cornell University Press, 1957. xv, 404 p.

A collection of essays surveying the state of culture in Canada. There is a selective bibliography, as well as a separate bibliography for the chapter on poetry and the novel.

Parker, George Lawrence. "A History of a Canadian Publishing House: A Study of the Relation between Publishing and the Profession of Writing, 1890-1940." Ph.D. thesis, University of Toronto, 1969.

Pelletier, Francine L. "The Search for Identity in Modern Canadian Poetry." M.A. thesis, University of Alberta, Edmonton, 1971.

Percival, W.P., ed. LEADING CANADIAN POETS. Toronto: Ryerson, 1948. x, 271 p.

See the entry in chapter II, section B, for commentary.

Phelps, Arthur L. CANADIAN WRITERS. Toronto: McClelland & Stewart, 1951. vii, 119 p.

A series of radio talks that attempt to be "friendly and positive without denial of literary standards." Phelps deals with E.J. Pratt, A.M. Klein, and Earle Birney in modern poetry.

Pierce, Lorne. AN OUTLINE OF CANADIAN LITERATURE (FRENCH AND ENGLISH). Toronto: Ryerson, 1927. 251 p.

A general history that includes a few critical biographies of modern Canadian writers.

Rashley, Richard Ernest. "Canadian Literature, A Survey and Evolution." M.A. thesis, University of Saskatchewan, Saskatoon, 1936.

_____. POETRY IN CANADA: THE FIRST THREE STEPS. Toronto: Ryerson, 1958. xvii, 166 p.

A sound survey of the development of Canadian poetry in English.

Rhodenizer, Vernon Blair. CANADIAN LITERATURE IN ENGLISH. Montreal: Quality Press, ca. 1965. 1,055 p.

See the entry in chapter II, section B, for commentary.

Ringrose, Christopher Xerxes. "PREVIEW: Anatomy of a Group." M.A. thesis, University of Alberta, Edmonton, 1969.

A critical history of the important magazine of the 1940's, PREVIEW.

Ross, Malcolm M., ed. THE ARTS IN CANADA. Toronto: Macmillan, 1958.

_____, ed. OUR SENSE OF IDENTITY. A BOOK OF CANADIAN ESSAYS.
Toronto: Ryerson, 1954. xii, 346 p.

> These essays, collected from books and magazines, are grouped
> under several headings: "Who We Are," "Where We Are," "The
> Two Nations," "The Larger Mosaic," "Faces and Figures," "Arts
> and Letters," and "Views and Values."

Roy, George Ross. "Symbolism in English-Canadian Poetry 1880-1939." Ph.D.
thesis, University of Montreal, 1959.

ROYAL COMMISSION STUDIES: A SELECTION OF ESSAYS PREPARED FOR
THE ROYAL COMMISSION ON NATIONAL DEVELOPMENT IN THE ARTS,
LETTERS AND SCIENCES. Ottawa: King's Printer, 1951. vii, 430 p.

> Twenty-eight studies selected from the many submitted to this
> Royal Commission. The authors were asked to shorten their origi-
> nal submissions to approximately five thousand words. The book
> stands as a document about Canadian cultural and scientific life
> as it was at the date of publication, with many suggestions in the
> essays for future developments in these areas.

Smith, A.J.M., ed. MASKS OF POETRY: CANADIAN CRITICS ON CANA-
DIAN VERSE. Toronto: McClelland & Stewart, 1962. xi, 143 p.

> The editor claims this book offers "in a conveniently portable form
> a representative sampling of critical and expository writing on Cana-
> dian poetry by Canadian scholars and men of letters from before
> Confederation to the present time." He further states that the es-
> says address themselves to what E.K. Brown has called "the prob-
> lem of a Canadian literature." About half of the essays are de-
> voted to modern English-Canadian poetry.

Stevens, Peter. "The Development of Canadian Poetry between the Wars and
Its Reflection of Social Awareness." Ph.D. thesis, University of Saskatchewan,
Saskatoon, 1968.

_____, ed. THE McGILL MOVEMENT: A.J.M. SMITH, F.R. SCOTT AND
LEO KENNEDY. Toronto: Ryerson, 1969. 146 p.

> A collection of critical essays devoted to these three writers, to-
> gether with a small selection of writings about these poets as a
> group. There is a select bibliography.

Stevenson, Lionel. APPRAISALS OF CANADIAN LITERATURE. Toronto:
Macmillan, 1926. xv, 272 p.

> Although it contains little about the poetry of the twentieth century
> in Canada, the book makes some passing references to such poets
> as E.J. Pratt, Marjorie Pickthall, Wilson MacDonald, and Tom

MacInnes. The essays in the book are on general themes such as Darwinism in Canadian poetry and the nature of Canadian literature.

Story, Norah. THE OXFORD COMPANION TO CANADIAN HISTORY AND LITERATURE. Toronto: Oxford University Press, 1967. xx, 935 p. Maps.

See entry in chapter II, section B, for commentary.

Sutherland, John. ESSAYS, CONTROVERSIES AND POEMS. Ed. with an introd. by Miriam Waddington. Toronto: McClelland & Stewart, 1972. 206 p.

John Sutherland was an important figure as editor and critic in the 1940's and 1950's. Miriam Waddington believes him to have had an authentic critical talent; these essays, she states, are still "full of fresh and living insights derived not from some over-worked academic generalization or cultural prejudice, but from the language and thought, from the words and rhythms which live and breathe in the works themselves."

The book is divided into three sections: "Opinion and Controversy," which consists of some essays of a general nature, including some of his famous replies to other critics; "Writers and Their Writing," devoted to individual, mainly modern poets; and "The Rule of Light: Poems and Sketches."

Thomas, Clara. OUR NATURE--OUR VOICES; A GUIDEBOOK TO ENGLISH-CANADIAN LITERATURE. Vol. 1. Toronto: New Press, 1972. ix, 175 p. Photographs.

See entry in chapter II, section B, for commentary.

Tisdall, Douglas Michael. "Continuity in Canadian Poetry; Some Recurrent Themes and Subjects." M.A. thesis, University of Toronto, 1961.

_____. "The Not Unfamiliar Face, a Comparative Study of the Influence of Culture, Religion and Locale in French-Canadian and English-Canadian Poetry." Ph.D. thesis, University of Toronto, 1971.

Toye, William, ed. SUPPLEMENT TO THE OXFORD COMPANION TO CANADIAN HISTORY AND LITERATURE. Toronto: Oxford University Press, 1973. v, 318 p.

Wainwright, Andy, ed. NOTES FOR A NATIVE LAND. Ottawa: Oberon Press, 1969. 155 p.

This work is a product of current Canadian nationalism. The contributors to this anthology try to define Canada in prose and poetry.

Waterston, Elizabeth. SURVEY: A SHORT HISTORY OF CANADIAN LITERATURE. Toronto: Methuen, 1973. 215 p. Photographs, illustrations.

A very interesting attempt at compiling a literary history by charting the emergence of recurrent themes in Canadian literature. Each section of the book has a very useful bibliography, and a survey chart places Canadian historical events in the context of Canadian and international literary events.

Wilson, Edmund. O CANADA: AN AMERICAN'S NOTES ON CANADIAN CULTURE. New York: Noonday Press, 1965. 245 p.

A quirky ramble through the thickets of Canadian writing by a noted American critic. Wilson devotes more space to French-Canadian writers than he does to English-Canadians, and he has little to say about twentieth-century Canadian poetry in English. He also includes speculative essays about the political situation of Quebec in relation to the rest of Canada.

Woodcock, George. ODYSSEUS EVER RETURNING, ESSAYS ON CANADIAN WRITERS AND WRITING. Introd. W.H. New. Toronto: McClelland & Stewart, 1970. xv, 158 p.

The author wishes these essays, written between 1954 and 1969, to be seen as "a developing commentary," so he has left the texts unchanged from their original appearance. He tackles fiction, nonfiction, and poetry; of particular interest are his essays on Irving Layton, Leonard Cohen, A.J.M. Smith, and Earle Birney.

_____, ed. THE SIXTIES: WRITERS AND WRITING OF THE DECADE. Vancouver: University of British Columbia Press, 1969. 138 p.

This symposium to celebrate the tenth anniversary of CANADIAN LITERATURE contains articles and a few poems by such poets as Dorothy Livesay, P.K. Page, Al Purdy, and James Reaney. It also includes separate surveys of poetry in English and of criticism. These essays originally appeared in the tenth-anniversary issue of the journal.

Chapter IV

MAJOR ANTHOLOGIES

Most anthologies cover the whole field of Canadian poetry in English, although those devoted to the twentieth century have proliferated during the last few years, keeping pace with the healthy development of modern poetry. Some anthologies surveying more than the twentieth century have been included if they have some historical importance. Anthologies assembled specifically as texts have been excluded (with one or two exceptions), although some of the volumes included are sometimes used as texts in schools and universities.

Collections of narrow range or directed at the topical tastes of a minority audience have been omitted--for example, T.O. NOW (Anansi, 1968); CANADA FIRST (Anansi, 1969); VOICES UNDERGROUND (New Press, 1972); and THE BROKEN ARK (Oberon Press, 1971), which offers Canadian poetry about animals but lacks sufficient examples to justify inclusion.

Anthologies included here, then, represent comprehensive approaches, although a few are admittedly restricted in method and approach.

Bennett, Ethel Hume, ed. NEW HARVESTING: CONTEMPORARY CANADIAN POETRY 1918-1938. Toronto: Macmillan, 1939. xi, 198 p.

> An uneven mixture of some well-known poets, some poets who had a measure of publishing success (Louise Moray Bowman, Arthur Bourinot), and some poor choices. Strangely, A.M. Klein is not represented in this book. There are brief biographical notes.

Benson, Nathaniel, ed. MODERN CANADIAN POETRY. Ottawa: Graphic, 1930. 227 p.

> An example of the anthology that refuses to have any dealings with so-called modern forms. The editor summarizes his approach as follows: "Of bizarre and grotesque affectations and practice of the ultra-modern 'isms,' a present-day mask and mockery worn by pseudo-poetry, there is no trace." Included are poems of some of the poets who operated within a rather traditional range: Audrey

Alexandra Brown, Dorothy Roberts Leisner, Charles Bruce, and Robert Finch, as well as the early, slight, imagistic poems of Dorothy Livesay.

Birney, Earle, ed. TWENTIETH CENTURY CANADIAN POETRY. Toronto: Ryerson, 1953. xvii, 169 p.

Gives a good cross-section of modern poetry in Canada. The poems are arranged in twelve sections under various subject headings. There are notes on individual poems.

Brown, Jim, and David Phillips, eds. WEST COAST SEEN. Vancouver, B.C.: Talonbooks, 1969. vii, 215 p.

Gives an overview of the younger west coast poets writing at the end of the 1960's. Includes selections, among others, by Bill Bissett, Patrick Lane, Pat Lowther, Seymour Mayne, Barry McKinnon, and Andreas Schroeder. Brown himself suggests that the range of poetry in the volume cannot lead to a narrowly limited concept of a west coast school. As he says, "There is no school of poetry, only pomes."

A CANADIAN ANTHOLOGY; POEMS FROM "THE FIDDLEHEAD," 1945-1959. Fredericton, N.B.: Fiddlehead, 1961. 76 p.

One of the longer-lived of Canadian literary magazines, the FIDDLEHEAD had an editorial board which showed an eclecticism sometimes leading to the inclusion of mediocre pieces but giving a more genuine spectrum of the current state of poetry (including work from outside Canada) than magazines with narrower editorial postures. This anthology gives a fair picture of the magazine's first fourteen years of publication.

Carman, Bliss, and Lorne Pierce, eds. OUR CANADIAN LITERATURE: REPRE-SENTATIVE VERSE, ENGLISH AND FRENCH. Toronto: Ryerson, 1934. xxvii, 361 p.

A large but generally uncritical anthology surveying literature up to the date of publication.

Carman, Bliss; Lorne Pierce; and Vernon Blair Rhodenizer, eds. CANADIAN POETRY IN ENGLISH. Rev. and enl. ed. Toronto: Ryerson, 1954. vi, 456 p.

Another somewhat uncritical anthology covering the whole genre. Contains some brief biographies of the poets represented.

Cogswell, Fred, comp. and trans. ONE HUNDRED POEMS OF MODERN QUEBEC. Fredericton, N.B.: Fiddlehead, 1970. 91 p.

_____. A SECOND HUNDRED POEMS OF MODERN QUEBEC. Fredericton, N.B.: Fiddlehead, 1971. 80 p.

These two books contain an English-Canadian poet's translation of recent French-Canadian poems.

Dudek, Louis, and Irving Layton, eds. CANADIAN POEMS 1850-1952. Rev. ed. Toronto: Contact Press, 1953. 160 p.

A somewhat polemical introductory note dismisses early poetry in Canada as a "poetry of an exhausted romanticism." The editors' claim for their anthology is that they have "preferred poems which show a dark grain of fact running through them, which are challenging and experimental, which shake up acquired prejudice and ingrained habit." The editors have included notes on individual poems.

Farmiloe, Dorothy, ed. CONTRA VERSE, NINE POETS. Windsor, Ont.: Concorde Press, 1971. x, 146 p.

Devoted to poets living in Windsor, Ontario, at the end of the 1960's (many of whom had published their own volumes), this volume includes not only Canadian writers but American Joyce Carol Oates. There are brief biographical notes and comments by the poets themselves on individual poems.

Geddes, Gary, and Phyllis Bruce, eds. 15 CANADIAN POETS. Toronto: Oxford University Press, 1970. xvi, 301 p.

A generally good selection of important Canadian poets from such older poets as Earle Birney and Irving Layton to younger poets Margaret Atwood and Michael Ondaatje. The editors have written short essays on each poet, with some bibliographic information elaborated in a section titled "Supplementary Materials."

_____. TWENTIETH CENTURY POETRY AND POETICS. Toronto: Oxford University Press, 1969. xxvi, 606 p.

Includes selections from Canadian, English, and American poets.

Gill, John, ed. NEW AMERICAN AND CANADIAN POETRY. Boston: Beacon Press, 1971. xxxvii, 280 p. Photographs.

A somewhat idiosyncratic view of worthwhile Canadian and American poets; Gill's choices come out of his editorship of the magazine NEW: AMERICAN AND CANADIAN POETRY. The editor is interested in presenting Canadian poets in North American context. He includes such well-known poets as Margaret Atwood, George Bowering, Irving Layton, John Newlove, and Alden Nowlan, as well as lesser names such as Doug Fetherling, Ray Fraser, Len Gasparini, and Ian Young. His presentation has a propagandist aim; he states, "Canadian poets are (1) fantastically good and (2) practically unknown in the States. . . . If American publishers are pretty stupid about American poets, they are literally blind to Canadian ones." There are some biographical and bibliographic notes.

Glassco, John, ed. THE POETRY OF FRENCH CANADA IN TRANSLATION. Toronto: Oxford University Press, 1970. 260 p.

The most comprehensive collection of translations of French-Canadian poetry from its beginning, rendered in the main by English-Canadian poets, many by the editor himself.

Godbout, Jacques, and John Robert Colombo, eds. POESIE/POETRY 64. Montreal: Editions du Jour; Toronto: Ryerson, 1963. 157 p.

One of the first anthologies to include some of the new experimental Canadian poetry in both English and French. The English side of the anthology features among others some of the young poets associated with the Tish group of Vancouver, British Columbia.

Granatstein, J.L., and Peter Stevens, eds. FORUM: CANADIAN LIFE AND LETTERS 1920-70: SELECTIONS FROM THE CANADIAN FORUM. Toronto: University of Toronto Press, 1972. xv, 431 p. Illustrated.

See the entry in chapter III for commentary.

Gustafson, Ralph, ed. A LITTLE ANTHOLOGY OF CANADIAN POETS. Norfolk, Conn.: New Directions, 1943. 26 p.

This anthology came out of Gustafson's work for the magazine VOICES: A QUARTERLY OF POETRY (see below, this chapter).

_____. THE PENGUIN BOOK OF CANADIAN VERSE. Rev. ed. Harmondsworth, Engl.: Penguin Books, 1967. 282 p.

One of the first to try to carry Canadian poetry beyond the boundaries of Canada, the editor originally compiled this book as a small collection, THE PELICAN BOOK OF CANADIAN POETRY, published in 1942. The book has since been enlarged and revised considerably, with an emphasis on the twentieth century.

_____. VOICES: A QUARTERLY OF POETRY, (Spring 1943), 3-43.

The first thirty pages of this issue are devoted to modern Canadian poems as an introduction for American readers.

Hambleton, Ronald, ed. UNIT OF FIVE. Toronto: Ryerson, 1944. xi, 87 p.

A good selection of the early work of five poets, all under the age of thirty at the time of publication: Louis Dudek, Ronald Hambleton, P.K. Page, Raymond Souster, and James Wreford. Each selection is preceded by a very brief biographical note.

Kirkconnell, Watson. CANADIAN OVERTONES: AN ANTHOLOGY OF CANADIAN POETRY WRITTEN ORIGINALLY IN ICELANDIC, SWEDISH, HUNGARIAN, ITALIAN, GREEK AND UKRANIAN, AND NOW TRANSLATED. Winnipeg, Man.: Columbia Press, 1935. 104 p.

Kirkconnell translated these poems as a record of the persistence of the culture of these various ethnic groups in Canada.

Klinck, Carl E., and R[eginald] E[yre] Watters, eds. CANADIAN ANTHOLOGY. Rev. ed. Toronto: Gage, 1965. xiv, 626 p.

An authoritative text by two distinguished scholars, this collection surveys the whole field of Canadian literature, both in prose and poetry. The selections of individual authors are very thorough, with biographical notes and sound bibliographies on each.

Layton, Irving, ed. LOVE WHERE THE NIGHTS ARE LONG: CANADIAN LOVE POEMS. Illus. Harold Town. Toronto: McClelland & Stewart, 1962. 78 p.

Early in his career Layton was considered something of an enfant terrible. In this volume he selected poems which he hoped would rise above the puritanism he so often berated. The illustrations for the book are by the Canadian artist Harold Town.

Livesay, Dorothy, ed. 40 WOMEN POETS. Montreal: Ingluvin, 1971. 141 p.

A good selection of practicing women poets in Canada, though the book spreads the representation so widely that little space is devoted to each poet.

Lochhead, Douglas, and Raymond Souster, eds. MADE IN CANADA: NEW POEMS OF THE SEVENTIES. Ottawa: Oberon Press, 1970. 192 p.

Compiled under the auspices of the then newly formed League of Canadian Poets, this anthology contains a good cross-section of the work of practicing poets, including many younger ones. Each poet provides autobiographical comment.

Ludwig, Jack, and Andy Wainwright, eds. SOUNDINGS: NEW CANADIAN POETS. Toronto: Anansi, 1969. 129 p.

Uneven in quality. An example of several anthologies produced by this publisher, but more eclectic in its choices than the others. This work concentrates on some younger Canadian poets, including Tom Wayman and Sid Marty.

Mandel, Eli, ed. POETS OF CONTEMPORARY CANADA 1960–1970. Toronto: McClelland & Stewart, 1972. xvi, 141 p.

Containing a good selection of "the new boundaries of contemporary poetry," this volume includes work by ten of the most well known poets writing in Canada. The editor's introduction is a sound critical summary of trends, with comments on each author. There are brief biographical notes.

Mandel, Eli, and Jean-Guy Pilon, eds. POETRY 62. Toronto: Ryerson, 1961. 116 p.

An attempt to catch the distinctive flavor of English and French poetry in Canada at that specific moment in time.

nichol, b p, ed. the cosmic chef: an evening of concrete. Ottawa: Oberon Press, 1970. 80 p. Illustrated.

A boxed set of loose leaves of concrete poetry by a wide representation of those Canadian poets who have experimented within what has been called "borderblur." In the words of the editor, these pieces come "from that point where language and/or the image blur together into the inbetween and become concrete objects."

Purdy, Al, ed. STORM WARNING: THE NEW CANADIAN POETS. Toronto: McClelland & Stewart, 1971. 152 p. Photographs.

A personal choice of younger Canadian poets by a well-known older poet. Idiosyncratic and uneven by trying to cover too wide a spectrum, the anthology shows the variety of styles and themes prevalent in Canadian poetry in the early 1970's. It also includes short personal statements by most of the poets represented.

Scott, F.R., ed. NEW PROVINCES: POEMS OF SEVERAL AUTHORS. Toronto: Macmillan, 1936. 77 p.

The most significant collection of modern poetry to be published in the 1930's in Canada, containing the work of several practitioners of the new poetry: Robert Finch, Leo Kennedy, A.M. Klein, E.J. Pratt, F.R. Scott, and A.J.M. Smith. Smith's original preface to this volume was considered too radical by Pratt and was withdrawn in favor of a short and inoffensive piece by Scott. Smith's piece was later published as "A Rejected Preface" (see under Smith in chapter VI).

Smith, A.J.M., ed. THE BOOK OF CANADIAN POETRY. Chicago: University of Chicago Press, 1943. 452 p. Rev. ed., Toronto: Gage, 1957. xxv, 532 p.

> A comprehensive selection of the whole field of Canadian poetry in English, this anthology was originally published by the University of Chicago Press in 1943 and included the editor's introduction in which he divided Canadian poetry into two strains, "native" and "cosmopolitan," a division which spawned much critical discussion and which gave rise to another anthology edited by John Sutherland (see below, this chapter). Subsequent editions of Smith's anthology have included revisions of this introduction. His book also contains brief biographical bibliographic notes.

_____. MODERN CANADIAN VERSE. Toronto: Oxford University Press, 1967. xxvi, 426 p.

> A good selection of modern Canadian poetry in English and French, though representations of some poets are rather skimpy. The brief preface defines the scope of the anthology: "This collection aims at variety, and it seeks to be representative." The editor modifies even further his twofold division of Canadian poetry (see THE BOOK OF CANADIAN POETRY, above).

_____. THE OXFORD BOOK OF CANADIAN VERSE. Toronto: Oxford University Press, 1960. lvi, 445 p.

> This anthology covers Canadian poetry in English and French from its beginnings, though much of it is devoted to the twentieth century. The editor's long introduction is a good critical summary of trends and themes in Canadian poetry.

Smith, A.J.M., and F.R. Scott, eds. THE BLASTED PINE: AN ANTHOLOGY OF SATIRE, INVECTIVE, AND DISRESPECTFUL VERSE, CHIEFLY BY CANADIAN WRITERS. Rev. and enl. ed. Toronto: Macmillan, 1967. 186 p.

> A good collection of poems in the satiric and humorous vein.

Souster, Raymond, ed. NEW WAVE CANADA. Toronto: Contact Press, 1966. vii, 172 p.

> As the last book to be published by his Contact Press, Souster chose an anthology of poetry by young poets. The book contains newer and more experimental work, with the inclusion of poets who have since achieved wider recognition, such as George Jonas, b p nichol, and Michael Ondaatje. The listing of poetry magazines is now outdated.

Sutherland, John, ed. OTHER CANADIANS: AN ANTHOLOGY OF THE NEW POETRY IN CANADA, 1940-1946. Montreal: First Statement Press, 1947. 113 p.

Sutherland issued this anthology as an alternative to Smith's THE BOOK OF CANADIAN POETRY (see above, this chapter), and in his introduction particularly takes Smith to task for his generalizations about Canadian poetry. Sutherland tends toward a Marxist interpretation. His choice of poets is, in general, very sound.

Toye, William, ed. A BOOK OF CANADA. Toronto: Collins, 1962. 416 p.

This "partial portrait of a country" (the editor's summary) concentrates more on prose, though it contains some poems on the Canadian themes around which the anthology is organized.

Wall, Ann, ed. MINDSCAPES. Toronto: Anansi, 1971. 136 p.

Another of the anthologies produced by this new publishing company (see above, this chapter, under Ludwig). This one is the most successful because it concentrates on the work of four young and developing Canadian poets: Dale Zieroth, Paulene Jiles, Susan Musgrave, and Tom Wayman. Contains very brief biographical entries.

Weaver, Robert, ed. THE FIRST FIVE YEARS: A SELECTION FROM THE TAMARACK REVIEW. Introd. Robert Fulford. Toronto: Oxford University Press, 1962. 360 p.

TAMARACK REVIEW, one of Canada's leading literary magazines, published many of Canada's best writers. This anthology concentrates on prose, but includes some pieces by well-known poets as well as a critical article by Milton Wilson.

Wilson, Milton, ed. POETRY OF MIDCENTURY 1940-1960. Toronto: McClelland & Stewart, 1964. xvi, 237 p.

A perspicacious introduction explains how the editor came to choose the ten poets in this anthology--six poets whose work really began in the 1940's, four who emerged in the 1950's. This is a splendid representation of the poetry of this period, though two of the poets have not fulfilled their promise (Jay MacPherson and Kenneth McRobbie) and the work of two other poets has developed in directions not suggested by the anthology (James Reaney and Alden Nowlan). The editor's biographical introductions are good.

_____. POETS BETWEEN THE WARS. Toronto: McClelland & Stewart, 1967. x, 196 p.

An admirable companion volume to Wilson's POETRY OF MID-CENTURY 1940-1960 (see above) featuring the five dominant modern poets of the 1920's and 1930's in Canada: E.J. Pratt, F.R. Scott, A.J.M. Smith, Dorothy Livesay, and A.M. Klein.

_____. TO EVERY THING THERE IS A SEASON: ROLOFF BENY IN CANADA. Toronto: Longmans, 1967. 324 p. Photographs, maps, line drawings.

A magnificent evocation of Canada through the photographs of Roloff Beny with writings, mainly poems, selected by Milton Wilson.

Yates, J. Michael, ed. CONTEMPORARY POETRY OF BRITISH COLUMBIA. Port Clements, B.C.: Sono Nis Press, 1970. xv, 252 p.

Offers a wide but uneven selection of poetry written by poets living in British Columbia or closely associated with that province. This was intended as the first of a continuing series, but no other volume has appeared as yet.

_____. VOLVOX: POETRY FROM THE UNOFFICIAL LANGUAGES OF CANADA . . . IN ENGLISH TRANSLATION. Port Clements, B.C.: Sono Nis Press, 1971. 256 p.

A wide variety of representative poets writing in other languages is included, along with some poets who are now writing in English in Canada: George Faludy, Walter Bauer, Robert Zend, and Andreas Schroeder.

Chapter V

PERIODICALS

Literary and academic journals, little magazines, ephemeral series, and assorted pamphlets have played a significant part in the development of poetry in Canada during the twentieth century. Many of them cover a wide area of subject matter and devote much space to prose. The brief annotations below try to indicate the scope of the publications and their importance in English-Canadian poetry.

ALPHABET: A SEMI-ANNUAL DEVOTED TO THE ICONOGRAPHY OF THE IMAGINATION. London, Ont. Nos. 1-17, 1960-69. Ceased publication with no. 18/19, June 1971. Absorbed WATERLOO REVIEW in July 1961.

> The brainchild of poet James Reaney, this magazine's issues centered around individual themes and their extensions into myth. It printed poetry and critical articles. A short article by Margaret Atwood, "Eleven Years of ALPHABET" (CANADIAN LITERATURE, no. 49 [Summer 1971], pp. 60-64), gives a succinct summary of the life and themes of the magazine.

ANOTHER POETRY MAGAZINE. Toronto. No. 1-- . 1970-- .

> Occasionally issued, devoted to Canadian poetry. Originally edited by poet Dale Zieroth.

ANTIGONISH REVIEW. Antigonish, N.S. Vol. 1-- . 1970-- .

> Associated with St. Francis Xavier University, this quarterly journal offers a mixed bag of poetry, fiction, criticism, and reviews, both from Canadian and other sources.

THE ANT'S FOREFOOT. Toronto. No. 1-- . 1967-- .

> Devoted to experimental poetry principally out of the ideas of Charles Olson, Robert Duncan, and poets generally associated with them, this magazine features an unusual but attractive format. The poems are largely Canadian and American.

Periodicals

ARIEL: A REVIEW OF INTERNATIONAL ENGLISH LITERATURE. Calgary, Alta. Vol. 1-- . 1970-- .

> Occasionally features an issue devoted to Canadian prose and poetry. Includes both critical and creative writing.

B.C. LIBRARY QUARTERLY. Vancouver, B.C. Vol. 1-- . 1937-- .

> Occasionally features critical articles on Canadian authors.

BLACKFISH. Vancouver, B.C. No. 1-- . 1971-- .

> An interesting occasional magazine, with Canadian poems and review articles on Canadian poets. Also issues attractive but expensive portfolios of poems by Canadian authors, most notably Dorothy Livesay and Pat Lowther.

BLACK MOSS. Windsor, Ont. Vol. 1-- . 1969-- .

> Spasmodic issues include Canadian poetry. Occasionally issues chapbooks by Canadian poets, notably Bill Bissett. OTHER MATTER, an anthology of poems from the magazine, was published in 1970.

BLEW OINTMENT. Vancouver, B.C. No. 1-- . 1963-- .

> The most outrageously experimental poetry magazine in Canada, organized by Bill Bissett. Features concrete and sound poetry, adventurous poems by younger poets, and poetry by established authors. Issues are sometimes devoted to a specific subject. Bissett also runs the Blew Ointment Press which issues the same kinds of poetry by individual poets, including himself. Mimeographed and often difficult to read.

BOOKS IN CANADA. Toronto. Vol. 1-- . 1971-- .

> An attempt to produce a monthly review magazine. Very spotty, somewhat journalistic, allowing little space for individual reviews. Nevertheless, the only magazine of its kind in Canada.

BULLETIN OF THE HUMANITIES ASSOCIATION OF CANADA. Vol. 1-- . 1954-- .

> Reprints academic papers from various disciplines. In recent years it has been taken over by the Association of Canadian University Teachers of English and has published more literary articles, including some on Canadian literature. This journal is now called the HUMANITIES ASSOCIATION REVIEW. The place of publication changes to the location of the officers of the association.

CANADIAN AUTHOR AND BOOKMAN. Toronto. Vol. 1-43 [?]. 1922-68.
Suspended publication August 1941-November 1942.

> Formed by the union of the CANADIAN AUTHOR and the CANA-
> DIAN BOOKMAN. In 1968 it merged with CANADIAN POETRY,
> and publication continues under the title CANADIAN AUTHOR
> AND BOOKMAN AND CANADIAN POETRY (see below).
>
> The organ of the Canadian Authors' Association, very uneven in
> quality. Spasmodically includes a few good poems, but in general
> it is interesting only for the strange light it throws on the com-
> mercial market through its helpful hints to writers.

CANADIAN AUTHOR AND BOOKMAN AND CANADIAN POETRY. Toronto.
1968-- .

> Formed by the merger of CANADIAN AUTHOR AND BOOKMAN
> and CANADIAN POETRY. See entries under those titles.

CANADIAN FORUM. AN INDEPENDENT JOURNAL OF OPINION AND THE
ARTS. Toronto. Vol. 1-- . 1920-- .

> An established monthly of political and social comment, but also
> including poetry and review articles on Canadian literature. It
> has had a series of distinguished literary editors, among whom
> have been Earle Birney, Northrop Frye, and Milton Wilson. In
> 1972 an anthology of its first fifty years was published: FORUM:
> CANADIAN LIFE AND LETTERS 1920-70 (see entry under J.L.
> Granatstein in chapter III).

CANADIAN LIBRARY JOURNAL. Ottawa. Vol. 27-- . 1970-- .

> Continues CANADIAN LIBRARY, volumes 1-26, 1944-69. Contains
> occasional articles on topics related to Canadian literature.

CANADIAN LITERATURE. Vancouver, B.C. No. 1-- . 1959-- .

> The premier critical quarterly devoted exclusively to all aspects
> of Canadian literature. Principally in English, though it includes
> some articles in French about Quebec writing.

CANADIAN MAGAZINE. Toronto. Vols. 1-63. 1893-1939.

> Carried the title CANADIAN MAGAZINE OF POLITICS, SCIENCE,
> ART AND LITERATURE from 1893 to 1925. Somewhat journalistic,
> this magazine contains some articles of general interest on Cana-
> dian authors.

CANADIAN MERCURY. Montreal. Vol. 1. 1928-29.

> A short-lived attempt to produce a lively political-literary maga-

zine, killed off by the advent of the depression. Some of the writers associated with the McGILL FORTNIGHTLY REVIEW contributed to this magazine.

CANADIAN NOTES AND QUERIES. See entry in chapter II, section A.

CANADIAN POETRY. Toronto. Vols. 1-31. 1936-68.

Merged in 1968 with CANADIAN AUTHOR AND BOOKMAN to form CANADIAN AUTHOR AND BOOKMAN AND CANADIAN POETRY.

Began as a serious attempt to be a forum of contemporary poetry in Canada under the sponsorship of the Canadian Authors' Association, but it restricted the editors too severely, rapidly deteriorated, and became a medium mainly for the publication of very ordinary verse.

CATAPULT. Montreal. Nos. 1-2. 1964-65.

A short-lived poetry magazine used principally as a medium for younger poets living in Montreal at the time. It superseded another short-lived magazine, CATARACT.

CIV/n. Montreal. Nos. 1-7. 1953-54.

Has similar interests to COMBUSTION and CONTACT (see below). See INDEX TO CIV/n in chapter II, section C.

COMBUSTION. Toronto. Nos. 1-15. 1957-60.

An important little magazine of newer trends in poetry. One further issue was published in 1966 in conjunction with the magazine ISLAND (see below, this chapter).

CONTACT. Toronto. Nos. 1-10. 1952-54.

Probably the most significant attempt in the 1950's to show Canadian poetry in the context of new ideas in the North American press. Out of this little magazine arose Contact Press, the single most important publisher of contemporary poetry in Canada between 1956 and 1967. See CONTACT 1952-1954; BEING AN INDEX TO THE CONTENTS OF CONTACT, cited in chapter II, section C.

CONTEMPORARY VERSE. A CANADIAN QUARTERLY. Victoria, B.C. Nos. 1-39. 1941-52.

An important magazine which published many of the poets whose work was part of the blossoming of Canadian poetry during the 1940's.

COPPERFIELD: AN INDEPENDENT CANADIAN LITERARY MAGAZINE OF THE LAND AND THE NORTH. Vol. 1-- . 1969-- .

The subtitle suggests the nature of this spasmodically appearing magazine of poems and prose.

CULTURE: REVUE TRIMESTRIELLE, SCIENCES RELIGIEUSES ET SCIENCES PROFANES AU CANADA. Quebec City, Que. Vols. 1-31. 1940-70.

Contains good critical articles and reviews on all aspects of Canadian literature written in both English and French.

DALHOUSIE REVIEW. Halifax, N.S. Vol. 1-- . 1923-- .

An academic quarterly of Dalhousie University which publishes articles covering a wide variety of subject matter. It includes some literary criticism devoted to Canadian poetry. A few poems appear in each issue.

DELTA: A MAGAZINE OF POETRY AND CRITICISM. Montreal. Nos. 1-24. 1957-66.

Interesting and lively poetry magazine guided by poet Louis Dudek. From this enterprise arose Delta Press which published poetry books by individual authors quite regularly through the late 1960's and early 1970's and less regularly up to the present.

DIALOG. Toronto. Vol. 1-- . 1970-- .

Edited by poet Joe Rosenblatt, this magazine features fiction and poetry chiefly by Canadian writers. Format is confusing, with advertisements appearing side by side with poems, but the literary content is good. There are occasional special issues on selected topics or writers.

DIRECTION. Outremont, Que. Nos. 1-10. 1945-46.

A small mimeographed magazine under the general editorship of Raymond Souster.

EDGE: AN INDEPENDENT PERIODICAL. Edmonton, Alta. Nos. 1-9. 1963-69.

A journal that attempted controversy and antiestablishment comment, together with fiction and poetry. Edited with originality by poet Henry Beissel.

ELLIPSE. Sherbrooke, Que. No. 1-- . 1969-- .

A quarterly devoted to the interchange of poetry, fiction, and
criticism of English- and French-Canadian literature, concentrating
on contemporary writing in bilingual translations.

EVIDENCE. Toronto. Nos. 1-10. 1959-67.

A good literary magazine concentrating on some of the newer
names of the 1960's.

EXILE. Toronto. Vol. 1-- . 1972-- .

An attempt to focus on contemporary writing in Canada and abroad,
with no critical articles.

FAR POINT. Winnipeg, Man. No. 1-- . 1968-- .

Includes fiction, poetry, and criticism mainly in the field of
contemporary Canadian and American literature.

FIDDLEHEAD. Fredericton, N.B. No. 1-- . 1945-- .

One of the longest-lived literary magazines of English Canada,
starting with small mimeographed issues. This magazine has an
eclectic editorial choice of fiction and poetry, the work mainly
of Canadian and American writers. See also A CANADIAN
ANTHOLOGY; POEMS FROM "THE FIDDLEHEAD," cited in
chapter IV.

FIRST STATEMENT. Montreal. Vols. 1-6. 1942-47.

A very important magazine in the renaissance of English-Canadian
poetry in the 1940's, often at odds with PREVIEW (see below, this
chapter). Edited by John Sutherland.

GANGLIA. Toronto. Series 1, nos. 1-7, 1965-67; Series 2, no. 1-- .
1971-- .

A randomly issued series, edited by b p nichol and featuring con-
crete poetry and writing within the ambience of "the language
revolution."

GANTS DU CIEL. Montreal. Nos. 1-12. 1943-46.

A magazine of criticism that occasionally ran essays on English-
Canadian poetry.

grOnk. Toronto. No. 1-- . 1967-- .

One of b p nichol's spasmodically issued, mimeographed pamphlet magazines devoted in the main to concrete poetry.

HERE AND NOW. Toronto. Nos. 1-2. 1948-49.

A very short-lived literary journal of prose and poetry, containing important work by some English-Canadian writers. Some of that work has never been republished.

HUMANITIES ASSOCIATION REVIEW. See BULLETIN OF THE HUMANITIES ASSOCIATION OF CANADA.

IMAGO. Calgary, Alta. Nos. 1-20. 1964-73.

A magazine devoted to the long poem or poetic sequence, edited by George Bowering. Some issues concentrated on single authors and poems: Lionel Kearns's LISTEN GEORGE, Frank Davey's THE SCARRED HULL, and George Bowering's SITTING IN MEXICO.

IMPULSE. Toronto. No. 1-- . 1971-- .

Devoted exclusively to Canadian writing, this magazine features the work of both new and established writers in prose, poetry, and criticism.

INGLUVIN. Montreal. No. 1. 1970.

A very short-lived poetry magazine edited by Seymour Mayne. It gave rise to Ingluvin Press.

INSCAPE: A QUARTERLY REVIEW OF LITERATURE AND LITERARY CRITICISM. Ottawa. No. 1-- . 1959-- .

Starting as a somewhat local journal, this publication has published some rather recondite essays on literary-technical matters, but in recent years has put more emphasis on poetry.

IS. Toronto. Vol. 1--. 1966-- .

A small offshoot of ISLAND (see below).

ISLAND. Toronto. No. 1-- . 1964-- .

Devoted to new and experimental poetry, this magazine is edited by poet Victor Coleman. A number of issues were entirely devoted to individual poets.

JOURNAL OF CANADIAN STUDIES. REVUE D'ETUDES CANADIENNES. Peterborough, Ont. Vol. 1-- . 1966-- .

An academic journal from Trent University which publishes occasional critical pieces on Canadian literature.

JOURNAL OF COMMONWEALTH LITERATURE. Leeds, Engl. Vol. 1-- .
1965-- .

> Publishes some critical articles on Canadian literature. Some
> issues contain annual bibliographies (see entry under journal title
> in chapter II, section A).

LAKEHEAD UNIVERSITY REVIEW. Thunder Bay (formerly Port Arthur), Ont.
Vol. 1-- . 1968-- .

> An academic journal publishing articles from a wide variety of
> disciplines, including literary studies. It also includes some poems,
> and on occasions devotes a whole issue to Canadian topics.

McGILL FORTNIGHTLY REVIEW. Montreal. Vols. 1-2. 1925-27.

> A formative influence in the development of modern Canadian
> poetry, the FORTNIGHTLY was a university magazine run princi-
> pally by poets A.J.M. Smith and F.R. Scott and publishing their
> early poems (under a variety of pseudonyms) and critical articles.
> Another poet, Earle Birney, has suggested that this short-lived re-
> view was "eventually to influence, by stimulus or reaction, most
> of what poetry has succeeded it in the country."

MAINLINE. Windsor, Ont. No. 1-- . 1967-- .

> A spasmodically issued poetry magazine, published in a variety
> of formats.

MALAHAT REVIEW. Victoria, B.C. No. 1-- . 1967-- .

> Concentrates on writing from many countries, both prose and
> poetry. Often includes reproductions of paintings.

NEW: AMERICAN AND CANADIAN POETRY. No. 1-- . 1966-- .

> An interesting attempt to show a perspective of North American
> poetry. This magazine gave rise to the anthology of the same
> name (see chapter IV under John Gill, ed.). It also runs occa-
> sional special issues, the most notable showing the response of
> French-Canadian poets to the Quebec Crisis of October 1970.

NEW FRONTIER. Toronto. Vols. 1-2. 1936-37.

> A left-wing periodical which included some essential critical
> articles and some radical poetry of the 1930's.

NORTHERN JOURNEY. Ottawa. No. 1-- . 1972-- .

A lively, at times juvenile and controversial, literary magazine in the new militant-nationalist mold. Irregular publication.

NORTHERN REVIEW. Toronto. Vols. 1-7. 1946-56.

Probably the most consistently readable and significant literary review in English Canada. Under the editorship of John Sutherland, this magazine was the result of the merging of FIRST STATEMENT, PREVIEW (see separate entries for these magazines in this chapter), and the CANADIAN REVIEW OF MUSIC AND ART.

OPEN LETTER. Toronto. Series 1, nos. 1-9, 1966-69; Series 2, no. 1-- . 1971-- .

A somewhat polemical journal which invites exchange of ideas and includes some poetry and reviews.

PREVIEW. Montreal. Vols. 1-4. 1942-45.

A literary magazine with left-wing leanings, started by poet Patrick Anderson. It tended to concentrate on the work of a few poets. See the M.A. thesis about this magazine and its writers by Christopher Ringrose, cited in chapter III.

PRISM INTERNATIONAL. Vancouver, B.C. Vol. 1-- . 1959-- .

A magazine associated with the creative writing department at the University of British Columbia. As its name suggests, it publishes work from outside Canada. In recent years it has tended to concentrate on rather derivative work based on eastern European and Germanic models.

QUARRY. Kingston, Ont. No. 1-- . 1952-- .

Originally started as a student publication at Queen's University, this has now become one of the best little magazines of poetry in English Canada.

QUEEN'S QUARTERLY. Kingston, Ont. Vol. 1-- . 1893-- .

One of the longest-established academic journals in Canada, it publishes articles and reviews on various topics. Each issue includes a few poems and occasional short stories along with critical articles.

QUILL & QUIRE. Toronto. Vol. 1-- . 1935-- .

This publication of booksellers contains short uneven reviews in each issue, with occasional articles of a general nature about Canadian books and publishing.

ROYAL SOCIETY OF CANADA. PROCEEDINGS AND TRANSACTIONS. 3rd Series, vol. 1-- . 1921-- .

Obviously covers a whole range of topics but occasionally includes some literary papers.

SALT. Moose Jaw, Sask. No. 1-- . 1969-- .

A lively, mimeographed little magazine of poetry. It has included some interesting autobiographical material of Canadian poets.

SATURDAY NIGHT. Toronto. Vol. 1-- . 1887-- .

Canada's oldest established monthly magazine, it has in recent years included two or three poems in each issue. An anthology derived from it (A SATURDAY NIGHT SCRAPBOOK, ed. Morris Wolfe, New Press, 1973) concentrates on aspects of social history and trivia.

STUFFED CROCODILE. London, Ont. No. 1-- . 1973-- .

A small mimeographed poetry magazine, each issue of which concentrates on the work of three or four poets. The magazine is complemented by a series of chapbooks, each devoted to the work of one poet.

TALON. Vancouver, B.C. Vols. 1-5. 1964-71.

A lively poetry magazine from the west coast. It developed into Talonbooks, a small press concentrating on poetry and drama.

TAMARACK REVIEW. Toronto. No. 1-- . 1956-- .

Generally regarded as English Canada's most prestigious literary magazine, it has sometimes been accused of being too conservative, too much an establishment publication. See also entry in chapter IV under Robert Weaver, for the TAMARACK REVIEW anthology.

TISH. Vancouver, B.C. No. 1-- . 1962-- .

Often smudged, occasionally unreadable, this is a seminal magazine associated with the new movement in poetry on the west coast. It saw the first publication of such poets as George Bowering, Frank Davey, and Lionel Kearns. See also the entry under Beverley Jean Mitchell in chapter III.

TUATARA. Victoria, B.C. No. 1-- . 1969-- .

Edited by poet Mike Doyle, this magazine shows an interesting

mixture of Canadian and American poetry, especially in the
Williams-Olson mold.

UNIVERSITY OF TORONTO QUARTERLY. Toronto. Vol. 1-- . 1931-- .

Another academic journal with a wide spectrum of critical essays
on all areas of literature. The QUARTERLY is of particular in-
terest to students of Canadian literature for its section titled
"Letters in Canada," a critical survey of the creative and criti-
cal works published each year in Canada. See also the entry under
chapter II, section A.

UNIVERSITY OF WINDSOR REVIEW. Windsor, Ont. Vol. 1-- . 1965-- .

An academic journal which has a little more fiction and poetry
than most others of its kind. Sometimes includes photographs and
reproductions of drawings and paintings.

WASCANA REVIEW. Regina, Sask. Vol. 1-- . 1966-- .

Associated with the University of Saskatchewan, this journal
features short stories and poetry as well as critical essays on
literature.

WHITE PELICAN. Edmonton, Alta. Vol. 1-- . 1971-- .

This magazine operates under a kind of rotating editorship, and
each editor is free to choose a topic around which the contents
of an issue are gathered. It usually contains illustrations and
photographs. The magazine has also produced occasional chap-
books of poetry, most notably by Wilfred Watson and Miriam
Mandel.

YES. Montreal. Vol. 1-- . 1956-- .

Becoming very irregular in publication in its later years, this
magazine of poetry and literary criticism is associated with the
Montreal school under Louis Dudek. Dudek has become a kind
of conservative patriarch of a poetry derived from Pound.

Chapter VI

THE BEGINNINGS: 1900-1940

In this chapter the entries under each individual author are arranged in three sections. The first two sections, poetry and prose, list the primary works of the author in chronological order; the third section lists criticism about the author in alphabetical order. Collections edited by the author are listed under Prose.

BAILEY, ALFRED GOLDSWORTHY (1905-)

Bailey is a historian and anthropologist and has written scholarly monographs and articles in these disciplines. His concerns with roots, race, place, and the past inform his poetry, which is written in a rather uneven mixture of the modern and traditional. Sometimes a tone from Eliot appears, as well as imagistic notations. Too often his diction becomes quirky and archaic, so that a clutter of rhetoric obscures the genuine pulse of his poetry which is occasionally lightened by flashes of dry humor. He has a Maritimer's feel for the sea; though born in Quebec, he has lived most of his adult life in New Brunswick. He was a cofounder of the important magazine the FIDDLEHEAD. There has been little critical work on his poetry, though it is a good example of that peculiar mode of transition between tradition and modernism.

1. Poetry

SONGS OF THE SAGUENAY AND OTHER POEMS. Quebec: Chronicle-Telegraph, 1927. 34 p.

TAO. Toronto: Ryerson, 1930. 8 p.

BORDER RIVER. Toronto: McClelland & Stewart, 1952. 61 p.

THANKS FOR A DROWNED ISLAND. Toronto: McClelland & Stewart, 1973. 96 p.

A selection spanning Bailey's poetic career.

2. Criticism

Beattie, [A.] Munro. "Poetry 1935-1950." In LITERARY HISTORY OF CANADA; CANADIAN LITERATURE IN ENGLISH. Ed. Carl F. Klinck et al. Toronto: University of Toronto Press, 1965, pp. 757-59.

Frye, Northrop. "From 'Letters in Canada.'" In his THE BUSH GARDEN: ESSAYS ON THE CANADIAN IMAGINATION. Toronto: Anansi, 1971, pp. 17-18.

A brief review of BORDER RIVER in which Frye asserts that Bailey is in "the front rank of Canadian poets."

BOURINOT, ARTHUR STANLEY (1893-1969)

Arthur Bourinot was one of the first practitioners of free verse in Canada, though he did not rid himself of the leftovers of an English Victorian conscious- ness in most of his poetry. The references to Canadian place and past are never more than obvious, for the diction and form are usually imitative of En- glish romanticism. His books also contain ringing paeans to some Canadian heroes, but these poems rarely rise above patriotic mush. His significance may well be measured not by his poetry but by his editing (somewhat haphazard) of the correspondence of Canadian writers of the close of the nineteenth century, particularly the correspondence he coedited with D.C. Scott. Both showed a much more thorough and sympathetic understanding of the newer forms in Bouri- not's poetry, even though Scott himself remains more closely associated with nineteenth-century Canadian poetry than Bourinot.

1. Poetry

LAURENTIAN LYRICS AND OTHER POEMS. Toronto: Copp Clark, 1915. 30 p.

POEMS. Toronto: Best, 1921. 47 p.

LYRICS FROM THE HILLS. Ottawa: Hope, 1923. 40 p.

PATTERING FEET; A BOOK OF CHILDHOOD VERSES. Ottawa: Graphic, 1925. 77 p.

OTTAWA LYRICS AND VERSES FOR CHILDREN. Ottawa: Graphic, 1929. 71 p.

SONNETS IN MEMORY OF MY MOTHER. Ottawa: Hope, 1931. 18 p.

SELECTED POEMS (1915-1935). Note by Sir Andrew Macphail. Toronto: Macmillan, 1935. 90 p.

ELEVEN POEMS. Ottawa: Author, 1937. 9 p.

LASALLE. WRITTEN ON THE 250TH ANNIVERSARY. Ottawa: Author, 1937. 4 p.
> A revised version was published in RHYMES OF THE FRENCH REGIME, below.

RHYMES OF THE FRENCH REGIME. Toronto: Nelson, 1937. 44 p.

UNDER THE SUN. Toronto: Macmillan, 1939. 69 p.

DISCOVERY. Toronto: Ryerson, 1940. 11 p.

WHAT FAR KINGDOM. Toronto: Ryerson, 1941. 66 p.

CANADA AT DIEPPE. Toronto: Ryerson, 1942. 16 p.

FIVE POEMS. Toronto: Ryerson, 1943. 8 p.

NINE POEMS. Toronto: Ryerson, 1944. 12 p.

TRUE HARVEST. Toronto: Ryerson, 1945. 56 p.

LINES FROM DEEPWOOD. Toronto: Heaton Printing, 1946. 8 p.

THE COLLECTED POEMS. Toronto: Ryerson, 1947. 222 p.

MORE LINES FROM DEEPWOOD. Toronto: Shepard Printing, 1949. 16 p.

THE TREASURES OF THE SNOW. Toronto: Ryerson, 1950. 16 p.

THIS GREEN EARTH. Gananoque, Ont.: Author, 1953. 52 p.

TOM THOMSON AND OTHER POEMS. Toronto: Ryerson, 1954. 10 p.

EVERYTHING ON EARTH MUST DIE. Ottawa: Author, 1955. 3 p.

TEN NARRATIVE POEMS. Ottawa: Author, 1955. 32 p.

A GATHERING. Ottawa: Author, 1958. 14 p.

PAUL BUNYAN, THREE LINCOLN POEMS, AND OTHER VERSE. Ottawa: Author, 1961. 40 p.

HARVEST FROM DEEPWOOD (POEMS 1962). Ottawa: Author, 1962. Unpaged.

TO AND FRO IN THE EARTH (POEMS 1963). Ottawa: Author, 1963. 37 p.

JOHN DONNE WAS RIGHT; POEMS, 1964. Ottawa: Author, 1964. 33 p.

HE WHO HAS LOOKED ON BEAUTY; SIX POEMS, 1965. Ottawa: Author, 1965. 8 p.

2. Prose

"An Editor's Notebook." CANADIAN POETRY, 14 (Spring 1951), 24-28.

FIVE CANADIAN POETS: DUNCAN CAMPBELL SCOTT, ARCHIBALD LAMPMAN, WILLIAM E. MARSHALL, CHARLES SANGSTER, GEORGE FREDERICK CAMERON. Ottawa: Author, 1954. 26 p. Rev. ed., Montreal: Quality, 1956. 26 p.

"George Frederick Cameron--Some Notes on His Opera and His Life." CANADIAN AUTHOR AND BOOKMAN, 29 (Winter 1954), 3-5.

"A Neglected Field in Canadian Literature." CANADIAN FORUM, 34 (December 1954), 198-99.

EDWARD WILLIAM THOMSON (1849-1924). A BIBLIOGRAPHY WITH NOTES AND SOME LETTERS. Ottawa: Author, 1955. 28 p.

THE QUICK AND THE DEAD. VIEWS AND REVIEWS ON POETRY. Ottawa: Author, 1955. 21 p.

Ed. ARCHIBALD LAMPMAN'S LETTERS TO EDWARD WILLIAM THOMSON (1890-1898). Ottawa: Author, 1956. 74 p.

> Contains an introduction, annotations, bibliography with notes, and Lampman's essay on happiness.

Ed. THE LETTERS OF EDWARD WILLIAM THOMSON TO ARCHIBALD LAMP-
MAN (1891-1897). Ottawa: Author, 1957. 49 p.

> Contains notes, bibliography, and other material on Thomson and
> Lampman.

Ed. AT THE MERMAID INN, CONDUCTED BY A. LAMPMAN, W.W. CAMP-
BELL, DUNCAN C. SCOTT. BEING SELECTIONS FROM ESSAYS WHICH AP-
PEARED IN THE TORONTO "GLOBE," 1892-1893. Ottawa: Author, 1958.
96 p.

Ed. SOME LETTERS OF DUNCAN CAMPBELL SCOTT, ARCHIBALD LAMPMAN
AND OTHERS. Ottawa: Author, 1959. 63 p.

Ed. MORE LETTERS OF DUNCAN CAMPBELL SCOTT, ARCHIBALD LAMPMAN
AND OTHERS. Ottawa: Author, 1960. 104 p.

> Includes some personal recollections by Bourinot.

3. Criticism

King, Amabel. "New Editor for 'Poetry Magazine.'" CANADIAN AUTHOR
AND BOOKMAN, 24 (June 1948), 16-17.

Martin, Burns. "Arthur S. Bourinot." EDUCATIONAL RECORD (QUEBEC), 63
(October-December 1947), 225-31.

Pomeroy, Elsie. "The Sonnets of Arthur S. Bourinot." DALHOUSIE REVIEW,
29 (October 1949), 310-13.

BROWN, AUDREY ALEXANDRA (1904-   )

Audrey Alexandra Brown is a thoroughgoing romanticist, probably the best ex-
ample in Canadian poetry of the persistence of the influence of English romanti-
cism well into the twentieth century. She is the Canadian equivalent, perhaps,
of the minor poets of the English Georgian group. Her poetry makes no con-
cessions to modernism; her poems derive mainly from Keatsian modes and are
technically adroit. Pelham Edgar, a sound academic critic, in his preface to
A DRYAD IN NANAIMO, called her long Keatsian poem "Laodamia" "one of
the most beautiful decorative narrative poems that has come out of America."
The word "decorative" here gives the clue to the strength and weakness of this
poet's work.

1. Poetry

A DRYAD IN NANAIMO. Pref. Pelham Edgar. Toronto: Macmillan, 1931.

vi, 70 p. Rev. ed. with new poems, Toronto: Macmillan, 1934. 120 p.

THE TREE OF RESURRECTION AND OTHER POEMS. Toronto: Macmillan, 1937. 151 p.

CHALLENGE TO TIME AND DEATH. Toronto: Macmillan, 1943. 55 p.

V-E DAY. Toronto: Ryerson, 1947. 5 p.

ALL FOOL'S DAY. Toronto: Ryerson, 1948. 56 p.

2. Prose

THE LOG OF A LAME DUCK. Toronto: Macmillan, 1938. 292 p.

POETRY AND LIFE. AN ADDRESS. Toronto: Macmillan, 1941. 10 p.

3. Criticism

Burrell, Martin. "Audrey Alexandra Brown." In his CRUMBS ARE ALSO BREAD. Toronto: Macmillan, 1934, pp. 313-27.

Clarke, George Herbert. "Audrey Alexandra Brown." EDUCATIONAL RECORD (Quebec), 60 (October-December 1944), 230-33. Rpt. in LEADING CANADIAN POETS. Ed. W.P. Percival. Toronto: Ryerson, 1948, pp. 30-36.

MacKay, L.A. "Audrey Alexandra Brown." CANADIAN FORUM, 12 (June 1932), 342-43.

BRUCE, CHARLES TORY (1906-71)

Charles Bruce's poetry is filled with a direct and honest treatment of themes, mainly of the Maritimes, written with an unpretentious realism. He presents his scenes with descriptive detail without overloading the poems. He retains a feeling for the use of traditional forms, but at times his poetry falls flat and the rhythmic pulse becomes flabby. His writing fits into the category which some critics have suggested is a peculiarly Canadian genre: the documentary poem. Wilfred Gibson, in his introduction to GREY SHIP MOVING, summarizes Bruce's poetry as being "uncontaminated by the contagion of cosmopolitan obscurantism."

1. Poetry

WILD APPLES. Sackville, N.B.: Tribune Press, 1927. 23 p.

TOMORROW'S TIDE. Toronto: Macmillan, 1932. 28 p.

PERSONAL NOTE. Toronto: Ryerson, 1941. 8 p.

GREY SHIP MOVING. Introd. Wilfred Gibson. Toronto: Ryerson, 1945. vii, 34 p.

THE FLOWERING SUMMER. Toronto: Ryerson, 1947. 31 p. Illustrated.

THE MULGRAVE ROAD. Toronto: Macmillan, 1951. 39 p.
    Contains some poems from GREY SHIP MOVING.

2. Prose

THE CHANNEL SHORE. Toronto: Macmillan, 1954. 398 p.

THE TOWNSHIP OF TIME. A CHRONICLE. Toronto: Macmillan, 1959. 234 p.
    Related short stories about a Nova Scotia family during the years 1786 and 1950.

NEWS AND THE SOUTHAMS. Toronto: Macmillan, 1968. vii, 429 p. Illustrated.
    History of the family which started and continues a newspaper empire in Canada.

3. Criticism

Beattie, [A.] Munro. "Poetry 1935-1950." In LITERARY HISTORY OF CANADA; CANADIAN LITERATURE IN ENGLISH. Ed. Carl F. Klinck et al. Toronto: University of Toronto Press, 1965, pp. 756-57.

Haughton, Kathryn Parker. "John Frederic Herbin and Charles Tory Bruce; Two Generations of Regional Literature." M.A. thesis, University of New Brunswick, Fredericton, 1970.

COATES, ALICE CAROL (? -)

Carol Coates, only a minor figure in twentieth-century Canadian poetry, brings into her work a feeling for imagism derived from her early life in Japan rather than from the North American experience. W.H. New suggests (see citation in section 3, Criticism, below) that her genuine talent became obscured by her confusion between the significance of form and the demands of content.

1. Poetry

FANCY FREE. Toronto: Ryerson, 1939. 15 p.

THE RETURN AND SELECTED POEMS. Toronto: Caronell Press, 1941. 34 p.

INVITATION TO MOOD. Toronto: Ryerson, 1949. 54 p.

2. Prose

SHANLING; OR THE TALE OF THE CELESTIAL TEAPOT. A CHRISTMAS FANTASY. Oakville, Ont.: Barber, 1944. 13 p.

THE JADE HEART. New York: Junior Leagues of America, 1946.

3. Criticism

New, W.H. "Carol Coates Cassidy and the Form Dispute." CANADIAN LITERATURE, 48 (Spring 1971), pp. 51-60. Rpt. in his ARTICULATING WEST: ESSAYS ON PURPOSE AND FORM IN MODERN CANADIAN LITERATURE. Toronto: New Press, 1972, pp. 20-31.

FINCH, ROBERT DUER CLAYDON (1900-)

Robert Finch was for many years a professor of French at the University of Toronto, and his studies in French poetry have influenced his poetry. His early work reflected an interest in French symbolist techniques filtered through imagism and the work of Wallace Stevens. In the 1920's and 1930's, Finch's work was unique in its stylistic wit and its technical adroitness in form and diction. In his later work his poetry loses its tightness and clarity and exhibits a rather facile imagery and an almost sentimental tone.

1. Poetry

Scott, F.R., ed. NEW PROVINCES: POEMS OF SEVERAL AUTHORS. Toronto: Macmillan, 1936. 77 p.

Finch's poems appear on pages 1-11.

POEMS. Toronto: Oxford, 1946. 51 p.

THE STRENGTH OF THE HILLS. Toronto: McClelland & Stewart, 1948. 132 p.

A CENTURY HAS ROOTS. A MASQUE PERFORMED AT HART HOUSE THEATRE TO COMMEMORATE THE ONE HUNDREDTH ANNIVERSARY OF THE FOUNDATION OF UNIVERSITY COLLEGE, TORONTO, 1853. Toronto: University of Toronto Press, 1953. 28 p.

ACIS IN OXFORD AND OTHER POEMS. Toronto: University of Toronto Press, 1961. 46 p.

Originally printed privately at Oxford: New Bodleian, 1959.

DOVER BEACH REVISITED. Toronto: Macmillan, 1961. 111 p.

SILVERTHORN BUSH AND OTHER POEMS. Toronto: Macmillan, 1966. 86 p.

2. Prose

THE SIXTH SENSE. INDIVIDUALISM IN FRENCH POETRY, 1686-1760. Toronto: University of Toronto Press, 1966. x, 411 p.

3. Criticism

Beattie, [A.] Munro. "Poetry 1920-1935." In LITERARY HISTORY OF CANADA; CANADIAN LITERATURE IN ENGLISH. Ed. Carl F. Klinck et al. Toronto: University of Toronto Press, 1965, pp. 738-40.

Daniells, Roy. "Earle Birney et Robert Finch." GANTS DU CIEL, 11 (Spring 1946), 83-96.

Pacey, Desmond. "Modern Canadian Poetry." In his CREATIVE WRITING IN CANADA; A SHORT HISTORY OF ENGLISH-CANADIAN LITERATURE. Rev. ed. Toronto: Ryerson, 1961, pp. 145-47.

Smith, A.J.M. "Turning New Leaves." CANADIAN FORUM, 27, no. 316 (May 1947), 42-43.

Stevens, Peter. "The Development of Canadian Poetry between the Wars and Its Reflection of Social Awareness. Ph.D. thesis, University of Saskatchewan, Saskatoon, 1968.

A section on Finch's early poems is on pages 39-42.

Sutherland, John. "Robert Finch and the Governor-General's Award." NORTHERN REVIEW, 1 (August-September 1947), 38-40. Rpt. in his ESSAYS, CONTROVERSIES AND POEMS. Ed. Miriam Waddington. Toronto: McClelland & Stewart, 1972.

A scathing review of Finch's POEMS (1946) aimed at the standards by which the Governor-General's Awards are chosen, because his book had won the award that year. The review provoked a reply by P.K. Page (NORTHERN REVIEW, 2 [October-November 1947], 40), who resigned from the magazine's editorial board, as did A.M. Klein and F.R. Scott.

KENNEDY, JOHN LEO (1907-)

Leo Kennedy, born in Liverpool, came to Canada as a child and lived in Montreal for many years before moving to the United States. During his time in Montreal, he was associated with other Montreal poets writing in the newer, modern vein. Initially, Kennedy was much influenced by T.S. Eliot, and the poetry in THE SHROUDING is a kind of pastiche of Eliot, written under the influence of THE GOLDEN BOUGH. During the 1930's, however, his views about poetry changed considerably. He rejected his own early poetry and that of his fellow poets in favor of a more radical, politically oriented poetry written under a variety of pseudonyms. This poetry is interesting mainly as an example of 1930's propagandist, political poetry, though an occasional poem makes an impact. These poems have never been collected, though one or two have been included in anthologies, including NEW PROVINCES (see entry under F.R. Scott in chapter IV). For the last thirty years or so, no new poems of his seem to have appeared in magazines or books.

1. Poetry

THE SHROUDING. Toronto: Macmillan, 1933. 59 p.

Scott, F.R., ed. NEW PROVINCES: POEMS OF SEVERAL AUTHORS. Toronto: Macmillan, 1936. 77 p.

Kennedy's poems appear on pages 15-25.

2. Prose

"Raymond Knister." CANADIAN FORUM, 12 (September 1932), 459-61.

"Archibald Lampman." CANADIAN FORUM, 13 (May 1933), 301-3.

3. Criticism

Brown, E.K. ON CANADIAN POETRY. Rev. ed. Toronto: Ryerson, 1944. 172 p.
> Kennedy is discussed on pages 70-73.

Collin, W.E. "This Man of April." In his THE WHITE SAVANNAHS. Toronto: Macmillan, 1936, pp. 267-84.

McMullen, Lorraine. "Leo Kennedy." LE CHIEN D'OR/THE GOLDEN DOG, (January 1972), pp. 46-62.

Ross, G. Arthur. "Three Minor Canadian Poets: Leo Kennedy, L.A. MacKay and Raymond Knister." M.A. thesis, University of Alberta, Edmonton, 1969.

Schultz, Gregory Peter. "The Periodical Poetry of A.J.M. Smith, F.R. Scott, Leo Kennedy, A.M. Klein and Dorothy Livesay (1925-1950)." M.A. thesis, University of Western Ontario, London, 1957.

Stevens, Peter, ed. THE McGILL MOVEMENT: A.J.M. SMITH, F.R. SCOTT AND LEO KENNEDY. Toronto: Ryerson, 1969. 146 p.
> A collection of critical essays (pp. 21-50) sets Kennedy in the context of other McGill-Montreal poets, F.R. Scott and A.J.M. Smith. Included is one of Kennedy's own polemical essays about socially conscious verse as well as an early working of ideas by W.E. Collin before he published the chapter on Kennedy in THE WHITE SAVANNAHS (above, this section, under Collin).

Watt, Frank W. "Radicalism in English Canadian Literature since Confederation." Ph.D. thesis, University of Toronto, 1957.
> Brief discussion of Kennedy's political poetry in the context of radical writing in Canada.

KLEIN, ABRAHAM MOSES (1909-72)

A.M. Klein's reputation has increased steadily, and he is now considered a major Canadian poet. He was raised in Montreal; after some education toward becoming a rabbi, he eventually chose law as his profession. He was actively involved in Zionism and in left-wing politics.

His earliest poetry rehearses many Jewish themes in a rhetorically exuberant language. His poetry turned to political subjects in the 1930's as he recognized the plight of the persecuted Jew and the disastrous effects of the depression. His radical poems of the 1930's were never collected in book form until some appeared in FORUM: CANADIAN LIFE AND LETTERS 1920-70. His last volume of poetry moves to French-Canadian themes. He seems to have become disillusioned with writing poetry and remained silent for the last twenty years of his life.

Klein's poetry is characterized by great erudition, technical mastery, and, above all, a uniquely and richly varied language which was sometimes experimental, even though the form of his poetry remained generally within traditional modes.

1. Poetry

Scott, F.R., ed. NEW PROVINCES: POEMS OF SEVERAL AUTHORS. Toronto: Macmillan, 1936. 77 p.

  Klein's poems appear on pages 29-48.

"Hershel of Ostropol." CANADIAN JEWISH CHRONICLE, 31 March 1939, pp. 19-27.

  A short play not published in the poetry volumes.

HATH NOT A JEW. Foreword by Ludwig Lewisohn. New York: Behrman's Jewish Book House, 1940. 116 p.

THE HITLERIAD. New York: New Directions, 1944. 30 p.

POEMS. Philadelphia: Jewish Publishing Society, 1944. 82 p.

SEVEN POEMS. Montreal: Author, 1947. 8 p.

HUIT POEMES CANADIENS (EN ANGLAIS). Montreal: Author, 1948. 16 p.

THE ROCKING CHAIR AND OTHER POEMS. Toronto: Ryerson, 1948. 56 p.

Wilson, Milton, ed. POETS BETWEEN THE WARS. Toronto: McClelland & Stewart, 1967. x, 196 p.

An anthology of poems by five poets: A.M. Klein, Dorothy Livesay, E.J. Pratt, F.R. Scott, A.J.M. Smith. It contains brief biographies. Klein's biography and poems appear on pages 155-94.

Granatstein, J.L., and Peter Stevens, eds. FORUM: CANADIAN LIFE AND LETTERS 1920-70: SELECTIONS FROM THE CANADIAN FORUM. Toronto: University of Toronto Press, 1972. xv, 431 p. Illustrated.

This edition of selections from the CANADIAN FORUM contains the first publication in book form of some of Klein's political poetry of the 1930's. The poems appear on pages 162, and 164-67.

2. Prose

"A Shout in the Street." In NEW DIRECTIONS IN PROSE AND POETRY. New York: New Directions, 1941, pp. 327-45.

"The Poetry of A.J.M. Smith." CANADIAN FORUM, 23 (February 1944), 257-58.

"Annotations on Shapiro's Essay on Rime." NORTHERN REVIEW, 1 (October-November 1946), 30-38.

"The Oxen of the Sun." HERE AND NOW, 3 (January 1949), 28-48.

"On Criticism: And the Mome Raths Outgrabe." HERE AND NOW, 4 (June 1949), 31-37.

"The Black Panther." ACCENT, 10 (Spring 1950), 139-55.

Klein wrote many short articles on writers as well as on other matters for the CANADIAN JEWISH CHRONICLE between 1937 and 1954, but the articles cited above represent his best criticism. Three of the above articles are from the book he started to write on James Joyce's ULYSSES: "A Shout in the Street," "The Oxen of the Sun," and "The Black Panther."

THE SECOND SCROLL. New York: Knopf, 1951. 198 p. Rpt., introd. M.W. Steinberg. New Canadian Library Series. Toronto: McClelland & Stewart, 1961. 142 p.

This is Klein's only novel.

3. Criticism

"A.M. Klein--A Tribute." JEWISH DIALOG, Passover 1973, entire issue.

> This special issue contains a variety of articles covering many aspects of Klein's work. It includes criticism on his prose and poetry as well as some poetic tributes. There is also a full bibliography prepared by Glen Siebrasse.

Beattie, [A.] Munro. "Poetry 1920-1935." In LITERARY HISTORY OF CANADA; CANADIAN LITERATURE IN ENGLISH. Ed. Carl F. Klinck et al. Toronto: University of Toronto Press, 1965, pp. 735-37.

Bell, Merirose. "The Image of French Canada in the Poetry of William Henry Drummond, Emile Coderre and A.M. Klein." M.A. thesis, McGill University, Montreal, 1967.

Brown, E.K. "The Immediate Present in Canadian Literature." SEWANEE REVIEW, 41 (October 1933), 430-32.

_____. ON CANADIAN POETRY. Rev. ed. Toronto: Ryerson, 1944. 172 p.

> Klein is discussed on pages 73-78.

CANADIAN LITERATURE, 25 (Summer 1965), entire issue.

> This special issue contains four essays devoted to Klein, one each by his later editors, Tom Marshall and Miriam Waddington, and others by Dorothy Livesay and M.W. Steinberg.

Edel, Leon. "Abraham M. Klein." CANADIAN FORUM, 12 (May 1932), 300-302.

Esco, Helen. "Symbol and Tradition in the Poetry of A.M. Klein." M.A. thesis, Queen's University, Kingston, Ont., 1973.

Fischer, G.K. "A.M. Klein's Forgotten Play." CANADIAN LITERATURE, 43 (Winter 1970), 42-53.

Marshall, Tom. "The Poetry of A.M. Klein: A Thematic Analysis of the Poetry of Abraham Moses Klein in the Light of the Major Themes of the Second Scroll." M.A. thesis, Queen's University, Kingston, Ont., 1965.

_____. "Poetry of a People: Some Afterthoughts about the Landscape of A.M. Klein." JEWISH DIALOG, Rosh Hashanah 1972, pp. 32-33.

_____, ed. A.M. KLEIN. Toronto: Ryerson, 1970. xxv, 165 p.

Tom Marshall, a poet himself, has spent many years in the study of Klein. He wrote his M.A. thesis on Klein (see above), and this collection includes the best critical survey of Klein's work. Marshall has gathered some of the early reviews and articles (notably W.E. Collin's essay from THE WHITE SAVANNAHS) together with reactions by other poets to Klein's work of the 1940's. Some of the later reassessments included here also appear in the special issue of CANADIAN LITERATURE (above, this section) devoted to Klein. This collection also contains a bibliography denoting the dates and places of Klein's individual poems.

Pacey, Desmond. "A.M. Klein." In his TEN CANADIAN POETS; A GROUP OF BIOGRAPHICAL AND CRITICAL ESSAYS. Toronto: Ryerson, 1958, pp. 254-92.

Phelps, Arthur L. "Two Poets: Klein and Birney." In his CANADIAN WRITERS. Toronto: McClelland & Stewart, 1951, pp. 111-19.

Schultz, Gregory Peter. "The Periodical Poetry of A.J.M. Smith, F.R. Scott, Leo Kennedy, A.M. Klein and Dorothy Livesay (1925-1950)." M.A. thesis, University of Western Ontario, London, 1957.

Scullion, John. "Abraham Moses Klein Poet and Novelist." M.A. thesis, University of Montreal, 1953.

Stevens, Peter. "The Development of Canadian Poetry between the Wars and Its Reflection of Social Awareness. Ph.D. thesis, University of Saskatchewan, Saskatoon, 1968.

Klein's poetry is discussed on pages 277-318. An abbreviated version appears in "A.M. Klein--A Tribute" (cited above, this section).

Waddington, Miriam. A.M. KLEIN. Toronto: Copp Clark, 1970. vi, 145 p.

_____. "The Cloudless Day: The Radical Poems of A.M. Klein." TAMARACK REVIEW, 45 (Autumn 1967), 65-92.

KNISTER, RAYMOND (1899-1932)

Raymond Knister was one of the first modern Canadian authors to devote his energies to writing as a full-time profession. He wrote a great deal of journalism in his hard-working short life, and produced a copious amount of material, much of which still remains unprinted. He published stories and poems outside Canada and seemed reasonably optimistic about his own chances of success within the context of Canadian literature.

He spent much of his early life in farming areas in southwestern Ontario, and many of his stories reflect that experience. His poetry, collected and published after his death, is also derived mainly from that life. His poetic work tends to be realistic and sparse in its diction and open in its use of free verse forms.

There has been a renewed interest in Knister recently, and his writings are being reassessed. Publication of previously unpublished work is being proposed. It now seems that Knister will be seen to have played a more significant part in the development of literature in twentieth-century Canada than has usually been assigned to him.

1. Poetry

COLLECTED POEMS OF RAYMOND KNISTER. Ed. with a memoir by Dorothy Livesay and a bibliog. by Margaret Ray. Toronto: Ryerson, 1949. xli, 45 p.

2. Prose

"The Poetical Works of Wilfred Campbell." QUEEN'S QUARTERLY, 31 (May 1924), 435-49.

"The Poetry of Archibald Lampman." DALHOUSIE REVIEW, 7 (October 1927), 348-61. Rpt. in ARCHIBALD LAMPMAN. Ed. Michael Gnarowski. Toronto: Ryerson, 1970, pp. 100-118.

> These two essays are Knister's most detailed criticism of other poets and shed some light on his own poetic principles.

Ed. CANADIAN SHORT STORIES. Toronto: Macmillan, 1928. xix, 340 p.

WHITE NARCISSUS. A NOVEL. New York: Harcourt, 1929. 250 p. Rpt., introd. Philip Child. New Canadian Library Series. Toronto: McClelland & Stewart, 1962. 135 p.

MY STAR PREDOMINANT. Toronto: Ryerson, 1934. 319 p.

> This novel based on the life of John Keats was awarded a prize by a publisher who went bankrupt. Knister received only part of the prize money, and the novel was published after his death.

SELECTED STORIES OF RAYMOND KNISTER. Ed. with an introd. Michael

Gnarowski. Ottawa: University of Ottawa Press, 1972. 119 p.

> Stories first published in magazines in Canada, the United States, and France in the mid-1920's. Collected in book form for the first time.

3. Criticism

Beattie, [A.] Munro. "Poetry 1920-1935." In LITERARY HISTORY OF CANADA; CANADIAN LITERATURE IN ENGLISH. Ed. Carl F. Klinck et al. Toronto: University of Toronto Press, 1965, pp. 728-30.

Everard, Doris Edna. "Tragic Dimensions in Selected Short Stories of Raymond Knister." M.A. thesis, Sir George Williams University, Montreal, 1972.

Kennedy, Leo. "Raymond Knister." CANADIAN FORUM, 12 (September 1932), 459-61.

Ross, G. Arthur. "Three Minor Canadian Poets: Leo Kennedy, L.A. Mackay and Raymond Knister." M.A. thesis, University of Alberta, Edmonton, 1969.

Stevens, Peter. "The Development of Canadian Poetry between the Wars and Its Reflection of Social Awareness." Ph.D. thesis, University of Saskatchewan, Saskatoon, 1968.

> Knister's poetry is discussed on pages 80-98; this section of the thesis is an elaboration of Stevens' article cited below.

_____. "The Old Futility of Art: Knister's Poetry." CANADIAN LITERA-TURE, 23 (Winter 1965), 45-52.

LESLIE, KENNETH (1892-1974)

Kenneth Leslie was born in Picton, Nova Scotia, and lived in the Maritimes for most of his life, apart from some years studying at the University of Nebraska and at Harvard. Much of his poetry draws on detail from Maritimes life, and he occasionally reflects the political concerns of his age. His poetry adheres to traditional form, though he used free verse at times. THE POEMS OF KENNETH LESLIE (1971) contains an addendum of new poems, though the bulk of that volume is devoted to the four books published in the 1930's. His position is best summarized in Munro Beattie's phrase, "a minor writer who now and again surpassed himself."

1. Poetry

WINDWARD ROCK. New York: Macmillan, 1934. 61 p.

SUCH A DIN. Halifax, N.S.: Author, 1935. 45 p.

LOWLANDS LOW. Halifax, N.S.: McCurdy, 1936. 47 p.

BY STUBBORN STARS, AND OTHER POEMS. Toronto: Ryerson, 1938. 64 p.

THE POEMS OF KENNETH LESLIE. Ladysmith, Que.: Ladysmith Press, 1971. 182 p.

2. Criticism

Beattie, [A.] Munro. "Poetry 1935-1950." In LITERARY HISTORY OF CANADA; CANADIAN LITERATURE IN ENGLISH. Ed. Carl F. Klinck et al. Toronto: University of Toronto Press, 1965, pp. 755-56.

LIVESAY, DOROTHY (1909-)

Dorothy Livesay was born in Winnipeg and educated at the University of Toronto and the Sorbonne. She was a social worker in New Jersey and Montreal in the 1930's, moving to Vancouver after her marriage in 1937. She was associated with the magazine CONTEMPORARY VERSE in the 1940's. During the 1960's she worked for UNESCO in Africa; her experiences there gave rise to her poem THE COLOUR OF GOD'S FACE, later revised, titled "Zambia," and included in THE UNQUIET BED. On her return to Canada she was caught up in the new linguistic openness of the west coast poets in the 1960's; her poetry, after starting with brief imagistic lyrics and moving through poems of social awareness, turned to more open forms and direct response to private experience.

1. Poetry

GREEN PITCHER. Toronto: Macmillan, 1928. 16 p.

SIGNPOST. Toronto: Macmillan, 1932. 61 p.

POEMS FOR PEOPLE. Toronto: Ryerson, 1947. 40 p.

CALL MY PEOPLE HOME. Toronto: Ryerson, 1950. 24 p.

NEW POEMS. Toronto: Emblem Books, 1955. 15 p.

SELECTED POEMS 1926-1956. Introd. Desmond Pacey. Toronto: Ryerson, 1957. xxii, 82 p.

THE COLOUR OF GOD'S FACE. Vancouver, B.C.: Author, 1964. 12 p.

THE UNQUIET BED. Toronto: Ryerson, 1967. 65 p.

Wilson, Milton, ed. POETS BETWEEN THE WARS. Toronto: McClelland & Stewart, 1967. x, 196 p.

> Livesay's poems appear on pages 125-54.

THE DOCUMENTARIES. Toronto: Ryerson, 1968. 56 p.

PLAINSONGS. Rev. and enl. ed. Fredericton, N.B.: Fiddlehead Poetry Books, 1971. 48 p.

DISASTERS OF THE SUN. Burnaby, B.C.: Blackfish, 1971. 7 p.

COLLECTED POEMS: THE TWO SEASONS. Toronto: McGraw-Hill, Ryerson, 1972. xvi, 368 p.

> This volume is a full collection of her poetry, including some previously unpublished poems as well as poems only previously published in magazines and journals. The poet has also written a foreword for this collection.

NINE POEMS OF FAREWELL. Windsor, Ont.: Black Moss, 1973. Unpaged.

2. Prose

Dorothy Livesay has contributed numerous articles of a literary and political nature to many journals. The few below were selected for being of particular relevance to her career and poetry.

Ed. RAYMOND KNISTER: COLLECTED POEMS. Toronto: Ryerson, 1949. 45 p.

"Song and Dance." CANADIAN LITERATURE, 41 (Summer 1969), 40-48.

"A Prairie Sampler." MOSAIC, 3 (Spring 1970), 85-92.

"The Early Days." CANADIAN FORUM, 50 (April-May 1970), 34-36.

Ed. 40 WOMEN POETS. Montreal: Ingluvin, 1971. 141 p.

A WINNIPEG CHILDHOOD. Winnipeg, Man.: Peguis Publications, 1973.

> These stories, although fictional in form, are to some extent auto-biographical.

3. Criticism

Beattie, [A.] Munro. "Poetry 1935-1950." In LITERARY HISTORY OF CANADA; CANADIAN LITERATURE IN ENGLISH. Ed. Carl F. Klinck et al. Toronto: University of Toronto Press, 1965, pp. 740-41.

Boylan, Charles. "The Social and Lyric Voices of Dorothy Livesay." M.A. thesis, University of British Columbia, Vancouver, 1969.

Collin, W.E. "My New Found Land." In his THE WHITE SAVANNAHS. Toronto: Macmillan, 1936, pp. 147-73.

Crawley, Alan. "Dorothy Livesay--An Intimate Biography." EDUCATIONAL RECORD (Quebec), 61 (July-September 1945), 169-73. Rpt. in LEADING CANADIAN POETS. Ed. W.P. Percival. Toronto: Ryerson, 1948, pp. 117-24.

Frye, Northrop. "From 'Letters in Canada.'" In his THE BUSH GARDEN: ESSAYS ON THE CANADIAN IMAGINATION. Toronto: Anansi, 1971, pp. 84-86.

Lane, Patrick. "The Collected Poems of Dorothy Livesay." BLACKFISH, 4-5 (Winter-Spring 1972/73), unpaged.

O'Donnell, Kathleen. "Dorothy Livesay." D.L. thesis, University of Montreal, 1959.

Pacey, Desmond. "The Poetry of Dorothy Livesay." In his ESSAYS IN CANA-DIAN CRITICISM 1938-1968. Toronto: Ryerson, 1969, pp. 135-44.

> This is a reprint of his introduction to SELECTED POEMS (see above, under Poetry, section 1), with the addition of a review of THE UNQUIET BED.

Pratt, E.J. "Dorothy Livesay." GANTS DU CIEL, 11 (Spring 1946), 61-65.

Schultz, Gregory Peter. "The Periodical Poetry of A.J.M. Smith, F.R. Scott, Leo Kennedy, A.M. Klein and Dorothy Livesay (1925-1950)." M.A. thesis, University of Western Ontario, London, 1957.

Steinberg, M.W. "Dorothy Livesay: Poet of Affirmation." B.C. LIBRARY QUARTERLY, 24 (October 1960), 9-13.

Stephan, Ruth. "A Canadian Poet." POETRY (Chicago), 65 (January 1945), 220-22.

Stevens, Peter. "The Development of Canadian Poetry between the Wars and Its Reflection of Social Awareness." Ph.D. thesis, University of Saskatchewan, Saskatoon, 1968.

    Livesay's poetry is discussed on pages 140-48 and 247-69.

_____. "Dorothy Livesay: The Love Poetry." CANADIAN LITERATURE, 47 (Winter 1971), 26-43.

_____. "Out of the Silence and across the Distance." QUEEN'S QUARTERLY, 78 (Winter 1971), 579-91.

Weaver, Robert. "The Poetry of Dorothy Livesay." CONTEMPORARY VERSE, 26 (Fall 1948), 18-22.

MacDONALD, WILSON PUGSLEY (1880-1967)

Wilson MacDonald's work can be linked with that of Audrey Alexandra Brown: it is a poetry of romanticism, ornate and rhetorical. His poetry echoes many other romantic figures in literature. His reputation, based on a popularity derived from his public readings in the 1920's and 1930's, has suffered a decline. At times, however, his poetry is touched with genuine lyric feeling, and he has written some satiric verse.

1. Poetry

SONG OF THE PRAIRIE LAND, AND OTHER POEMS. Toronto: McClelland & Stewart, 1918. 144 p.

THE MIRACLE SONGS OF JESUS. Toronto: Privately Printed by the Author, 1921. 12 p.

THE MIRACLE SONGS OF JESUS. Toronto: Ryerson, 1921. 26 p.

OUT OF THE WILDERNESS. Ottawa: Graphic, 1926. 209 p. 9th printing, Toronto: Ryerson, 1957.

AN ODE ON THE DIAMOND JUBILEE OF CONFEDERATION. Toronto: Warwick, 1927. 14 p.

CAW-CAW BALLADS. Toronto: MacDonald, 1930. 44 p.

A FLAGON OF BEAUTY. Toronto: Pine Tree Publishing Co., 1931. 217 p.

PAUL MARCHAND, AND OTHER POEMS. Toronto: Pine Tree Publishing Co., 1933. 46 p.

QUINTRAINS OF "CALLANDER", AND OTHER POEMS. Toronto: Saunders, 1935. 46 p.

THE SONG OF THE UNDERTOW, AND OTHER POEMS. Toronto: Saunders, 1935. 175 p.

COMBER COVE. Toronto: Saunders, 1937. 91 p.

GREATER POEMS OF THE BIBLE: METRICAL VERSIONS, BIBLICAL FORMS, AND ORIGINAL POEMS. Toronto: Macmillan, 1943. 277 p.

ARMAND DUSSAULT, AND OTHER POEMS. Buffalo, N.Y.: Broadway Press, 1946. 46 p.

PUGWASH. Toronto: Pine Tree Publishing Co., 1957. 15 p.

OLD SAMUEL CASHSWIGGER. Willowdale, Ont.: Author, 1958. 3 p.

2. Criticism

Fraser, A. Ermatinger. "Who's Who in Canadian Literature: Wilson MacDonald." CANADIAN BOOKMAN, 9 (January 1927), 3-6.

Hughes, J.M. "Wilson MacDonald: A Sketch of Personality." ACTA VICTORIANA, 55 (February-March 1931), 9-14.

Knister, Raymond. "A Poet in Arms for Poetry." CANADIAN MAGAZINE, 68 (October 1927), 28, 38-39.

MacKay, L.A. "Wilson MacDonald." CANADIAN FORUM, 13 (April 1933), 262-63.

Pacey, Desmond. "Modern Canadian Writing." In his CREATIVE WRITING IN CANADA; A SHORT HISTORY OF ENGLISH-CANADIAN LITERATURE. Rev. ed. Toronto: Ryerson, 1961, pp. 126-28.

Quinlan, Anna. "A Survey of Wilson MacDonald." M.A. thesis, University of Ottawa, 1936.

Roberts, Joan. "Wilson MacDonald." EDUCATIONAL RECORD (Quebec), 59 (January-March 1943), 35-40. Rpt. in LEADING CANADIAN POETS. Ed. W.P. Percival. Toronto: Ryerson, 1948, pp. 125-34.

MacINNES, THOMAS ROBERT EDWARD (1867-1951)

Born in Dresden, Ontario, educated at the University of Toronto, Tom MacInnes became a lawyer in British Columbia. He participated in the Klondike gold rush and often visited China.

A very uneven poet, MacInnes lived an active life, and much of his vital brashness gets into his verse. Very romantic in his propounding of the bohemian life, he still manages to show a clear craftsmanship in his use of French forms, such as the ballade and villanelle. Often his verse descends to doggerel, but at times it exhibits a racy humor. His poetry is of a very minor kind, part of the latter-day romanticism that existed in early twentieth-century Canadian poetry in English. William Arthur Deacon summarizes his work as a "combination of French poetic form, Chinese philosophy and the incurably optimistic Canadian temperament."

1. Poetry

A ROMANCE OF THE LOST. Montreal: Desbarats, 1908. 175 p.

LONESOME BAR, A ROMANCE OF THE LOST, AND OTHER POEMS. Montreal: Desbarats, 1909. 205 p.

IN AMBER LANDS. New York: Broadway Publishing Co., 1910. 202 p.

RHYMES OF A ROUNDER. New York: Broadway Publishing Co., 1913. 79 p. 2nd ed., Vancouver, B.C.: Sasamat Publishing Co., 1935. 136 p.

THE FOOL OF JOY. Toronto: McClelland & Stewart, 1918. 83 p.

COMPLETE POEMS OF TOM MacINNES. Toronto: Ryerson, 1923. 298 p.

ROUNDABOUT RHYMES. Foreword by Charles G.D. Roberts. Toronto: Ryerson, 1923. 80 p.

HIGH LOW ALONG. A DIDACTIC POEM. Vancouver, B.C.: Clarke & Stuart, 1934. 68 p.

IN THE OLD OF MY AGE, A NEW BOOK OF RHYMES. Toronto: Ryerson, 1947. 55 p.

2. Prose

MacInnes' three books of prose bear only an indirect relevance to his poetry. His life in China is evident in two books: THE TEACHING OF THE OLD BOY, a translation and investigation of the ideas of Lao-Tse, and ORIENTAL OCCUPATION OF BRITISH COLUMBIA, his response to the new political regime in China as it related to the Chinese population of British Columbia. CHINOOK DAYS is devoted to a mishmash of ideas and fictions about life in British Columbia.

CHINOOK DAYS. Vancouver, B.C.: Sun Publishing Co., 1926. 206 p.

ORIENTAL OCCUPATION OF BRITISH COLUMBIA. Vancouver, B.C.: Sun Publishing Co., 1927. 170 p.

THE TEACHING OF THE OLD BOY. London: Dent, 1927. 227 p.

3. Criticism

Brown, E.K. ON CANADIAN POETRY. Rev. ed. Toronto: Ryerson, 1944. 172 p.

> MacInnes is discussed on pages 62-64.

Deacon, William Arthur. "Tom MacInnes." EDUCATIONAL RECORD (Quebec), 63 (July-September 1947), 161-66. Rpt. in LEADING CANADIAN POETS. Ed. W.P. Percival. Toronto: Ryerson, 1948, pp. 135-44.

Pacey, Desmond. "The Early Twentieth Century." In his CREATIVE WRITING IN CANADA; A SHORT HISTORY OF ENGLISH-CANADIAN LITERATURE. Rev. ed. Toronto: Ryerson, 1961, pp. 95-98.

_____ . "Service and MacInnes." NORTHERN REVIEW, 4 (February-March 1951), 12-17.

Pound, A.M. "Who's Who in Canadian Literature: Tom MacInnes." CANA-DIAN BOOKMAN, 8 (December 1926), 363-64.

Prouty, William Howard. "Tom MacInnes: Biography and Poetic Myth." M.A. thesis, University of New Brunswick, Fredericton, 1956.

MacKAY, LOUIS ALEXANDER (1901-)

Born in Hensall, Ontario, MacKay was educated at the University of Toronto and Oxford University. He became professor of Latin at the University of California, where he taught for the greater part of his academic career.

His poetry has been strangely neglected. It shows the influence of the classics in the use of rhyme, diction, and form. He employs the devices of classical satire to fire off witty poems about Canadian life. In the 1930's he wrote a series of caustic critical essays about earlier Canadian authors; these essays show a keen perception of the faults of these authors and are full of implications about the state and development of Canadian poetry in English in the twentieth century.

1. Poetry

Smalacombe, John (pseud.). VIPER'S BUGLOSS. Toronto: Ryerson, 1938. 7 p.

THE ILL-TEMPERED LOVER, AND OTHER POEMS. Toronto: Macmillan, 1948. 72 p.

2. Prose

"Audrey Alexandra Brown." CANADIAN FORUM, 12 (June 1932), 342-43.

"Bliss Carman." CANADIAN FORUM, 13 (February 1933), 182-83.

"James Gay." CANADIAN FORUM, 13 (September 1933), 457-58.

"W.W. Campbell." CANADIAN FORUM, 14 (November 1933), 66-67.

"The Poetry of E.J. Pratt." CANADIAN FORUM, 24 (December 1944), 208-9.

THE WRATH OF HOMER. Toronto: University of Toronto Press, 1948. 131 p.

3. Criticism

Pacey, Desmond. "Modern Canadian Poetry." In his CREATIVE WRITING IN CANADA; A SHORT HISTORY OF ENGLISH-CANADIAN LITERATURE. Rev. ed. Toronto: Ryerson, 1961, pp. 178-79.

Ross, G. Arthur. "Three Minor Canadian Poets: Leo Kennedy, L.A. MacKay and Raymond Knister." M.A. thesis, University of Alberta, Edmonton, 1969.

Stevens, Peter. "The Development of Canadian Poetry between the Wars and Its Reflection of Social Awareness." Ph.D. thesis, University of Saskatchewan, Saskatoon, 1968.

   MacKay's poetry is discussed on pages 170-74 and 209-15.

Sutherland, John. "Louis McKay: The Critic Is to Blame." In his ESSAYS, CONTROVERSIES AND POEMS. Ed. Miriam Waddington. Toronto: Mc-Clelland & Stewart, 1972, pp. 114-19.

MARRIOTT, ANNE (1913-)

Anne Marriott was born in Victoria, British Columbia, and she has lived most of her life in that province. She had a considerable reputation in the 1940's, particularly for her poems dealing with prairie life during the drought and the depression of the 1930's, especially her sequence THE WIND OUR ENEMY. She has returned to the publication of poetry; some has been included in recent magazines.

1. Poetry

THE WIND OUR ENEMY. Toronto: Ryerson, 1939. 8 p.

CALLING ADVENTURERS. Toronto: Ryerson, 1941. 8 p.

SALT MARSH. Toronto: Ryerson, 1942. 16 p.

SANDSTONE, AND OTHER POEMS. Toronto: Ryerson, 1945. 42 p.

2. Criticism

Collin, W.E. "Drought on the Prairies." POETRY (Chicago), 58 (April 1941), 53-54.

DeBruyn, Jan. "Anne Marriott, Poet of Joy." BRITISH COLUMBIA LIBRARY QUARTERLY, 22 (January 1959), 23-29.

Stevens, Peter. "The Development of Canadian Poetry between the Wars and Its Reflection of Social Awareness." Ph.D. thesis, University of Saskatchewan, Saskatoon, 1968.

Marriott's poetry is discussed on pages 187-93.

PICKTHALL, MARJORIE (1883-1922)

Born in England, Marjorie Pickthall came to Canada as a child and was educated in Toronto. She returned to England for some time before settling in Vancouver in the final years of her life.

Marjorie Pickthall is another of those Canadian poets who indulged in an imitative romanticism. The language of her poems is derived in large measure from the Pre-Raphaelites and the poets of the Celtic Twilight. Many of her poems are based on a simple religious view of life. What distinguishes them are their delicacy of movement and her technical competence, though the rather self-conscious literary quality of her work and its dreaminess and avoidance of reality militate against its genuine success. Pacey's summary is most apt: "She was a genuine if minor artist, and easily the best poetic craftsman of her Canadian generation."

1. Poetry

THE DRIFT OF PINIONS. Montreal: University Magazine, 1913. 94 p.

THE LAMP OF POOR SOULS, AND OTHER POEMS. New York: Lane, 1916. 140 p.

Includes those poems which made up THE DRIFT OF PINIONS.

MARY TIRED. London: Stonebridge Press, 1922. 4 p.

THE WOODCARVER'S WIFE, AND LATER POEMS. Toronto: McClelland & Stewart, 1922. 105 p.

TWO POEMS. Toronto: Ryerson, 1923. 5 p.

THE COMPLETE POEMS OF MARJORIE PICKTHALL. Toronto: McClelland & Stewart, 1925.   250 p.

LITTLE SONGS. Toronto: McClelland & Stewart, 1925.   88 p.

THE NAIAD AND FIVE OTHER POEMS. Toronto: Ryerson, 1931.   11 p.

>   These poems were selected by Lorne Pierce from a manuscript and
>   issued in a limited printing of fourteen copies.

THE SELECTED POEMS OF MARJORIE PICKTHALL.   Ed. with an introd. by
Lorne Pierce.   Toronto: McClelland & Stewart, 1957.   104 p.

2. Prose

Marjorie Pickthall wrote novels and short stories as well as three juvenile books;
these juvenile books are not included here.

THE WORKER IN SANDALWOOD. New York: Everyland, 1914.   16 p.

LITTLE HEARTS. London: Methuen, 1915.   309 p.

THE BRIDGE: A STORY OF THE GREAT LAKES. London: Hodder, 1922.
320 p.

3. Criticism

Adcock, A. St. John.   "Marjorie Pickthall."   BOOKMAN (London), 62 (June
1922), 127-29.

Brown, E.K.   ON CANADIAN POETRY. Rev. ed. Toronto: Ryerson, 1944.   172 p.

>   Pickthall's poetry is discussed on pages 64-67.

Collin, W.E.   "Dream Gardens."   In his THE WHITE SAVANNAHS.   Toronto:
Macmillan, 1936, pp. 43-79.

Hassard, Albert R.   "The Dawn of Marjorie Pickthall's Genius."   CANADIAN
BOOKMAN, 4 (May 1922), 159-61.

Logan, J.D.   "The Genius of Marjorie Pickthall: An Analysis of Aesthetic
Paradox."   CANADIAN MAGAZINE, 59 (June 1922), 154-61.

_____. MARJORIE PICKTHALL: HER POETIC GENIUS AND ART. Halifax, N.S.: Allen, 1922. 44 p.

MacDonald, John Harry. "Marjorie Pickthall." M.A. thesis, Dalhousie University, Halifax, N.S., 1927.

Pacey, Desmond. "The Early Twentieth Century." In his CREATIVE WRITING IN CANADA; A SHORT HISTORY OF ENGLISH-CANADIAN LITERATURE. Rev. ed. Toronto: Ryerson, 1961, pp. 98-102.

Pierce, Lorne. "Marjorie Pickthall." ACTA VICTORIANA, 67 (June 1943), 21-30.

_____. "Marjorie Pickthall." EDUCATIONAL RECORD (Quebec), 63 (January-March 1947), 31-35. Rpt. in LEADING CANADIAN POETS, ed. W.P. Percival. Toronto: Ryerson, 1948, pp. 168-76.

_____. MARJORIE PICKTHALL: A BOOK OF REMEMBRANCE. Toronto: Ryerson, 1925. 217 p.

St. Cecilia, Sister. "Marjorie Pickthall, the Ethereal Minstrel of Canada." M.A. thesis, University of Ottawa, 1941.

Scott, D.C. "Poetry and Progress." CANADIAN MAGAZINE, 60 (January 1923), 187-95.

Stevenson, O.J. "A Golden Page." In his A PEOPLE'S BEST. Toronto: Musson, 1927, pp. 159-68.

Toye, D.E. "The Poetry of Marjorie Pickthall." ACTA VICTORIANA, 47 (January 1923), 15-18.

Whitney, V.L. "Marjorie Pickthall." ACTA VICTORIANA, 39 (March 1915), 332-41.

PRATT, EDWIN JOHN (1883-1964)

E.J. Pratt has long been singled out as the only major Canadian poet; the list of criticism of his work is probably the longest devoted to any individual poet in Canadian literature. In the main, criticism has been adulatory; but in recent years new critical voices have begun to cast doubt on Pratt's reputation, generally on two main grounds: (1) that he is divorced from modern trends and is simply a twentieth-century holdover dealing with essentially Victorian themes (mainly evolution) in basically Victorian forms (the verse narrative); and (2) that his development and elucidation of ideas is ambiguous to the point of fuzziness. The critical debate continues, and it is apparent that still further criticism will attempt to decide finally Pratt's place in the development of modern poetry in Canada.

Pratt was born in Newfoundland and was at one time training to become a Methodist clergyman. After his study of philosophy and psychology at the University of Toronto, however, he seems to have had a crisis of faith which remains unsolved in his work. He taught English from 1920 to 1953.

Pratt's early work reflects his feelings for the sea, part of his Newfoundland background. The sea remains one of the dominant threads of his work, from his earliest poem, RACHEL, to BEHIND THE LOG (1947). His two long poems, BREBEUF AND HIS BRETHREN and TOWARDS THE LAST SPIKE, were attempts to transform specifically Canadian stories into poetic myth. His diction and control of verse rhythms give his work a rhetorical exuberance which is emphasized by his use of humor. Pratt is one of the few Canadian poets writing in English to have produced a substantial body of work as a basis for a critical discussion about his status as a major poet, however debatable that status may be.

1. Poetry

RACHEL: A SEA STORY OF NEWFOUNDLAND IN VERSE. New York: Privately Printed, 1915. 15 p. Rpt. in HERE THE TIDES FLOW. Ed. E.J. Pratt. Toronto: Macmillan, 1962, pp. 41-58.

NEWFOUNDLAND VERSE. Toronto: Ryerson, 1923. 140 p.

THE WITCHES' BREW. London: Selwyn & Blount, 1925. 32 p.

TITANS. London: Macmillan, 1926; rpt. London: Macmillian, 1961. 67 p.

THE IRON DOOR: AN ODE. Toronto: Macmillan, 1927. 30 p.

THE ROOSEVELT AND THE ANTINOE. New York: Macmillan, 1930. 44 p.

VERSES OF THE SEA. Introd. Charles G.D. Roberts. Toronto: Macmillan, 1930. 97 p.

MANY MOODS. Toronto: Macmillan, 1932. 53 p.

THE TITANIC. Toronto: Macmillan, 1935. 42 p.

Scott, F.R., ed. NEW PROVINCES: POEMS OF SEVERAL AUTHORS. Toronto: Macmillan, 1936. 77 p.

Pratt's poetry appears on pages 41–48.

THE FABLE OF THE GOATS AND OTHER POEMS. Toronto: Macmillan, 1937. 47 p.

BREBEUF AND HIS BRETHREN. Toronto: Macmillan, 1940. 65 p.

DUNKIRK. Toronto: Macmillan, 1941. 13 p.

STILL LIFE AND OTHER VERSE. Toronto: Macmillan, 1943. 40 p.

COLLECTED POEMS. Toronto: Macmillan, 1944. 314 p.

THEY ARE RETURNING. Toronto: Macmillan, 1945. 15 p.

BEHIND THE LOG. Toronto: Macmillan, 1947. 47 p.

TEN SELECTED POEMS. Toronto: Macmillan, 1947. 149 p.

Includes notes by the poet.

TOWARDS THE LAST SPIKE. Toronto: Macmillan, 1952. 53 p.

MAGIC IN EVERYTHING. Toronto: Macmillan, 1955. 6 p.

THE COLLECTED POEMS OF E.J. PRATT. Introd. Northrop Frye. 2nd ed. Toronto: Macmillan, 1958. xxviii, 395 p.

HERE THE TIDES FLOW. Introd., notes, and questions by D[avid] G. Pitt. Toronto: Macmillan, 1962. 169 p.

Wilson, Milton, ed. POETS BETWEEN THE WARS. Toronto: McClelland & Stewart, 1967. x, 196 p.

Pratt's poems appear on pages 1–80.

2. Prose

STUDIES IN PAULINE ESCHATOLOGY, AND ITS BACKGROUND. Toronto: Briggs, 1917. 203 p.

3. Criticism

Beattie, [A.] Munro. "E.J. Pratt." In LITERARY HISTORY OF CANADA; CANA-
DIAN LITERATURE IN ENGLISH. Ed. Carl F. Klinck et al. Toronto: Uni-
versity of Toronto Press, 1965, pp. 742-50.

Benet, William Rose. Introduction to COLLECTED POEMS BY E.J. PRATT.
New York: Knopf, 1945.

Birney, Earle. "E.J. Pratt and His Critics." In OUR LIVING TRADITION,
2nd and 3rd ser. Ed. Robert L. McDougall. Toronto: University of Toronto
Press, 1959, pp. 123-47.

Brown, E.K. ON CANADIAN POETRY. Rev. ed. Toronto: Ryerson, 1944. 172 p.
 Pratt's poetry is discussed on pages 143-64.

_____. "The Originality of E.J. Pratt." In CANADIAN ACCENT. Ed.
Ralph Gustafson. Harmondsworth, Engl.: Penguin Books, 1944, pp. 32-44.

Buitenhuis, Peter. Introduction to SELECTED POEMS OF E.J. PRATT. To-
ronto: Macmillan, 1968, pp. ix-xxx.

CANADIAN LITERATURE, 19 (Winter 1964), entire issue.
 A special issue devoted to Pratt, including essays by Vincent
 Sharman discussing Pratt's religious views, Fred Cogswell on
 Pratt's place in Canadian literature, and Paul West on the
 whale in Pratt's narrative.

Clark, James Murray. "E.J. Pratt and the Will to Believe: An Examination
of His Unpublished 'Clay' and His Poetry." M.A. thesis, University of New
Brunswick, Fredericton, 1972.

Coles, Baxter Matthew. "Man as Hero: A Study of E.J. Pratt's Concept of
Heroism." M.A. thesis, Acadia University, Wolfville, N.S., 1971.

Davey, Frank. "E.J. Pratt: Apostle of Corporate Man." CANADIAN LITERA-
TURE, 43 (Winter 1970), 54-66.

Edgar, Pelham. "E.J. Pratt." EDUCATIONAL RECORD (Quebec), 59 (July-
September 1943), 178-80. Rpt. in LEADING CANADIAN POETS. Ed. W.P.
Percival. Toronto: Ryerson, 1948, pp. 177-83.

_____. "Edwin John Pratt." GANTS DU CIEL, 11 (Spring 1946), 31-45.

English version, "The Poetry of E.J. Pratt." In ACROSS MY PATH. Ed. Northrop Frye. Toronto: Ryerson, 1952, pp. 109-17.

Frye, Northrop. "From 'Letters in Canada.'" In his THE BUSH GARDEN: ESSAYS ON THE CANADIAN EXPERIENCE. Toronto: Anansi, 1971, pp. 10-14.

_____. Introduction to THE COLLECTED POEMS OF E.J. PRATT. 2nd ed. Toronto: Macmillan, 1958, pp. xiii-xxviii.

_____. "La Tradition Narratif dans la Poesie Canadienne-Anglaise." GANTS DU CIEL, 11 (Spring 1946), 19-30. Rpt. (English version) in his THE BUSH GARDEN: ESSAYS ON THE CANADIAN EXPERIENCE. Toronto: Anansi, 1971, pp. 145-55.

Frye, Northrop, and Roy Daniells. "Ned Pratt: Two Recollections." CANADIAN LITERATURE, 21 (Summer 1964), 6-12.

Gibbs, Robert. "Aspects of Irony in the Poetry of E.J. Pratt." Ph.D. thesis, University of New Brunswick, Fredericton, 1970.

_____. "Knocking in the Clay." CANADIAN LITERATURE, 55 (Winter 1973), 50-64.

_____. "The Living Contour: The Whale Symbol in Melville and in Pratt." CANADIAN LITERATURE, 40 (Spring 1969), 17-25.

Gustafson, Ralph. "Portrait of Ned." QUEEN'S QUARTERLY, 74 (Autumn 1967), 437-51.

Jones, D.G. "The Courage to Be." In his BUTTERFLY ON ROCK; A STUDY IN THEMES AND IMAGES IN CANADIAN LITERATURE. Toronto: University of Toronto Press, 1970, pp. 111-20.

Keyworth, Vida. "Irony in the Poetry of E.J. Pratt." Ph.D. thesis, University of Montreal, 1962.

Livesay, Dorothy. "The Polished Lens: Poetic Techniques of Pratt and Klein." CANADIAN LITERATURE, 25 (Summer 1965), 33-42.

MacLeod, Denise Anne. "The Narrative Technique of E.J. Pratt." M.A. thesis, Mount St. Vincent University, Halifax, N.S., 1969.

MacPherson, Jay. PRATT'S ROMANTIC MYTHOLOGY: THE WITCHES' BREW.

St. John's, Newfoundland: Memorial University Press, 1972. 18 p.

Marie, Sister St. Dorothy. "The Epic Note in the Poetry of Edwin John Pratt." M.A. thesis, University of Ottawa, 1956.

_____. "The Poetic Imagery of Edwin Pratt." Ph.D. thesis, University of Ottawa, 1958.

Mensch, Fred. "Aspects of Heroism and Evolution in Some Poems by E.J. Pratt." M.A. thesis, Simon Fraser University, Burnaby, B.C., 1972.

New, W.H. "The Identity of Articulation: Pratt's TOWARDS THE LAST SPIKE." In his ARTICULATING WEST: ESSAYS ON PURPOSE AND FORM IN MODERN CANADIAN LITERATURE. Toronto: New Press, 1972, pp. 32-42.

Pacey, Desmond. "E.J. Pratt." In his TEN CANADIAN POETS; A GROUP OF BIOGRAPHICAL AND CRITICAL ESSAYS. Toronto: Ryerson, 1958, pp. 165-93.

Paisley, Alixe Catherine. "Epic Features of Brebeuf and His Brethren by E.J. Pratt." M.A. thesis, University of Windsor, Windsor, Ont., 1960.

Phelps, Arthur L. "E.J. Pratt." In his CANADIAN WRITERS. Toronto: McClelland & Stewart, 1951, pp. 1-9.

Pitt, David G., ed. E.J. PRATT. Toronto: Ryerson, 1969.

> A collection of criticism, which includes an introduction by Pitt, reviews of Pratt's work on first publication, and significant essays by such critics as W.E. Collin, E.K. Brown, John Sutherland, James Reaney, Louis Dudek, Northrop Frye, and A.J.M. Smith.

Pratt, Mildred Claire. THE SILENT ANCESTORS: THE FOREBEARS OF E.J. PRATT. Toronto: McClelland & Stewart, 1971.

Rashley, R[ichard] E[rnest]. POETRY IN CANADA: THE FIRST THREE STEPS. Toronto: Ryerson, 1958. xvii, 166 p.

Rosalinda, Sister Mary. "Brebeuf and His Brethren: A Great Canadian Poem." M.A. thesis, University of Ottawa, 1959.

Sharman, Vincent Douglas. "Patterns of Imagery and Symbolism in the Poetry of E.J. Pratt." M.A. thesis, University of British Columbia, Vancouver, 1963.

Stevens, Peter. "The Development of Canadian Poetry between the Wars and Its Reflection of Social Awareness." Ph.D. thesis, University of Saskatchewan, Saskatoon, 1968.

Pratt is discussed on pages 127-40.

Stonehewer, Lila Lavinia. "An Interpretation of Symbols in the Work of E.J. Pratt." M.A. thesis, McGill University, Montreal, 1970.

Story, G.M. "The Newfoundlander Who is Canada's Greatest Poet." NEWFOUNDLAND RECORD, 1 (September-October 1962), 7-8.

Sutherland, John. "Foremost Poet of Canada." POETRY (Chicago), 82 (September 1953), 350-54.

_____. THE POETRY OF E.J. PRATT: A NEW INTERPRETATION. Toronto: Ryerson, 1956.

TAMARACK REVIEW, 6 (Winter 1958), entire issue.

Features "A Garland for E.J. Pratt," a collection of critical and personal articles about Pratt by such writers as Louis Dudek, Murdo MacKinnon, and A.J.M. Smith.

Thorpe, John B.M. "Man and Religion in the Poetry of E.J. Pratt." M.A. thesis, McGill University, Montreal, 1970.

Tietze, Edna Elizabeth. "Edwin John Pratt and the Epic Quality of his Poetry." M. Phil. thesis, University of Waterloo, Waterloo, Ont., 1968.

Watt, Frank W. "Edwin John Pratt." UNIVERSITY OF TORONTO QUARTERLY, 29, no. 1 (October 1959), 77-84.

Wells, H.W. "Canada's Best-Known Poet: E.J. Pratt." COLLEGE ENGLISH, 7 (May 1946), 452-56.

Wells, H.W., and Carl F. Klinck. EDWIN J. PRATT: THE MAN AND HIS POETRY. Toronto: Ryerson, 1947. viii, 197 p.

Wilson, Milton. E.J. PRATT. Toronto: McClelland & Stewart, 1969. 64 p.

_____. "Pratt's Comedy." JOURNAL OF CANADIAN STUDIES, 3 (1968), 21-30.

ROSS, WILLIAM WRIGHTSON EUSTACE (1894-1966)

Called the "father of modern poetry in Canada" by Raymond Souster, W.W.E. Ross was born and educated in Ontario. He worked as a geophysicist for the Dominion Magnetic Observatory.

His poetry, published in the 1920's in Europe and the United States, was often written in an unadorned imagistic style. He also wrote some poems in traditional forms and meters, but it is for his uncluttered, freer poetry that he is now remembered. He remained a somewhat forgotten figure in Canadian poetry until Raymond Souster published some of his early work in 1956. That small publication brought Ross to the attention of some other poets; but his work still remained largely unnoticed, although one or two critical notices appeared just before his death. SHAPES & SOUNDS, the selection of his poems published after his death, contains some previously unpublished poems and shows that he is a poet of a wider range of subject matter and style than had been generally acknowledged.

1. Poetry

LACONICS. Ottawa: Overbrook Press, 1930. 92 p.

SONNETS. Toronto: Heaton Publishing Co., 1932. 72 p.

EXPERIMENT 1923-1929. Toronto: Contact Press, 1956. 23 p.

SHAPES & SOUNDS: POEMS OF W.W.E. ROSS. Ed. Raymond Souster and John Robert Colombo. Memoir by Barry Callaghan. Toronto: Longmans, 1968. 145 p.

2. Criticism

Gerber, Philip. "The Surface and the Terror: Poetry of Eustace Ross." FAR POINT, 5 (Winter 1970), 46-54.

Moore, Marianne. "Experienced Simplicity." POETRY (Chicago), 38 (August 1931), 280-81.

Stevens, Peter. "The Development of Canadian Poetry between the Wars and Its Reflection of Social Awareness." Ph.D. thesis, University of Saskatchewan, Saskatoon, 1968.

   Ross is discussed on pages 98-122.

_____. "On W.W.E. Ross." CANADIAN LITERATURE, 39 (Winter 1969),

43-61.

Sutherland, John.   "An Unpublished Introduction to the Poetry of W.W.E.
Ross."   In his ESSAYS, CONTROVERSIES AND POEMS.   Ed. Miriam Wad-
dington.   Toronto: McClelland & Stewart, 1972, pp. 162-64.

SCOTT, FRANCIS REGINALD (1899-)

Often referred to as a kind of renaissance man in Canada because of his wide-
ranging legal, social, and political interests, F.R. Scott was born in the city
of Quebec and, after some education in Canada, became a Rhodes scholar at
Oxford.   He trained as a lawyer and taught for almost forty years on the fac-
ulty of law at McGill University, where he was dean of law from 1961 to
1964.   He was a participant in political activities of the left for much of his
life--a founding member of both the C.C.F. party (now the New Democratic
party) and the League for Social Reconstruction.   He wrote many books on
Canadian political life and constitutional law.   He also worked for the United
Nations in Burma in 1952.

These myriad interests find an outlet in Scott's poetry in its clearly defined
diction and in its use of satire.   His early poetry showed the influence of the
imagists and the metaphysical poets, an influence also showing in the work of
his friend A.J.M. Smith, with whom he was associated in early poetic endeav-
ors in the McGILL FORTNIGHTLY REVIEW.   Scott and Smith also worked to-
gether in editing THE BLASTED PINE: AN ANTHOLOGY OF SATIRE, INVEC-
TIVE, AND DISRESPECTFUL VERSE and NEW PROVINCES: POEMS OF SEV-
ERAL AUTHORS.

Scott has also shown himself to be open to newer trends, and published a
volume of "found" poetry, TROUVAILLES.   His is a unique voice in Canadian
poetry, with a feeling for the northern landscape, an eye for the follies of
Canadian society, a rational approach to human progress, and a satirical and
genuine wit.   All of these qualities are expressed in precise and often elegant
poems which never, however, attain greatness.   He is, in Robin Skelton's
phrase, "a poet of the middle slopes."

1. Poetry

Ed. NEW PROVINCES: POEMS OF SEVERAL AUTHORS.   Toronto: Macmillan,
1936.   77 p.

     Scott's own poems appear on pages 51-61.

OVERTURE.   Toronto: Ryerson, 1945.   79 p.

EVENTS AND SIGNALS. Toronto: Ryerson, 1954. 58 p.

THE EYE OF THE NEEDLE. Montreal: Contact Press, 1957. 71 p.

Trans. ST.-DENYS GARNEAU AND ANNE HEBERT. Vancouver, B.C.: Klanak Press, 1962. 49 p.

SIGNATURE. Vancouver, B.C.: Klanak Press, 1964. 56 p.

SELECTED POEMS. Toronto: Oxford, 1966. 177 p.

TROUVAILLES. Introd. Louis Dudek. Montreal: Delta, 1967. 43 p.

Wilson, Milton, ed. POETS BETWEEN THE WARS. Toronto: McClelland & Stewart, 1967. x, 196 p.

    Scott's poems appear on pages 81-102.

2. Prose

Ed., with A.J.M. Smith. THE BLASTED PINE: AN ANTHOLOGY OF SATIRE, INVECTIVE, AND DISRESPECTFUL VERSE, CHIEFLY BY CANADIAN WRITERS. Rev. and enl. ed. Toronto: Macmillan, 1967. 186 p.

3. Criticism

Adelman, Seymour. "Elements of Social Criticism in Canadian Poetry with Emphasis on the Poetry of F.R. Scott and A.J.M. Smith." M.A. thesis, University of Montreal, 1961.

Beattie, [A.] Munro. "Poetry 1920-1935." In LITERARY HISTORY OF CANADA; CANADIAN LITERATURE IN ENGLISH. Ed. Carl F. Klinck et al. Toronto: University of Toronto Press, 1965, pp. 732-34.

Collin, W.E. "Pilgrim of the Absolute." In his THE WHITE SAVANNAHS. Toronto: Macmillan, 1936, pp. 177-204.

Frye, Northrop. "From 'Letters in Canada.'" In his THE BUSH GARDEN: ESSAYS ON THE CANADIAN IMAGINATION. Toronto: Anansi, 1971, pp. 37-39.

Martin, Jane. "F.R. Scott." M.A. thesis, Carleton University, Ottawa, 1966.

Pacey, Desmond. "F.R. Scott." In his TEN CANADIAN POETS; A GROUP OF BIOGRAPHICAL AND CRITICAL ESSAYS. Toronto: Ryerson, 1958, pp. 223-53.

Schultz, Gregory Peter. "The Periodical Poetry of A.J.M. Smith, F.R. Scott." Leo Kennedy, A.M. Klein and Dorothy Livesay (1925-1950)." M.A. thesis, University of Western Ontario, London, 1957.

Scobie, Stephen. "The Road Back to Eden: The Poetry of F.R. Scott." QUEEN'S QUARTERLY, 79 (Autumn 1972), 314-23.

Stevens, Peter. "The Development of Canadian Poetry between the Wars and Its Reflection of Social Awareness." Ph.D. thesis, University of Saskatchewan, Saskatoon, 1968.

Scott is discussed on pages 67-76.

_____, ed. THE McGILL MOVEMENT: A.J.M. SMITH, F.R. SCOTT AND LEO KENNEDY. Toronto: Ryerson, 1969. 146 p.

This collection of critical essays focuses on the work of Leo Kennedy, F.R. Scott, and A.J.M. Smith. The section on Scott (pp. 51-94) includes essays by Scott himself as well as by E.K. Brown, Louis Dudek, Milton Wilson, Chester Duncan, Robin Skelton, and A.J.M. Smith. There is also a selected bibliography.

SERVICE, ROBERT WILLIAM (1874-1958)

Robert Service was born in England and as a young man came to Canada, where he worked as a bank clerk in the Yukon. Though the gold rush had passed, much of Service's writing is based upon that frontier period.

His poetry derives from Kipling's jingoistic and colloquial ballads and has little or nothing to do with modern poetry in Canada, though his verse was enormously popular and was printed widely in many editions. The listing below includes the principal volumes, excluding reprints of editions appearing in other countries. Roy Daniells has suggested that although "no case can be made for Service as a poet, no history of Canadian letters can fail to find him a place," for his verses are "an ineradicable part of Canadian tradition," achieving "effects outside the ordinary canons of performance."

1. Poetry

SONGS OF A SOURDOUGH. Toronto: Briggs, 1907. 116 p.

BALLADS OF A CHEECHAKO. Toronto: Briggs, 1909. 137 p.

RHYMES OF A ROLLING STONE. Toronto: Briggs, 1912. 195 p.

RHYMES OF A RED-CROSS MAN. London: Unwin, 1916. 192 p.

SELECTED POEMS OF ROBERT SERVICE. London: Unwin, 1917. 28 p.

THE SHOOTING OF DAN McGREW, AND OTHER VERSES. New York: Bane & Hopkins, 1920.

BALLADS OF A BOHEMIAN. New York: Barse, 1921. 220 p.

COMPLETE POETICAL WORKS. New York: Barse, 1921. 855 p.

TWENTY BATH-TUB BALLADS. London: Francis, Day & Hunter, 1939. 48 p.

BAR-ROOM BALLADS. New York: Dodd, Mead, 1940. 169 p.

THE COMPLETE POEMS. New York: Dodd, Mead, 1940. 735 p.

THE COMPLETE POEMS. New York: Dodd, Mead, 1942. 1032 p.

SONGS OF A SUN-LOVER. London: Benn, 1949. 191 p.

RHYMES OF A ROUGHNECK. New York: Dodd, Mead, 1950. 207 p.

LYRICS OF A LOW BROW. New York: Dodd, Mead, 1951. 182 p.

RHYMES OF A REBEL. New York: Dodd, Mead, 1952. 213 p.

SONGS FOR MY SUPPER. New York: Dodd, Mead, 1953. 192 p.

CAROLS OF AN OLD CODGER. New York: Dodd, Mead, 1954. 190 p.

LATER COLLECTED VERSE. New York: Dodd, Mead, 1954. 477 p.

MORE COLLECTED VERSE. London: Benn, 1955. Var. pag.

RHYMES FOR MY RAGS. London: Benn, 1956. 191 p.

SONGS OF THE HIGH NORTH. Toronto: Ryerson, 1958. 125 p.

COLLECTED POEMS. New York: Dodd, Mead, 1958. 735 p.

BEST OF ROBERT SERVICE. Toronto: Ryerson, 1963. 216 p.

MORE SELECTED VERSE. Toronto: McGraw-Hill, Ryerson, 1971. vii, 215 p.

2. Prose

THE TRAIL OF '98. Toronto: Briggs, 1911. 514 p.

THE PRETENDER. New York: Dodd, Mead, 1914. 349 p.

THE POISONED PARADISE. New York: Dodd, Mead, 1922. 412 p.

THE ROUGHNECK. New York: Barse, 1923. 448 p.

THE MASTER OF THE MICROBE. New York: Barse, 1926. 424 p.

THE HOUSE OF FEAR. New York: Dodd, Mead, 1927. 408 p.

WHY NOT GROW YOUNG? New York: Barse, 1928. 266 p.

PLOUGHMAN OF THE MOON. New York: Dodd, Mead, 1945. 472 p.

HARPER OF HEAVEN. New York: Dodd, Mead, 1948. 452 p.

3. Criticism

Atherton, Stanley S. "The Klondike Muse." CANADIAN LITERATURE, 47 (Winter 1971), 67-72.

Bolla, Raymond Peter. "The Northern Ballads of Robert Service." M.A. thesis, University of Montreal, 1952.

Bucco, Martin. "Folk Poetry of Robert W. Service." ALASKA REVIEW, 2 (Fall 1965), 16-26.

Hamer-Jackson, Celesta. "Robert W. Service." EDUCATIONAL RECORD (Quebec), 59 (October-December 1943), 226-28. Rpt. in LEADING CANA-DIAN POETS. Ed. W.P. Percival. Toronto: Ryerson, 1948, pp. 227-33.

Hellman, G.T. "Whooping It Up." NEW YORKER, 31 March 1946, pp. 34-38; 6 April 1946, pp. 32-36.

Horning, L.E. "Robert W. Service." ACTA VICTORIANA, 41 (June 1917), 295-301.

Migone, Pietro. "Robert Service, Poet of the Canadian North." M.A. thesis, University of Ottawa, 1949.

Pacey, Desmond. "Service and MacInnes." NORTHERN REVIEW, 4 (February-March 1951), 12-17.

Phelps, Arthur L. "R.W. Service." In his CANADIAN WRITERS. Toronto: McClelland & Stewart, 1951, pp. 28-35.

Stouffer, R.P. "Robert W. Service." ACTA VICTORIANA, 39 (November 1914), 55-63.

SMITH, ARTHUR JAMES MARSHALL (1902-)

A.J.M. Smith, born in Montreal and educated there before leaving to study at the University of Edinburgh, has devoted his life to the writing, criticism, and teaching of literature. He was one of the first critics of Canada to demand strict critical standards as a prerequisite for the production of good Canadian literature. His own criticism has attempted to establish such standards, though he has sometimes been at the center of controversy, most notably in the case of his distinction between the cosmopolitan and native strains in Canadian poetry. He has been an indefatigable anthologist, particularly in poetry, and has edited collections that include both English- and French-Canadian poetry.

Smith's poetry is based on a kind of classical strictness, with an additional symbolic mode, derived in part from Yeats and the metaphysical poets. He uses some traditional structures together with some freer verse derived from imagism. His hard intellectual stance also brings into his poetry some witty themes and developments, but this same intellectualism has been the source of a good deal of critical reaction against his work. He has been accused of writing an overly literary poetry with no real self-involvement. It may be that his place in modern Canadian literature will depend more on his editing and anthologizing than on his poetic effort.

1. Poetry

Scott, F.R., ed. NEW PROVINCES: POEMS OF SEVERAL AUTHORS. Toronto: Macmillan, 1936. 77 p.

Smith's poems appear on pages 65-77.

NEWS OF THE PHOENIX AND OTHER POEMS. Toronto: Ryerson, 1943. 42 p.

A SORT OF ECSTASY. POEMS: NEW AND SELECTED. Toronto: Ryerson, 1954. 55 p.

COLLECTED POEMS. Toronto: Oxford, 1962. 124 p.

POEMS: NEW AND COLLECTED. Toronto: Oxford, 1967. 160 p.

Wilson, Milton, ed. POEMS BETWEEN THE WARS. Toronto: McClelland & Stewart, 1967. 196 p.

Smith's poems appear on pages 103-24.

Ed. with F.R. Scott. THE BLASTED PINE: AN ANTHOLOGY OF SATIRE, INVECTIVE, AND DISRESPECTFUL VERSE, CHIEFLY BY CANADIAN WRITERS. Rev. and enl. ed. Toronto: Macmillan, 1967. 186 p.

2. Prose

Smith usually wrote critical introductions to his anthologies, some of which are listed here, along with a selection of his many critical articles. Items which reveal Smith's critical and creative ideas about Canadian literature and about his own poetry have been selected.

"Symbolism in Poetry." McGILL FORTNIGHTLY REVIEW, 1 (5 December 1925), 11-12, 16.

"Contemporary Poetry." McGILL FORTNIGHTLY REVIEW, 2 (15 December 1926), 31-32.

"Wanted--Canadian Criticism." CANADIAN FORUM, 8 (April 1928), 600-601.

"A Note on Metaphysical Poetry." CANADIAN MERCURY, 1 (February 1929), 61-62.

The four articles above give a clear view of Smith's critical and poetic interests at the beginning of his career.

"A Rejected Preface." CANADIAN LITERATURE, 24 (Spring 1965), 6-9.

Though published in 1965, this preface was originally written for
the anthology NEW PROVINCES in 1936, but E.J. Pratt objected
to its content. F.R. Scott wrote a shorter preface for the an-
thology.

"Canadian Poetry--A Minority Report." UNIVERSITY OF TORONTO QUAR-
TERLY, 8 (January 1939), 125-38.

Smith castigates critics who unthinkingly praise Canadian poetry
which he judges "provincial." He maintains that more stringent
regulation of selections in anthologies and more rigorous standards
of criticism are necessary--two ideas which seem to be a program
Smith himself attempted to adopt in his later career.

"Our Poets." UNIVERSITY OF TORONTO QUARTERLY, 11 (July 1942), 457-
74.

"Canadian Anthologies, New and Old." UNIVERSITY OF TORONTO QUAR-
TERLY, 11 (July 1942), 457-74.

Ed. THE BOOK OF CANADIAN POETRY. Chicago: University of Chicago
Press, 1943. 452 p. Rev. ed., Toronto: Gage, 1957. xxv, 532 p.

Smith's introduction to this critical and historical anthology pro-
voked critical controversy. He used the terms "native" and "cos-
mopolitan" as labels for two divisions of Canadian poetry. He
was bitterly attacked for this view, particularly by John Suther-
land, who assembled his own anthology, OTHER CANADIANS, as
an opposing statement (see in Criticism, section 3, below and under
Sutherland in chapter IV).

"Colonialism and Nationalism in Canadian Poetry before Confederation." In
PROCEEDINGS OF THE CANADIAN HISTORICAL ASSOCIATION. Ottawa:
C.H.A., 1944, pp. 74-84.

"Nationalism and Canadian Poetry." NORTHERN REVIEW, 1 (December-
January 1945-46), 33-42.

"The Fredericton Poets." Founders' Day Address, University of New Brunswick,
Fredericton, 1946.

"Poet." In WRITING IN CANADA. Ed. George Whalley. Toronto: Mac-
millan, 1956, pp. 13-24.

Ed. THE OXFORD BOOK OF CANADIAN VERSE. Toronto: Oxford University

Press, 1960. lvi, 445 p.

> This anthology represents Smith's selection of both English- and French-Canadian poetry. His introduction links the developments of the two poetries, still using the split between "native" and "cosmopolitan," though in a moderate vein, and suggesting that a distinctive quality of contemporary Canadian poetry is its "eclectic detachment," an idea he pursues in the article "Poet" (1956, see above, this section), and in "Eclectic Detachment" (1961, see below).

"Eclectic Detachment: Aspects of Identity in Canadian Poetry." CANADIAN LITERATURE, 9 (Summer 1961), 6-14.

Ed. MASKS OF POETRY: CANADIAN CRITICS ON CANADIAN VERSE. Toronto: McClelland & Stewart, 1962. xi, 143 p.

"The Poetic Process: On the Making of Poems." In THE CENTENNIAL REVIEW OF ARTS AND SCIENCES. East Lansing: Michigan State University Press, 1964, pp. 353-71.

"The Critic's Task: Frye's Latest Work." CANADIAN LITERATURE, 20 (Spring 1964), 6-12.

"A Survey of English-Canadian Letters--A Review." UNIVERSITY OF TORONTO QUARTERLY, 35 (October 1965), 107-16.

Ed. with F.R. Scott. THE BLASTED PINE: AN ANTHOLOGY OF SATIRE, INVECTIVE, AND DISRESPECTFUL VERSE, CHIEFLY BY CANADIAN WRITERS. Rev. and enl. ed. Toronto: Macmillan, 1967. 186 p.

Ed. MODERN CANADIAN VERSE IN ENGLISH AND FRENCH. Toronto: Oxford University Press, 1967.

"F.R. Scott and Some of His Poems." CANADIAN LITERATURE, 31 (Winter 1967), 25-39.

"Impromptu Remarks Spoken at the International Poetry Conference." ETUDES LITTERAIRES, 1 (December 1968), 411-13.

> The whole of the proceedings of the conference were published in this issue on pages 331-425.

Ed. THE COLLECTED POEMS OF ANNE WILKINSON, AND A PROSE MEMOIR. Toronto: Macmillan, 1968. xxi, 212 p.

"The Canadian Poet: Part I: To Confederation." CANADIAN LITERATURE, 37 (Summer 1968), 6-14.

"The Canadian Poet: Part II: After Confederation." CANADIAN LITERA-TURE, 38 (Autumn 1968), 41-49.

3. Criticism

Adelman, Seymour. "Elements of Social Criticism in Canadian Poetry with Emphasis on the Poetry of F.R. Scott and A.J.M. Smith." M.A. thesis, University of Montreal, 1961.

Brinnin, John Malcolm. "Views of Favorite Mythologies." POETRY (Chicago), 65 (December 1944), 157-60.

Brown, E.K. Review of NEWS OF THE PHOENIX. UNIVERSITY OF TORONTO QUARTERLY, 13 (April 1944), 308-9.

CANADIAN LITERATURE, 15 (Winter 1963), entire issue.
    This special issue devoted to Smith contains essays and tributes by Earle Birney, Roy Fuller, and Milton Wilson, and an editorial by George Woodcock.

Collin, W.E. "Difficult Lonely Music." In his THE WHITE SAVANNAHS. Toronto: Macmillan, 1936, pp. 235-63.

Dudek, Louis. "Smith's COLLECTED POEMS." DELTA, 20 (February 1963), 27-28.

Frye, Northrop. "From 'Letters in Canada.'" In his THE BUSH GARDEN: ESSAYS ON THE CANADIAN IMAGINATION. Toronto: Anansi, 1971, pp. 36-37.

Klein, A.M. "The Poetry of A.J.M. Smith." CANADIAN FORUM, 23 (February 1944), 257-58.

Livesay, Dorothy. "NEWS OF THE PHOENIX." FIRST STATEMENT, 2 (April 1944), 18-19.

Pacey, Desmond. CREATIVE WRITING IN CANADA; A SHORT HISTORY OF ENGLISH-CANADIAN LITERATURE. Rev. ed. Toronto: Ryerson, 1961. ix, 314 p.
    Comments on Smith appear on pages 135-39.

_____. TEN CANADIAN POETS; A GROUP OF BIOGRAPHICAL AND
CRITICAL ESSAYS. Toronto: Ryerson, 1958. ix, 350 p.

>The chapter on Smith's poetry appears on pages 194-222.

Schultz, Gregory Peter. "The Periodical Poetry of A.J.M. Smith,
    F.R. Scott, Leo Kennedy, A.M. Klein and Dorothy Livesay (1925-
    1950)." M.A. thesis, University of Western Ontario, London, 1957.

Scott, F.R. "A.J.M. Smith." EDUCATIONAL RECORD (Quebec), 64
(January-March 1948), 24-29. Rpt. in LEADING CANADIAN POETS. Ed.
W.P. Percival. Toronto: Ryerson, 1948, pp. 234-44.

Stevens, Peter. "The Development of Canadian Poetry between the Wars and
Its Reflection of Social Awareness." Ph.D. thesis, University of Saskatchewan,
Saskatoon, 1968.

>Smith is discussed on pages 42-65, 160-62, and 225-29.

_____, ed. THE McGILL MOVEMENT: A.J.M. SMITH, F.R. SCOTT AND
LEO KENNEDY. Toronto: Ryerson, 1969. 146 p.

>This collection of critical essays concentrates on the work of Leo
>Kennedy, F.R. Scott, and A.J.M. Smith. The section on Smith
>(pp. 95-143) includes essays by E.K. Brown, W.E. Collin, Pad-
>raig O Broin, George Woodcock, Lionel Kearns, and Milton Wil-
>son, as well as a self-review by Smith.

Sutherland, John. "Mr. Smith and 'The Tradition.'" In his OTHER
CANADIANA. AN ANTHOLOGY OF THE NEW POETRY IN CANADA, 1940-
1946. Montreal: First Statement Press, 1947, pp. 5-12.

>Sutherland's reply to Smith's labels of "cosmopolitan" and "native"
>for Canadian poetry. See also THE OXFORD BOOK OF CANA-
>DIAN VERSE (1960) and THE BOOK OF CANADIAN POETRY
>(1957) in Prose, section 2, above.

Chapter VII

POETIC RENAISSANCE: THE 1940'S AND BEYOND

In this chapter the listings under each individual author are arranged in three sections. The first two sections list the primary works of the author in chronological order; the third section contains criticism about the author, listed in alphabetical order. Collections edited by the author are listed under Prose.

ANDERSON, PATRICK JOHN McALISTER (1915-)

Patrick Anderson was born and educated in England. He came to New York to study at Columbia University and then moved to Montreal, where he founded the magazine PREVIEW. He left Canada in 1950 and has since lived principally in England, though he has travelled widely in Europe. These travels have been the basis of his prose writing in the last twenty-five years.

Anderson was a poet who brought into Canadian poetry a flamboyance of imagery deriving from Dylan Thomas. He has always been fascinated by landscape, and he applied his Thomas-like images to descriptions of the landscape around Montreal. He was also interested in leftist politics through the 1940's and adapted some of the techniques of 1930's English poets in an attempt to produce a politically oriented verse that might also be considered popular.

1. Poetry

A TENT FOR APRIL. Montreal: First Statement Press, 1945. 26 p.

THE WHITE CENTRE. Toronto: Ryerson, 1946. 72 p.

THE COLOUR AS NAKED. Toronto: McClelland & Stewart, 1953. 93 p.

2. Prose

SNAKE WINE. London: Chatto and Windus, 1955. 288 p. Photographs.

SEARCH ME: AN AUTOBIOGRAPHY--THE BLACK COUNTRY, CANADA AND SPAIN. London: Chatto and Windus, 1957. 237 p.

FIRST STEPS IN GREECE. London: Chatto and Windus, 1958. 212 p. Photographs.

FINDING OUT ABOUT THE ATHENIANS. London: Frederick Muller, 1961. 144 p. Illustrated.

Ed. with Alistair Sutherland. EROS: AN ANTHOLOGY OF FRIENDSHIP. London: Blond, 1961. 433 p.

THE CHARACTER BALL: CHAPTERS OF AUTOBIOGRAPHY. London: Chatto and Windus, 1963. 221 p. Photographs.

DOLPHIN DAYS: A WRITER'S NOTEBOOK OF MEDITERRANEAN PLEASURES. London: Gollancz, 1963. 224 p.

THE SMILE OF APOLLO: A LITERARY COMPANION TO GREEK TRAVEL. London: Chatto and Windus, 1964. 245 p. Maps.

OVER THE ALPS: REFLECTIONS ON TRAVEL AND TRAVEL WRITING WITH SPECIAL REFERENCE TO THE GRAND TOURS OF BOSWELL, BECKFORD AND BYRON. London: Hart-Davis, 1969. 224 p. Illustrated.

"A Poet Past and Future." CANADIAN LITERATURE, 56 (Spring 1973), 7-21.

3. Criticism

Beattie, [A.] Munro. "Poetry 1935-1950." In LITERARY HISTORY OF CANADA; CANADIAN LITERATURE IN ENGLISH. Ed. Carl F. Klinck et al. Toronto: University of Toronto Press, 1965, pp. 771-73.

Francis, Wynne. "Montreal Poets of the Forties." CANADIAN LITERATURE, 14 (Autumn 1962), 21-34.

Frye, Northrop. "From 'Letters in Canada.'" In his THE BUSH GARDEN: ESSAYS ON THE CANADIAN IMAGINATION. Toronto: Anansi, 1971, pp. 23-26.

Livesay, Dorothy. "This Canadian Poetry." CANADIAN FORUM, 24 (April 1944), 20-21.

North, Jessica N. "Mercurial." POETRY (Chicago), 69 (February 1947), 284-86.

Pacey, Desmond. "Modern Canadian Poetry 1920-1950." In his CREATIVE WRITING IN CANADA; A SHORT HISTORY OF ENGLISH-CANADIAN LITERATURE. Rev. ed. Toronto: Ryerson, 1961, pp. 154-58.

Ringrose, Christopher Xerxes. "Patrick Anderson and the Critics." CANADIAN LITERATURE, 43 (Winter 1970), 10-23.

_____. "Preview: Anatomy of a Group." M.A. thesis, University of Alberta, Edmonton, 1969.

Sutherland, John. "The Poetry of Patrick Anderson." NORTHERN REVIEW, 2 (April-May 1949), 8-20, 25-34.

_____. "The Writing of Patrick Anderson." FIRST STATEMENT, 1 (May 1943), 3-6.

Wreford, James. "Canadian Background." INDEX, 1 (July 1946), 6-10.

AVISON, MARGARET KIRKLAND (1918-)

Margaret Avison was born, raised, and educated in Ontario. She has worked in that province as librarian, lecturer, and social worker. Although her first collection of poetry was not published until 1960, her work appeared in magazines throughout the late 1940's and the 1950's. Her poetry is densely textured, using a language at times craggy, at times metaphysical. Her poems often spring from simple, personal experience opened out by her ability to shift historical and visual perspectives. Her poetry has moved increasingly to express her own religious vision of life. She has also contributed translations to an anthology of Hungarian writing.

1. Poetry

WINTER SUN. Toronto: University of Toronto Press, 1960. 89 p.

Duczynska, Ilona, and Karl Polyani, eds. THE PLOUGH AND THE PEN: WRITINGS FROM HUNGARY 1930-1956. Foreword by W.H. Auden. Toronto: McClelland & Stewart, 1963. 231 p.

Wilson, Milton, ed. POETRY OF MIDCENTURY 1940-1960. Toronto: Mc-Clelland & Stewart, 1964. xvi, 237 p.

>An anthology of the work of ten poets. Avison's poems appear on pages 84-111.

THE DUMBFOUNDING. New York: Norton, 1966. 99 p.

Geddes, Gary, and Phyllis Bruce, eds. 15 CANADIAN POETS. Toronto: Oxford University Press, 1970. xvi, 301 p.

>Avison's poetry appears on pages 129-43.

2. Prose

HISTORY OF ONTARIO. Toronto: Gage, 1951. v, 138 p. Illustrations, maps.

3. Criticism

Ade, Janet Elizabeth. "The Poetry of Margaret Avison." M.A. thesis, University of Toronto, 1966.

Beattie, [A.] Munro. "Poetry 1950-1960." In LITERARY HISTORY OF CANADA; CANADIAN LITERATURE IN ENGLISH. Ed. Carl F. Klinck et al. Toronto: University of Toronto Press, 1965, pp. 808-11.

Bowering, George. "Avison's Imitation of Christ the Artist." CANADIAN LITERATURE, 54 (Autumn 1972), 56-69.

Ghiselin, Brewster. "The Architecture of Vision." POETRY (Chicago), 70 (September 1947), 324-28.

Jones, Lawrence M. "A Core of Brilliance: Margaret Avison's Achievement." CANADIAN LITERATURE, 38 (Autumn 1968), 50-57.

New, W.H. "The Mind's Eyes (I's) (Ice): The Poetry of Margaret Avison." In his ARTICULATING WEST: ESSAYS ON PURPOSE AND FORM IN MODERN CANADIAN LITERATURE. Toronto: New Press, 1972, pp. 234-58.

Pacey, Desmond. "The Literature of the Fifties." In his CREATIVE WRITING IN CANADA; A SHORT HISTORY OF ENGLISH-CANADIAN LITERATURE. Rev. ed. Toronto: Ryerson, 1961, pp. 240-41.

Redekop, Ernest. MARGARET AVISON. Toronto: Copp Clark, 1970. 152 p.

_____. "The Only Political Duty: Margaret Avison's Translations of Hungarian Poems." LITERARY HALF YEARLY, 13 (July 1972), 157-70.

Smith, A.J.M. "Critical Improvisations on Margaret Avison's WINTER SUN." TAMARACK REVIEW, 18 (Winter 1961), 81-86.

_____. "Margaret Avison's New Book." CANADIAN FORUM, 46 (September 1966), 132-34.

BIRNEY, ALFRED EARLE (1904-)

Earle Birney was born and brought up in Alberta. He attended universities in Canada and the United States and has also taught at various universities. He established the first department of creative writing at a Canadian university (University of British Columbia).

He has been publishing poetry volumes consistently since the early 1940's. His poems are wide ranging in both subject matter and technique. His travels have given him opportunities to report his Canadian consciousness in relation to other lands and peoples and to transcribe in dramatic monologues the voices of some of the people he has encountered. A restless experimenter, Birney has rewritten many of his poems in the light of later ideas about punctuation in poetry. He has also indulged his playful and satiric sense in many poems, and tried the new forms of concrete and sound poetry.

1. Poetry

DAVID AND OTHER POEMS. Toronto: Ryerson, 1942. 40 p.

NOW IS TIME. Toronto: Ryerson, 1945. 56 p.

THE STRAIT OF ANIAN: SELECTED POEMS. Toronto: Ryerson, 1948. 84 p.

TRIAL OF A CITY AND OTHER VERSE. Toronto: Ryerson, 1952. 71 p.

ICE COD BELL OR STONE. Toronto: McClelland & Stewart, 1962. 62 p.

NEAR FALSE CREEK MOUTH. Toronto: McClelland & Stewart, 1964. Unpaged.

Wilson, Milton, ed. POETRY OF MIDCENTURY 1940-1960. Toronto: McClelland & Stewart, 1964. xvi, 237 p.

Birney's poems appear on pages 19-46.

SELECTED POEMS: 1940-1966. Toronto: McClelland & Stewart, 1966. 222 p.

MEMORY NO SERVANT. Trumansburg, N.Y.: New Books, 1968. 52 p.

THE POEMS OF EARLE BIRNEY. Toronto: McClelland & Stewart, 1969. 64 p.

PNOMES JUKOLLAGES AND OTHER STUNZAS. grOnk, ser. 4, no. 3. Introd. b p nichol. Toronto: Ganglia Press, 1969. Unpaged.

Geddes, Gary, and Phyllis Bruce, eds. 15 CANADIAN POETS. Toronto: Oxford University Press, 1970. xvi, 301 p.

Birney's poems appear on pages 1-23.

RAG AND BONE SHOP. Toronto: McClelland & Stewart, 1971. 59 p.

With Bill Bissett, Judith Copithorne, and Andrew Suknaski. FOUR PARTS SAND. Ottawa: Oberon Press, 1972. Unpaged.

Contains a few of Birney's experimental graphics.

WHAT'S SO BIG ABOUT GREEN? Toronto: McClelland & Stewart, 1973. Unpaged.

THE BEAR ON THE DELHI ROAD. London: Chatto and Windus, 1973.

2. Prose

Earle Birney has written fiction, political essays, critical articles, and academic essays. The following are selected entries which seem to have the most relevance to his own poetry.

Robertson, E. (pseud.). CONVERSATIONS WITH TROTSKY. London: Author, 1935.

"Chaucer's Irony." Ph.D. thesis, University of Toronto, 1936.

"Proletarian Literature: Theory and Practice." CANADIAN FORUM, 17 (May 1937), 58-60.

"Advice to Anthologists: Some Rude Reflections on Canadian Verse." CANADIAN FORUM, 21 (January 1942), 338-40.

"Has Poetry a Future in Canada?" MANITOBA ARTS REVIEW, 5 (Spring 1946), 7-15.

"Age Shall Not Wither Thee: Extracts from a Letter to Mr. Philip Child, Bursar of the Canadian Authors' Association, 15 November 1948." HERE AND NOW, 1 (January 1949), 86-87.

TURVEY. Toronto: McClelland & Stewart, 1952. 286 p. Rpt., introd. George Woodcock. Toronto: McClelland & Stewart, 1963.

> Birney's satiric novel about war and life in the Canadian army during the Second World War.

Ed. TWENTIETH CENTURY CANADIAN POETRY. Toronto: Ryerson, 1953. xvii, 169 p.

> See the entry in chapter IV, for commentary.

DOWN THE LONG TABLE. Toronto: McClelland & Stewart, 1955. 298 p.

> Birney's second novel, about political life during the 1930's.

"The Writer and the H-Bomb: Why Create?" QUEEN'S QUARTERLY, 62 (Spring 1955), 37-44.

"E.J. Pratt and His Critics." In OUR LIVING TRADITION, 2nd and 3rd ser. Ed. Robert L. McDougall. Toronto: University of Toronto Press, 1959, pp. 123-47.

"The Unknown Poetry of Malcolm Lowry." BRITISH COLUMBIA LIBRARY QUARTERLY, 24 (April 1961), 33-40.

"Preface to Poems by Malcolm Lowry." CANADIAN LITERATURE, 8 (Spring 1961), 17-19.

Ed. SELECTED POEMS OF MALCOLM LOWRY. Rev. ed. San Francisco: City Lights, 1963. 79 p. Illustrated.

THE CREATIVE WRITER. Toronto: CBC Publications, 1966. 85 p.

A series of seven radio talks in which Birney expounds his later ideas about poetry, often illustrating the ideas with examples from his own poems.

"The Canadian Writer vs. the Canadian Education." EVIDENCE, 10 (1967), pp. 97-113.

THE COW JUMPED OVER THE MOON: THE WRITING AND READING OF POETRY. Toronto: Holt, Rinehart and Winston, 1972. 112 p. Illustrated.

In some ways this book is an extension of THE CREATIVE WRITER (1966, above, this section), for Birney examines the responses of readers to his narrative poem "David" and also offers some personal exegesis of some of his other poems.

3. Criticism

Beattie, [A.] Munro. "Poetry 1935-1950." In LITERARY HISTORY OF CANADA: CANADIAN LITERATURE IN ENGLISH. Ed. Carl F. Klinck et al. Toronto: University of Toronto Press, 1965, pp. 761-65.

Belanger, Raynald. "Canadian Humorists: Stephen Leacock, Thomas Haliburton, Earle Birney and W.O. Mitchell." D.E.S. thesis, Laval University, Quebec City, Que. 1968.

Brown, E.K. ON CANADIAN POETRY. Rev. ed. Toronto: Ryerson, 1944. 172 p.

Birney's poetry is discussed on pages 76-78.

_____. "To the North: A Wall against Canadian Poetry." SATURDAY RE-VIEW OF LITERATURE, 29 April 1944, pp. 9-11.

CANADIAN LITERATURE, 30 (Autumn 1966), entire issue.

A special issue devoted to critical essays by A.J.M. Smith and Milton Wilson as well as an essay by Birney about the critical response to TURVEY. All of these essays are included in Nesbitt's collection (see below, this section).

Clay, Charles. "Earle Birney, Canadian Spokesman." EDUCATIONAL REC-ORD (Quebec), 61 (April-June 1945), 83-87. Rpt. in LEADING CANADIAN POETS. Ed. W.P. Percival. Toronto: Ryerson, 1948, pp. 23-29.

Davey, Frank. EARLE BIRNEY. Toronto: Copp Clark, 1971. 128 p.

A one-sided reading of Birney's work, developed according to Davey's poetic precepts, which do not necessarily apply as a critical approach to Birney's poetry.

Elliott, Brian. "Earle Birney: Canadian Poet." MEANJIN, 18 (1959), 338-47.

Nesbitt, Bruce, ed. EARLE BIRNEY. Toronto: McGraw-Hill, Ryerson, 1974. ix, 222 p.

The most useful collection of criticism of Birney's writing, spanning his whole career, including contemporary reviews of his books as well as more academic work on his output. Critics included are Northrop Frye, John Sutherland, Roy Daniells, E.K. Brown, George Woodcock, W.E. Fredeman, Paul West, D.G. Jones, and Milton Wilson. The editor's introduction is a thoughtful summary of the criticism as well as a sound reading of Birney's work. The book also contains some of Birney's own, often acerbic, answers to his critics.

New, W.H. "Maker of Order, Prisoner of Dreams: The Poetry of Earle Birney." In his ARTICULATING WEST: ESSAYS ON PURPOSE AND FORM IN MODERN CANADIAN LITERATURE. Toronto: New Press, 1972, pp. 259-69.

Noel-Bentley, Peter C. "A Study of the Poetry of Earle Birney." M.A. thesis, University of Toronto, 1966.

Noel-Bentley, Peter C., and Earle Birney. "Earle Birney: A Bibliography in Progress 1923-1969." WEST COAST REVIEW, 5 (October 1970), 45-53.

Pacey, Desmond. "Earle Birney." In his TEN CANADIAN POETS; A GROUP OF BIOGRAPHICAL AND CRITICAL ESSAYS. Toronto: Ryerson, 1958, pp. 293-326.

_____. "Modern Canadian Poetry 1920-1950." In his CREATIVE WRITING IN CANADA; A SHORT HISTORY OF ENGLISH-CANADIAN VERSE. Rev. ed. Toronto: Ryerson, 1961, pp. 150-53.

Phelps, Arthur L. "Two Poets: Klein and Birney." In his CANADIAN WRITERS. Toronto: McClelland & Stewart, 1951, pp. 111-19.

Robillard, Richard. EARLE BIRNEY. Toronto: McClelland & Stewart, 1971.

An interesting linguistic study of Birney's poetry in particular.

Woodcock, George. "Earle Birney." In CONTEMPORARY POETS OF THE

ENGLISH LANGUAGE. Ed. Rosalie Murphy. London: St. James Press, 1970, pp. 94-97.

BREWSTER, ELIZABETH WINIFRED (1922-)

Elizabeth Brewster was born in New Brunswick and went to a university in that province before studying in the United States. She was a librarian for many years but recently has been teaching in universities.

Her poetry reflects her early life in the Maritimes, dealing with landscape and with people in relation to their environment. The point of view behind the poems is often full of nostalgia and regret, but within the simple language the poet manages to alleviate the pervasive gloom by the directness of personal response and by some self-mockery and humor.

1. Poetry

EAST COAST. Toronto: Ryerson, 1951. 8 p.

LILLOOET. Toronto: Ryerson, 1954. 28 p.

ROADS AND OTHER POEMS. Toronto: Ryerson, 1957. 12 p.

FIVE NEW BRUNSWICK POETS: ELIZABETH BREWSTER, FRED COGSWELL, ROBERT GIBBS, ALDEN NOWLAN, KAY SMITH. Fredericton, N.B.: Fiddle-head Press, 1962. 64 p.

PASSAGE OF SUMMER: SELECTED POEMS. Toronto: Clarke, Irwin, 1969. 129 p.

SUNRISE NORTH. Toronto: Clarke, Irwin, 1972. 87 p.

2. Criticism

Beattie, [A.] Munro. "Poetry 1950-1960." In LITERARY HISTORY OF CANADA; CANADIAN LITERATURE IN ENGLISH. Ed. Carl F. Klinck et al. Toronto: University of Toronto Press, 1965, p. 800.

Pacey, Desmond. "The Poetry of Elizabeth Brewster." ARIEL, 4 (July 1973), 58-69.

COGSWELL, FREDERICK WILLIAM (1917-)

Fred Cogswell is a Maritimer; he has spent most of his life in the Maritimes, where he has taught English at the University of New Brunswick. Much of his energy has been devoted to the editing and publishing of poetry, first through the FIDDLEHEAD magazine, and second through his own Fiddlehead Press.

Cogswell's poetry is strongly traditional, though he does use free verse on occasions. He is very effective in his portrayal of Maritime life and people; his poems are touched with compassion, but also with sardonic and sometimes bitter humor.

Cogswell has been a great enthusiast for the encouragement of Canadian litera-ture; he has published the work of many poets through the Fiddlehead Press and has written many articles and reviews on a wide variety of Canadian subjects. He has translated some modern French-Canadian poetry.

1. Poetry

THE STUNTED STRONG. Fredericton: University of New Brunswick, 1954. 16 p.

THE HALOED TREE. Toronto: Ryerson, 1956. 16 p.

Trans. THE TESTAMENT OF CRESSEID, by Robert Henryson. Toronto: Ryerson, 1957. 24 p.

DESCENT FROM EDEN. Toronto: Ryerson, 1959. 38 p.

LOST DIMENSION. Dulwich Village, Engl.: Outposts Publications, 1960. 12 p.

STAR PEOPLE. Fredericton, N.B.: Fiddlehead Press, 1968. 48 p.

IMMORTAL PLOWMAN. Fredericton, N.B.: Fiddlehead Press, 1969. 38 p.

IN PRAISE OF CHASTITY. Fredericton, N.B.: Fiddlehead Press, 1970. 30 p.

Comp. and trans. ONE HUNDRED POEMS OF MODERN QUEBEC. Fredericton, N.B.: Fiddlehead Press, 1970. 91 p.

THE CHAINS OF LILIPUT. Fredericton, N.B.: Fiddlehead Press, 1971. 32 p.

Comp. and trans. A SECOND HUNDRED POEMS OF MODERN QUEBEC. Frederiction, N.B.: Fiddlehead Press, 1971. 80 p.

THE HOUSE WITHOUT A DOOR. Fredericton, N.B.: Fiddlehead Press, 1973. 32 p.

Trans. CONFRONTATION, by Gratien Lapointe. Fredericton, N.B.: Fiddlehead Press, 1973. 26 p.

2. Prose

Cogswell has devoted much of his career to reviewing and to the writing of scholarly articles on both poetry and prose. This brief list reflects his interest in the literature of the Maritimes, since it plays such an important part in his own poetry.

"E.J. Pratt's Literary Reputation." CANADIAN LITERATURE, 19 (Winter 1964), 6–12.

A critical reappraisal of the work of E.J. Pratt.

"Haliburton." In LITERARY HISTORY OF CANADA; CANADIAN LITERATURE IN ENGLISH. Ed. Carl F. Klinck et al. Toronto: University of Toronto Press, 1965, pp. 92–101.

"Literary Activity in the Maritime Provinces 1815–1880." In LITERARY HISTORY OF CANADA; CANADIAN LITERATURE IN ENGLISH. Ed. Carl F. Klinck et al. Toronto: University of Toronto Press, 1965, pp. 102–24.

"Settlement: I Newfoundland 1715–1880; II The Maritime Provinces 1720–1815." In LITERARY HISTORY OF CANADA; CANADIAN LITERATURE IN ENGLISH. Ed. Carl F. Klinck et al. Toronto: University of Toronto Press, 1965, pp. 68–83.

3. Criticism

Beattie, [A.] Munro. "Poetry 1950-1960." In LITERARY HISTORY OF CANADA; CANADIAN LITERATURE IN ENGLISH. Ed. Carl F. Klinck et al. Toronto: University of Toronto Press, 1965, pp. 800–802.

Pacey, Desmond. "The Literature of the Fifties." In his CREATIVE WRITING IN CANADA; A SHORT HISTORY OF ENGLISH-CANADIAN LITERATURE. Rev. ed. Toronto: Ryerson, 1961, pp. 248–49.

DUDEK, LOUIS (1918-)·

Louis Dudek was born and educated in Montreal. Apart from a period in New York (1943-51), he has lived in Montreal, teaching at McGill University, editing and publishing little magazines, and establishing small presses. He has been associated with magazines such as CONTACT and DELTA which burgeoned into small presses.

Dudek's early, realistic poetry is in the form of short lyrics, expressing precise observations. These detailed observations are often used as a basis for philosophical meditation. His gloomy view of human civilization finds expression in his later, longer poems, in which he develops his philosophic strain. He has also written some satirical poems. Dudek's views on poetry have become increasingly conservative, and are unsympathetic to the boisterous experimentation in contemporary Canadian poetry.

1. Poetry

Hambleton, Ronald, ed. UNIT OF FIVE. Toronto: Ryerson, 1944. xi, 87 p.
> Dudek's poems are on pages 3-18.

EAST OF THE CITY. Toronto: Ryerson, 1946. 51 p.

CERBERUS. Toronto: Contact Press, 1952. 98 p.
> Poems by Louis Dudek, Irving Layton, and Raymond Souster.

THE SEARCHING IMAGE. Toronto: Ryerson, 1952. 12 p.

TWENTY-FOUR POEMS. Toronto: Contact Press, 1952. 24 p.

EUROPE. Toronto: Laocoon (Contact) Press, 1954. 139 p.

THE TRANSPARENT SEA. Toronto: Contact Press, 1956. 114 p.

EN MEXICO. Toronto: Contact Press, 1958. 78 p.

LAUGHING STALKS. Toronto: Contact Press, 1958. 113 p.

ATLANTIS. Montreal: Delta, 1967. 151 p.

COLLECTED POETRY. Montreal: Delta, 1971. 327 p.

2. Prose

Louis Dudek has been an indefatigable propagandist for poetry and an expounder of his own ideas about its theory and practice. He has written many articles and reviews, of which the following entries give a sampling.

"The Montreal Poets." CULTURE, 18 (June 1957), 149-54.

"A Note on Metrics." DELTA, 5 (October 1958), 15-17.

LITERATURE AND THE PRESS: A HISTORY OF PRINTING, PRINTED MEDIA, AND THEIR RELATION TO LITERATURE. Toronto: Ryerson and Contact Press, 1960. 238 p.

"The Two Traditions: Literature and the Ferment in Quebec." CANADIAN LITERATURE, 12 (Spring 1962), 44-51.

"Art, Entertainment and Religion." QUEEN'S QUARTERLY, 70 (Autumn 1963), 413-30.

"Groundhog among the Stars: The Poetry of Raymond Souster." CANADIAN LITERATURE, 22 (Autumn 1964), 34-49.

"The New Vancouver Poetry." CULTURE, 25 (December 1964), 323-30.

THE FIRST PERSON IN LITERATURE. Toronto: CBC Publications, 1967. 69 p.

Ed. with Michael Gnarowski. THE MAKING OF MODERN POETRY IN CANADA: ESSENTIAL ARTICLES ON CONTEMPORARY CANADIAN POETRY IN ENGLISH. Toronto: Ryerson, 1967. ix, 303 p.

"Nationalism in Canadian Poetry." QUEEN'S QUARTERLY, 75 (Winter 1968), 557-67.

"The Writing of the Decade: Poetry." CANADIAN LITERATURE, 41 (Summer 1969), 111-20.

"Technology and Culture." In ROYAL SOCIETY OF CANADA, 4th ser., VII (Translations). Ottawa: R.S.C., 1969, pp. 57-72.

"The Mirror of Art: Relations between French and English Literature in Canada." CULTURE, 31 (September 1970), 225-31.

"The Misuses of Imagination: A Rib-Roasting of Some Recent Canadian Critics."
TAMARACK REVIEW, 60 (October 1973), 51-67.

3. Criticism

Barbour, Douglas. "Poet as Philosopher." CANADIAN LITERATURE, 53
(Summer 1972), 18-29.

Beattie, [A.] Munro. "Poetry 1935-1950." In LITERARY HISTORY OF CANADA;
CANADIAN LITERATURE IN ENGLISH. Ed. Carl F. Klinck et al. Toronto:
University of Toronto Press, 1965, pp. 776-78.

Francis, Wynne. "A Critic of Life: Dudek as Man of Letters." CANADIAN
LITERATURE, 22 (Autumn 1964), 5-23.

Frye, Northrop. "From 'Letters in Canada.'" In his THE BUSH GARDEN:
ESSAYS ON THE CANADIAN IMAGINATION. Toronto: Anansi, 1971, pp.
19-21, 53-54, 62-64, 98-100.

Gnarowski, Michael. "Louis Dudek: A Note." YES, 14 (September 1965),
4-6.

Livesay, Dorothy. "The Sculpture of Poetry." CANADIAN LITERATURE, 30
(Autumn 1966), 26-35.

Pacey, Desmond. "Modern Canadian Poetry." In his CREATIVE WRITING IN
CANADA; A SHORT HISTORY OF ENGLISH-CANADIAN LITERATURE. Rev.
ed. Toronto: Ryerson, 1961, pp. 170-74.

Smith, A.J.M. "Turning New Leaves." CANADIAN FORUM, 27 (May 1947),
42-43.

Wilson, Milton. "Review of EUROPE." CANADIAN FORUM, 35 (October
1955), 162-63; (November 1955), 182-84.

EVERSON, RONALD GILMOUR (1903-)

R.G. Everson was born in Oshawa, Ontario, and educated at the University of
Toronto. He was a practicing lawyer for several years until he became involved
in public relations work in Montreal. His poetry was first published in the
1920's in Canada and the United States, but he assembled a collection for book
publication only in 1957.

Everson's poetry often concentrates on simple incidents presented in short, fragmentary pieces with direct and imagistic diction. Although the surface of his writing appears simple, he unobtrusively weaves many literary and historical allusions into the texture of his poetry. He can be sardonic and ironic by turns and occasionally introduces a grotesque note into his work. Generally, his poetry is realistic and immediate, with a firm grip on time and place. Everson's poetry has been generally ignored by the critics.

1. Poetry

Everson's principal volumes of poetry follow. He has published some small leaflets of poems under the imprint of small press publishers in the United States, but the poems in these pamphlets are included in the volumes published in Canada.

THREE DOZEN POEMS. Montreal: Author, 1957. 51 p. Illustrated.

A LATTICE FOR MOMOS. Toronto: Contact Press, 1958. 58 p. Illustrated.

BLIND MAN'S HOLIDAY. Toronto: Ryerson, 1963. 34 p. Illustrated.

WRESTLE WITH AN ANGEL. Montreal: Delta, 1965. 48 p. Illustrated.

THE DARK IS NOT SO DARK. Montreal: Delta, 1969. 91 p. Illustrated.

SELECTED POEMS: 1920/1970. Montreal: Delta, 1970. 108 p. Illustrated.

2. Criticism

Beattie, [A.] Munro. "Poetry 1950-1960." In LITERARY HISTORY OF CANADA; CANADIAN LITERATURE IN ENGLISH. Ed. Carl F. Klinck et al. Toronto: University of Toronto Press, 1965, pp. 803-5.

Frye, Northrop. "From 'Letters in Canada.'" In his THE BUSH GARDEN: ESSAYS ON THE CANADIAN IMAGINATION. Toronto: Anansi, 1971, pp. 82-83, 93-95.

Gustafson, Ralph. "Everson's Half Century." CANADIAN LITERATURE, 49 (Summer 1971), 65-67.

GLASSCO, JOHN (1909-)

John Glassco was born and educated in Montreal. In the late 1920's he went to live in Paris (his autobiographical MEMOIRS OF MONTPARNASSE concentrates on this period of his life). Since the mid-1930's he has lived mainly in rural Quebec, devoting his energies to his own work, both in poetry and prose, to translating from French, and to editing.

Glassco's poetry is traditional in nature, rendering in a sophisticated elegance his feelings for the rural regions of Quebec, his sense of its past, and his feelings of regret and loss. He is another Canadian poet whose work has been subjected to little criticism apart from book reviews.

1. Poetry

CONAN'S FIG. Paris: Transition, 1928.

THE DEFICIT MADE FLESH. Toronto: McClelland & Stewart, 1958. 64 p.

Trans. THE JOURNAL OF SAINT-DENYS-GARNEAU. Toronto: McClelland & Stewart, 1962. 270 p.

A POINT OF SKY. Toronto: Oxford University Press, 1964. 78 p.

ENGLISH POETRY IN QUEBEC. Proceedings of the Foster Poetry Conference, 12-14 October 1963. Montreal: McGill University Press, 1965. 142 p.

SELECTED POEMS. Toronto: Oxford University Press, 1971. 96 p.

2. Prose

CONTES EN CRINOLINE. Paris: Gaucher, 1930.

> In French. Anon. German translation, MARCHEN IN KRINOLINE, Leipzig, 1931.

UNDER THE HILL. Paris: Olympia Press, 1959. 123 p. Illustrated.

> Completion of the unfinished novel by Aubrey Beardsley, with a critical introduction.

Underwood, Miles (pseud.). THE ENGLISH GOVERNESS. Paris: Olympia Press, 1960.

Gooch, Silas (pseud.). "A Season in Limbo." TAMARACK REVIEW, 23 (Spring 1962), 55–84.

MEMOIRS OF MONTPARNASSE. Introd. Leon Edel. Toronto: Oxford University Press, 1970. 254 p.

Ed. THE POETRY OF FRENCH CANADA IN TRANSLATION. Toronto: Oxford University Press, 1970. 260 p.

3. Criticism

Beattie, [A.] Munro. "Poetry 1950–1960." In LITERARY HISTORY OF CANADA; CANADIAN LITERATURE IN ENGLISH. Ed. Carl F. Klinck et al. Toronto: University of Toronto Press, 1965, pp. 797–99.

Frye, Northrop. "From 'Letters in Canada.'" In his THE BUSH GARDEN: ESSAYS ON THE CANADIAN IMAGINATION. Toronto: Anansi, 1971, pp. 91–93.

Gnarowski, Michael. "John Glassco: A Note." YES, 15 (September 1966), 12–14.

GRIER, ELDON (1917-)

Born in London, England, of Canadian parents and educated in Canada, Eldon Grier is a painter who has lived in Mexico, studying under Diego Rivera. He lived for some time in Europe where he first started writing poetry, which is painterly in its presentation of direct images. In his later work, however, he shows some effects of being influenced by surrealism, setting his directness against the irrational and the flux of life. His work has never been assessed critically, apart from book reviews.

1. Poetry

A MORNING FROM SCRAPS. Montreal: Author, ca. 1955. 22 p.

POEMS. Montreal: Author, 1956.

MANZILLO AND OTHER POEMS. Montreal: Author, 1957.

THE RING OF ICE. Montreal: Cambridge Press, 1957. 101 p.

A FRICTION OF LIGHTS. Toronto: Contact Press, 1963. 61 p.

PICTURES ON THE SKIN. Montreal: Delta, 1967. 61 p. Illustrated.

SELECTED POEMS 1955-1970. Montreal: Delta, 1971. 129 p. Illustrated.

GUSTAFSON, RALPH BARKER (1909-)

Ralph Gustafson was born near Sherbrooke, Quebec, and was educated in Canada and England. After living in New York for several years, he returned to Canada where he has been a professor at Bishop's University, Lennoxville, Quebec, for many years.

His early poetry was antimodernist until in the 1940's he began to forge his unique style, based on the work of Hopkins, Yeats, and the metaphysical poets in particular. His verse is often dense and craggy, sometimes to the point of being awkward and obscure. In recent years this roughness of surface and use of allusion has been tempered by a kind of jocular colloquialism.

Gustafson has always been a champion of Canadian poetry, and he has been an editor of anthologies which have been instrumental in introducing readers outside Canada to the world of Canadian poetry in English (see the annotations for Gustafson's anthologies in chapter IV). He has written some critical prose and some short stories, though these have never been collected.

1. Poetry

THE GOLDEN CHALICE. London: Nicholson & Watson, 1935. 105 p.

ALFRED THE GREAT. London: Joseph, 1937. 119 p.

EPITHALAMIUM IN TIME OF WAR. New York: Author, 1941. 11 p.

LYRICS UNROMANTIC. New York: Author, 1942. 19 p.

Ed. ANTHOLOGY OF CANADIAN POETRY. Harmondsworth, Engl. and New York: Penguin Books, 1942. 123 p.

Ed. A LITTLE ANTHOLOGY OF CANADIAN POETS. Norfolk, Conn.: New Directions, 1943. 26 p.

Ed. VOICES: A QUARTERLY OF POETRY, (Spring 1943), 3-43.

FLIGHT INTO DARKNESS. New York: Pantheon, 1944. 96 p.

Ed. CANADIAN ACCENT. A COLLECTION OF STORIES AND POEMS. Harmondsworth, Engl.: Penguin Books, 1944. 144 p.

RIVERS AMONG ROCKS. Toronto: McClelland & Stewart, 1960. 68 p.

ROCKY MOUNTAIN POEMS. Vancouver, B.C.: Klanak Press, 1960. 36 p.

SIFT IN AN HOURGLASS. Toronto: McClelland & Stewart, 1966. 93 p.

Ed. THE PENGUIN BOOK OF CANADIAN VERSE. Rev. ed. Harmondsworth, Engl.: Penguin Books, 1967. 282 p.

IXION'S WHEEL. Toronto: McClelland & Stewart, 1969. 128 p.

SELECTED POEMS. Toronto: McClelland & Stewart, 1972. 128 p.

THEME AND VARIATIONS FOR SOUNDING BRASS. Sherbrooke, Que.: Progressive Publications, 1972. 24 p.

2. Criticism

Beattie, [A.] Munro. "Poetry 1950-1960." In LITERARY HISTORY OF CANADA; CANADIAN LITERATURE IN ENGLISH. Ed. Carl F. Klinck et al. Toronto: University of Toronto Press, 1965, pp. 783-84.

Dudek, Louis. "Two Canadian Poets: Ralph Gustafson and Eli Mandel." CULTURE 22 (June 1961), 145-51.

Keitner, Wendy Joan Robbins. "Ralph Gustafson: Heir of Centuries in a Country without Myths." Ph.D. thesis, Queen's University, Kingston, Ont., 1973.

Mullins, S.G. "Ralph Gustafson's Poetry." CULTURE, 22 (December 1961), 417-22.

HINE, WILLIAM DARYL (1936-)

Born in Burnaby, British Columbia, Daryl Hine studied classics and philosophy at McGill University in Montreal. He served on the staff of the Canadian Legation in Paris in the early 1960's, also traveling throughout Europe at that time. He spent some time in Poland as an editor of subtitles for a Polish film, and has written an account of his Polish experiences in POLISH SUBTITLES (1963). He studied comparative literature at the University of Chicago on his return to this continent, and has taught at that university since 1967. In October 1969 he was appointed editor of POETRY (Chicago).

Hine's poetry was first published when he was fifteen, and he has published consistently since that time. His poetry is obviously influenced, in both form and content, by his readings in the classics. His main theme is the duality of art and life, although his poetry often examines the undersurfaces of life. His technique is very sophisticated, showing a masterly control of traditional meters and stanza forms. At times he writes in free verse, and this looser form has added a new liveliness to a poetry that otherwise seemed, occasionally, too arid and detached.

1. Poetry

FIVE POEMS, 1954. Toronto: Emblem Press, 1955. 13 p.

THE CARNAL AND THE CRANE. Montreal: McGill Poetry Series, 1957. 50 p.

THE DEVIL'S PICTURE BOOK. Toronto: Abelard-Schuman, 1960. 32 p.

THE WOODEN HORSE. New York: Atheneum, 1965. 58 p.

MINUTES; POEMS. New York: Atheneum, 1968. 53 p.

THE HOMERIC HYMNS AND THE BATTLE OF THE FROGS AND MICE. New York: Atheneum, 1972. xii, 94 p.

2. Prose

THE PRINCE OF DARKNESS & CO. Toronto: Abelard-Schuman, 1961. 190 p.

POLISH SUBTITLES: IMPRESSIONS FROM A JOURNEY. Toronto: Abelard-Schuman, 1963. 160 p.

3. Criticism

Beattie, [A.] Munro. "Poetry 1935-1950." In LITERARY HISTORY OF CANADA; CANADIAN LITERATURE IN ENGLISH. Ed. Carl F. Klinck et al. Toronto:

University of Toronto Press, 1965, pp. 812-14.

Frye, Northrop. "From 'Letters in Canada.'" In his THE BUSH GARDEN: ESSAYS ON THE CANADIAN IMAGINATION. Toronto: Anansi, 1971, pp. 55, 76-80.

Howard, Richard. "Daryl Hine." In his ALONE WITH AMERICA: ESSAYS IN THE ART OF POETRY IN THE UNITED STATES SINCE 1950. New York: Atheneum, 1969, pp. 174-86.

New, W.H. "Six Canadian Poets." In his ARTICULATING WEST: ESSAYS ON PURPOSE AND FORM IN MODERN CANADIAN LITERATURE. Toronto: New Press, 1972, pp. 149-51.

JONES, DOUGLAS GORDON (1929-)

D.G. Jones, born in Ontario and educated there and at McGill University, has taught in several educational institutions and is now with the Department of English at the University of Sherbrooke, Quebec.

His poetry is a mixture of sharp, clear imagist lyrics and some attempts at philosophic meditation. His interest in myths as the basis for literature led him to write a theoretical study of Canadian literature, BUTTERFLY ON ROCK. He has devoted his energies in recent years to editing the magazine ELLIPSE, which is concerned with an exchange of translations of and ideas about French- and English-Canadian literature. He has also continued to write review articles about French- and English-Canadian poetry.

1. Poetry

FROST ON THE SUN. Toronto: Contact Press, 1957. 46 p.

THE SUN IS AXEMAN. Toronto: University of Toronto Press, 1961. 70 p.

PHRASES FROM ORPHEUS. Toronto: Oxford University Press, 1967. 88 p.

Geddes, Gary, and Phyllis Bruce, eds. 15 CANADIAN POETS. Toronto: Oxford University, Press, 1970. xvi, 301 p.

    Jones's poems appear on pages 97-112.

2. Prose

"The Sleeping Giant: Or the Uncreated Conscience of the Race." CANA-
DIAN LITERATURE, 26 (Autumn 1965), pp. 3-21.

BUTTERFLY ON ROCK; A STUDY OF THEMES AND IMAGES IN CANADIAN
LITERATURE. Toronto: University of Toronto Press, 1970. x, 197 p.

For annotation, see the main entry in chapter III.

"Myth, Frye and Canadian Writers." CANADIAN LITERATURE, 55 (Winter
1973), 7-22.

3. Criticism

Frye, Northrop. "From 'Letters in Canada.'" In his THE BUSH GARDEN:
ESSAYS ON THE CANADIAN IMAGINATION. Toronto: Anansi, 1971,
pp. 80-81.

LAYTON, IRVING PETER [LAZAROVITCH] (1912-)

Irving Layton was born in Rumania in 1912 and was brought to Canada by his
parents the following year. He was educated in Montreal, receiving a B.S.
from MacDonald College and an M.A. from McGill University. For most of
his life Layton has been a teacher and poet-in-residence at a wide variety of
educational institutions. At the present time he is a professor at York Univer-
sity, Downsview, Ontario.

Layton has been publishing voluminously since his first poem was printed in
1931. His poetry is often flamboyant and rhetorically charged, centering on
the self-image of the poet. His poetry typically expresses the notion of polari-
ties, using Apollonian (order and rationality) and Dionysian (creativity and
ecstasy) symbols. His early work was condemned, ostensibly for its overt sex-
uality; and his later work has been dismissed, ostensibly for its repetitive nature
and its slackness. These condemnations have been recurrent, and Layton has
had a continual, often vituperative, dialogue with his critics, defending his
own poetry and attacking their myopia, brainlessness, and total confusion about
the poetic process. These prose skirmishes run through the pages of various
journals and newspapers and give a clear picture of the poetic temper of Canada
from the 1940's on. Much of this prose of contention, together with Layton's
short stories, has been collected in ENGAGEMENTS (see below, section 2).

1. Poetry

HERE AND NOW. Montreal: First Statement Press, 1945. 44 p.

NOW IS THE PLACE: POEMS AND STORIES. Montreal: First Statement Press, 1948. 57 p.

THE BLACK HUNTSMEN. Montreal: Author, 1951. 56 p.

CERBERUS. Toronto: Contact Press, 1952. 98 p.
    Poems by Louis Dudek, Irving Layton, and Raymond Souster.

LOVE THE CONQUEROR WORM. Toronto: Contact Press, 1953. 49 p.

IN THE MIDST OF MY FEVER. Palma de Mallorca, Spain: Divers Press, 1954. 39 p.

THE LONG PEA-SHOOTER. Montreal: Laocoon Press, 1954. 68 p.

THE BLUE PROPELLER. Toronto: Contact Press, 1955. 50 p.

THE COLD GREEN ELEMENT. Toronto: Contact Press, 1955. 56 p.

MUSIC ON A KAZOO. Toronto: Contact Press, 1956. 59 p.

THE BULL CALF AND OTHER POEMS. Toronto: Contact Press, 1956. 49 p.

THE IMPROVED BINOCULARS. Introd. William Carlos Williams. Highlands, N.C.: Jonathan Williams, 1956. 106 p.

THE IMPROVED BINOCULARS. 2nd ed., with 30 additional poems. Highlands, N.C.: Jonathan Williams, 1957. 139 p.

A LAUGHTER IN THE MIND. Highlands, N.C.: Jonathan Williams, 1958. 54 p.

A LAUGHTER IN THE MIND. 2nd ed., with 20 additional poems. Montreal: Editions d'Orphee, 1959. 97 p.

A RED CARPET FOR THE SUN. Toronto: McClelland & Stewart, 1959. 240 p.

THE SWINGING FLESH. Toronto: McClelland & Stewart, 1961. 189 p.

BALLS FOR A ONE-ARMED JUGGLER. Toronto: McClelland & Stewart, 1963. xxii, 121 p.

THE LAUGHING ROOSTER. Toronto: McClelland & Stewart, 1964. 112 p.

Wilson, Milton, ed. POETRY OF MIDCENTURY 1940-1960. Toronto: McClelland & Stewart, 1964. xvi, 237 p.

Layton's poetry appears on pages 47-83.

COLLECTED POEMS. Toronto: McClelland & Stewart, 1965. 354 p.

PERIODS OF THE MOON. Toronto: McClelland & Stewart, 1967. 127 p.

THE SHATTERED PLINTHS. Toronto: McClelland & Stewart, 1968. 95 p.

THE WHOLE BLOODY BIRD. Toronto: McClelland & Stewart, 1969. 155 p.

SELECTED POEMS. Ed. with a pref. Wynne Francis. Toronto: McClelland & Stewart, 1969. 140 p.

Geddes, Gary, and Phyllis Bruce, eds. 15 CANADIAN POETS. Toronto: Oxford University Press, 1970. xvi, 301 p.

Layton's poems appear on pages 45-61.

NAIL POLISH. Toronto: McClelland & Stewart, 1971. 87 p.

THE COLLECTED POEMS. Toronto: McClelland & Stewart, 1971. 589 p.

LOVERS AND LESSER MEN. Toronto: McClelland & Stewart, 1973. 109 p.

2. Prose

Ed. with Louis Dudek. CANADIAN POEMS 1850-1952. Rev. ed. Toronto: Contact Press, 1953. 126 p.

Ed. POEMS FOR 27 CENTS. Montreal: Authors, 1961. 30 p.

Layton also wrote an introduction to this collection of poetry by Lorna Chaisson, Maria Van Den Yssel, Stan Fisher, Gertrude Katz, Alan Pearson.

Ed. LOVE WHERE THE NIGHTS ARE LONG: CANADIAN LOVE POEMS. Illus. Harold Town. Toronto: McClelland & Stewart, 1962. 78 p.

Ed. ANVIL: A SELECTION OF WORKSHOP POEMS. Montreal: Authors, 1966. 67 p.

ENGAGEMENTS: THE PROSE OF IRVING LAYTON. Toronto: McClelland & Stewart, 1972. xvi, 336 p.

3. Criticism

Adams, Richard. "The Poetic Theories of Irving Layton: A Study in Polarities." M.A. thesis, University of New Brunswick, Fredericton, 1971.

Beattie, [A.] Munro. "Poetry 1935-1950." In LITERARY HISTORY OF CANADA; CANADIAN LITERATURE IN ENGLISH. Ed. Carl F. Klinck et al. Toronto: University of Toronto Press, 1965, pp. 781-83.

Bukowski, Charles. "The Corybant of Wit." EVIDENCE, 9 (1965), 112-17.

Carruth, Hayden. "That Heaven-Sent Lively Rope-Walker, Irving Layton." TAMARACK REVIEW, 39 (Spring 1966), 68-73.

Cogswell, Fred. "Eros or Narcissus: The Male Canadian Poet." MOSAIC, 1 (January 1968), 103-11.

Doyle, Mike. "The Occasions of Irving Layton." CANADIAN LITERATURE, 54 (Autumn 1972), 70-83.

Edelstein, George. "Irving Layton: A Study of the Poet in Revolt." M.A. thesis, University of Montreal, 1962.

Francis, Wynne. "Irving Layton." JOURNAL OF COMMONWEALTH LITERATURE, 3 (July 1967), 34-48.

_____. "Montreal Poets of the Forties." CANADIAN LITERATURE, 14 (Autumn 1962), 21-34.

Frye, Northrop. "From 'Letters in Canada.'" In his THE BUSH GARDEN: ESSAYS ON THE CANADIAN IMAGINATION. Toronto: Anansi, 1971, pp. 8, 31, 40-42, 52-53, 68-70, 95-97, 115-18.

Hope, A.D. Review of A RED CARPET FOR THE SUN. DALHOUSIE REVIEW,

40 (Summer 1960), 271-77.

Jones, D.G. BUTTERFLY ON ROCK; A STUDY OF THEMES AND IMAGES IN CANADIAN LITERATURE. Toronto: University of Toronto Press, 1970. x, 197 p.

    For discussion of Layton see pages 11-12, 21-23, 26, 83, 88, 111, 128-34, 136, 138-39, 163, 165, and 183.

Junkins, Donald. Review of SELECTED POEMS. FAR POINT, 3 (Fall/Winter 1969), 61-69.

Kenner, Hugh. "Beast-Type Sockdolagers." POETRY, 94 (September 1959), 413-18.

Lyons, Roberta. "Jewish Poets from Montreal: Concepts of History in the Poetry of A.M. Klein, Irving Layton and Leonard Cohen." M.A. thesis, Carleton University, Ottawa, 1966.

Mandel, Eli. IRVING LAYTON. Toronto: Forum House, 1969. 82 p.

_____. Review of A LAUGHTER IN THE MIND. DALHOUSIE REVIEW, 41, (Spring 1959), 119-23.

Mayne, Seymour. "Irving Layton: A Bibliography in Progress." WEST COAST REVIEW, 7 (January 1973), 23-32.

_____. "A Study of the Poetry of Irving Layton." Ph.D. thesis, University of British Columbia, Vancouver, 1972.

O Broin, Padraig. "Fire-Drake." TEANGADOIR, 2nd ser., 1 (November 1962), 73-80.

Ower, John. "An Over-Riding Metaphor: Images of Exile, Imprisonment and Home in Modern Canadian Poetry." MOSAIC, 4 (Summer 1971), 75-90.

Pacey, Desmond. "Modern Canadian Poetry." In his CREATIVE WRITING IN CANADA; A SHORT HISTORY OF ENGLISH-CANADIAN LITERATURE. Rev. ed. Toronto: Ryerson, 1961, pp. 163-67.

_____. Review of THE SWINGING FLESH. FIDDLEHEAD, 49 (Summer 1961), 61-72.

Reif, Eric Anthony. "Irving Layton: The Role of the Poet." M.A. thesis, University of Toronto, 1966.

Reznitsky, Laurence J. "Interview with Irving Layton." LE CHIEN D'OR/ THE GOLDEN DOG, 1 (January 1972), unpaged.

Ripley, J.D. Review of THE SWINGING FLESH. DALHOUSIE REVIEW, 41 (Winter 1961–62), 567–73.

Smith, A.J.M. "The Recent Poetry of Irving Layton: A Major Voice." QUEEN'S QUARTERLY, 62 (Winter 1955–56), 587–91.

Smith, Patricia Keeney. "Irving Layton and the Theme of Death." CANADIAN LITERATURE, 48 (Spring 1971), 6–15.

Thomas, Clara. "A Conversation about Literature: An Interview with Margaret Laurence and Irving Layton." JOURNAL OF CANADIAN FICTION, 1 (Winter 1972), 65–69.

Waterston, Elizabeth. "Apocalypse in Montreal." CANADIAN LITERATURE, 48 (Spring 1971), 16–24.

Wilson, Milton. "Turning New Leaves." CANADIAN FORUM, 35 (October 1955), 162–64.

   Review of IN THE MIDST OF MY FEVER and THE COLD GREEN ELEMENT.

Woodcock, George. "A Grab at Proteus." CANADIAN LITERATURE, 28 (Spring 1966), 5–21.

LePAN, DOUGLAS VALENTINE (1914-)

Douglas LePan was born and educated in Toronto. He also studied at Oxford University. After his war service, he joined the Department of External Affairs until 1959 when he returned to the teaching profession.

His poetry is restrained and smoothly flowing as he develops themes about the nature of the Canadian wilderness and the early adventurers who traveled through it. Some of his poems deal with war experiences in which he meditates on the once-noble grandeur of Europe, its destruction, and the place of the Canadian in relation to that European heritage.

1. Poetry

THE WOUNDED PRINCE AND OTHER POEMS. London: Chatto and Windus, 1948. 39 p.

THE NET AND THE SWORD. London: Chatto and Windus, 1953. 56 p.

2. Prose

THE DESERTER. Toronto: McClelland & Stewart, 1964. 298 p.

3. Criticism

Beattie, [A.] Munro. "Poetry 1950-1960." In LITERARY HISTORY OF CANADA;
CANADIAN LITERATURE IN ENGLISH. Ed. Carl F. Klinck et al. Toronto:
University of Toronto Press, 1965, pp. 795-97.

Davies, M. "The Bird of Heavenly Airs: Thematic Strains in Douglas LePan's
Poetry." CANADIAN LITERATURE, 15 (Winter 1963), 27-39.

Frye, Northrop. "From 'Letters in Canada.'" In his THE BUSH GARDEN:
ESSAYS ON THE CANADIAN IMAGINATION. Toronto: Anansi, 1971,
pp. 26-29.

Hamilton, S.C. "European Emblem and Canadian Image; A Study of Douglas
LePan's Poetry." MOSAIC, 3 (Winter 1970), 62-73.

Stewart, Hugh. "Literary Mining in the Canadian Shield." COPPERFIELD,
3 (November 1970), 57-64.

MacPHERSON, JAY (1931-)

Born in England and brought to Newfoundland as a child, Jay MacPherson was
educated in Ottawa and Toronto. She has been teaching at the University of
Toronto since completing her graduate work.

MacPherson's place in the history of Canadian poetry in the twentieth century
is based principally on her one full book of poetry, THE BOATMAN. Written
in a sophisticated style and using simple, traditional forms, it is a sequence of
interrelated poems about man's life expressed in universal terms drawn from
Biblical and mythological sources.

1. Poetry

NINETEEN POEMS. Deya, Mallorca: Seizin Press, 1952. 9 p.

O EARTH RETURN. Toronto: Emblem Books, 1954. 9 p.

THE BOATMAN. Toronto: Oxford, 1957. 70 p.

Wilson, Milton, ed. POETRY OF MIDCENTURY 1940-1960. Toronto: Mc-Clelland & Stewart, 1964. xvi, 237 p.

MacPherson's poems appear on pages 201-13.

POEMS. Toronto: Oxford, 1968. 86 p.

2. Prose

THE FOUR AGES OF MAN: THE CLASSICAL MYTHS. Toronto: Macmillan, 1962. 188 p.

3. Criticism

Beattie, [A.] Munro. "Poetry 1950-1960." In LITERARY HISTORY OF CANADA; CANADIAN LITERATURE IN ENGLISH. Ed. Carl F. Klinck et al. Toronto: University of Toronto Press, 1965, pp. 788-90.

Frye, Northrop. "From 'Letters in Canada.'" In his THE BUSH GARDEN: ESSAYS ON THE CANADIAN IMAGINATION. Toronto: Anansi, 1971, pp. 18, 55-56, 70-76.

Jones, D.G. BUTTERFLY ON ROCK; A STUDY OF THEMES AND IMAGES IN CANADIAN LITERATURE. Toronto: University of Toronto Press, 1970. x, 197 p.

For MacPherson see pages 7-8, 16-42, 75, 97, 117, 127, 138, 167.

Pacey, Desmond. "The Literature of the Fifties." In his CREATIVE WRITING IN CANADA; A SHORT HISTORY OF ENGLISH-CANADIAN LITERATURE. Rev. ed. Toronto: Ryerson, 1961, pp. 238-39.

Reaney, James. "The Third Eye: Jay MacPherson's THE BOATMAN." CANADIAN LITERATURE, 3 (Winter 1960), 22-34.

MANDEL, ELIAS WOLF (1922-)

Born in Estevan, Saskatchewan, Eli Mandel was educated in Saskatchewan and has taught at educational institutions across the country. He is now a professor at York University, Downsview, Ontario.

His early poetry is densely structured, arising out of his reading of Northrop Frye and using mythological legends as a basis. This work is sometimes tortured and obscure in style, but his more recent work has become looser and more colloquial. His poems nearly always center on the violence of modern civilization, and are full of the horrors of the twentieth century; the poetry abounds in generalized Gothic images expressed in a more personal voice.

Mandel's criticism was probably the most informative and important of the 1960's. He has published many critical articles and reviews embodying his ideas about the directions of Canadian poetry in relation to the process of literature.

1. Poetry

TRIO. Toronto: Contact Press, 1954. 89 p.

    First poems by Gael Turnbull, Phyllis Webb, and Eli Mandel.

FUSELI POEMS. Toronto: Contact Press, 1960. 66 p.

BLACK AND SECRET MAN. Toronto: Ryerson, 1964. 33 p.

AN IDIOT JOY. Edmonton, Alta.: Hurtig, 1967. 85 p.

Geddes, Gary, and Phyllis Bruce, eds. 15 CANADIAN POETS. Toronto: Oxford University Press, 1970. xvi, 301 p.

    Mandel's poems appear on pages 145-60.

CRUSOE: POEMS SELECTED AND NEW. Toronto: Anansi, 1973. 108 p.

STONY PLAIN. Toronto: Press Porcepic, 1973. 96 p.

2. Prose

Ed. with Jean-Guy Pilon. POETRY 62. Toronto: Ryerson, 1961. 116 p.

CRITICISM: THE SILENT-SPEAKING WORDS. Toronto: CBC Publications, 1966. 73 p.

IRVING LAYTON. Toronto: Forum House, 1969. 82 p.

Ed. FIVE MODERN CANADIAN POETS. Additional material by Roy Bentley. Toronto: Holt, Rinehart & Winston, 1970. 88 p.

Ed. CONTEXTS OF CANADIAN CRITICISM. Chicago: University of Chicago Press, 1971. vii, 304 p.

For annotation, see the main entry in chapter III.

Ed. with Desmond Maxwell. ENGLISH POEMS OF THE TWENTIETH CENTURY. Toronto: Macmillan, 1971. 221 p.

Ed. POETS OF CONTEMPORARY CANADA 1960-1970. Toronto: McClelland & Stewart, 1972. xvi, 141 p.

Ed. EIGHT MORE CANADIAN POETS. Toronto: Holt, Rinehart & Winston, 1972. 88 p.

3. Criticism

Beattie, [A.] Munro. "Poetry 1950-1960." In LITERARY HISTORY OF CANADA; CANADIAN LITERATURE IN ENGLISH. Ed. Carl F. Klinck et al. Toronto: University of Toronto Press, 1965, pp. 793-94.

Dudek, Louis. "Two Canadian Poets: Ralph Gustafson and Eli Mandel." CULTURE 22 (June 1961), 145-51.

Frye, Northrop. "From 'Letters in Canada.'" In his THE BUSH GARDEN: ESSAYS ON THE CANADIAN IMAGINATION. Toronto: Anansi, 1971, pp. 43-44.

McMaster, R.D. "The Unexplained Interior: A Study of E.W. Mandel's FUSELI POEMS." DALHOUSIE REVIEW, 40 (Fall 1960), 392-96.

Ower, John. "Black and Secret Poet, Notes on Eli Mandel." CANADIAN LITERATURE, 42 (Autumn 1969), 14-25.

Simms, Norman. "An Idiot Joy." FAR POINT, 2 (Spring/Summer 1969), 63-68.

PAGE, PATRICIA KATHLEEN (1916-)

Born in England, P.K. Page came to Alberta as a child with her parents. She studied art in Brazil and New York. She worked at a variety of jobs until settling in Montreal where she became associated with the new poetry centered in the magazine PREVIEW. In 1950 she married W.A. Irwin, and she has used her married name for her work as a visual artist. Between 1953 and 1964 she lived outside Canada in the various countries which figure in some of her poetry. Since returning, she has lived in Victoria, British Columbia.

Her early poetry was influenced by the socially concerned English writers of the 1930's, but soon her interests shifted more to a particular concern with the lives of individuals trapped by social circumstance, by family conditions, or by their own isolation. In recent years she has emphasized the painterly qualities of her work by meditating on scenes and their colors in order to achieve the essence of the experience. Such scenes and meditations often seem to represent entrapment and methods of escape from it. At times she expresses an enigmatic, almost mystical mood in the portrayal of scenes beyond reality, though her work maintains a controlled balance between these fantasies and the real world.

1. Poetry

Hambleton, Ronald, ed. UNIT OF FIVE. Toronto: Ryerson, 1944. xi, 87 p.

> Page's poems appear on pages 39-52.

AS TEN AS TWENTY. Toronto: Ryerson, 1946. 43 p.

THE METAL AND THE FLOWER. Toronto: McClelland & Stewart, 1954. 64 p.

Wilson, Milton, ed. POETRY OF MIDCENTURY 1940-1960. Toronto: McClelland & Stewart, 1964. xvi, 237 p.

> Page's poems appear on pages 167-82.

CRY ARARAT! POEMS NEW AND SELECTED. Toronto: McClelland & Stewart, 1967. 111 p.

2. Prose

Cape, Judith (pseud.). THE SUN AND THE MOON. Toronto: Macmillan, 1944. 200 p.

> This novel has been reprinted under her own name together with a brief introduction by Margaret Atwood, in a volume which also contains her short stories: THE SUN AND THE MOON AND OTHER FICTIONS (Toronto: Anansi, 1973. 204 p.).

"Questions and Images." CANADIAN LITERATURE, 41 (Summer 1969), 17-22.

"Traveller, Conjurer, Journeyman." CANADIAN LITERATURE, 46 (Autumn 1970), 35-40.

3. Criticism

Beattie, [A.] Munro. "Poetry 1935-1950." In LITERARY HISTORY OF CANADA; CANADIAN LITERATURE IN ENGLISH. Ed. Carl F. Klinck et al. Toronto: University of Toronto Press, 1965, pp. 770-71.

Frye, Northrop. "From 'Letters in Canada.'" In his THE BUSH GARDEN: ESSAYS ON THE CANADIAN IMAGINATION. Toronto: Anansi, 1971, pp. 39-40.

Macri, Francis M. "L'Alienation dans l'oeuvre de Anne Hebert et de P.K. Page." M.A. thesis, University of Sherbrooke, Sherbrooke, Que., 1970.

Meredith, W. "A Good Modern Poet and a Modern Poet." POETRY (Chicago), 70 (July 1947), 208-11.

Pacey, Desmond. "Modern Canadian Poetry." In his CREATIVE WRITING IN CANADA; A SHORT HISTORY OF ENGLISH-CANADIAN LITERATURE. Rev. ed. Toronto: Ryerson, 1961, pp. 158-61.

Shaw, Neufville. "The Poetry of P.K. Page." EDUCATIONAL RECORD (Quebec), 64 (July-September 1948), 152-56.

Smith, A.J.M. "New Canadian Poetry." CANADIAN FORUM, 26 (February 1947), 252.

_____. "The Poetry of P.K. Page." CANADIAN LITERATURE, 50 (Autumn 1971), 17-27.

Stevens, Peter. "Canadian Artists as Writers." CANADIAN LITERATURE, 46 (Autumn 1970), 19-34.

Sutherland, John. "The Poetry of P.K. Page." NORTHERN REVIEW, 1 (December-January 1946-47), 12-23.

PURDY, ALFRED WELLINGTON (1918-)

Al Purdy was born, raised, and educated in small settlements around Belleville, Ontario, an area of the country he has made uniquely his own in his poetry. He has maintained a small self-built house in Ameliasburgh, a settlement in the same area and one which figures in his poetry, together with nearby Roblin's Mills.

Purdy is a self-educated poet. His early writing grew out of traditional models, and it was not until the late 1950's that the characteristic colloquial approach surfaced in his work. His own idiosyncratically wide-ranging reading furnishes a broad spectrum of allusion in his poetry and, together with his travels in Canada and in many other countries, provides him with the necessary material for creating poems at once sensitive and tough, romantic and realistic, in forms which have broken with traditional modes in an attempt to catch the "nowness" of existence.

1. Poetry

THE ENCHANTED ECHO. Vancouver, B.C.: Clarke & Stuart, 1944. 62 p.

PRESSED ON SAND. Toronto: Ryerson, 1955. 16 p.

EMU, REMEMBER! Fredericton, N.B.: Fiddlehead Poetry Books, 1956. 16 p.

THE CRAFTE SO LONGE TO LERNE. Toronto: Ryerson, 1959. 23 p.

POEMS FOR ALL THE ANNETTES. Toronto: Contact Press, 1962. 64 p. 3rd ed., Toronto: Anansi, 1973. 108 p.

> This book is a key volume in Purdy's career because it contains the first extensive use of his changed style.

THE BLUR IN BETWEEN. Toronto: Emblem Books, 1963. 21 p.

THE CARIBOO HORSES. Toronto: McClelland & Stewart, 1965. 112 p.

NORTH OF SUMMER: POEMS FROM BAFFIN ISLAND. Oil sketches of the Arctic by A.Y. Jackson. Toronto: McClelland & Stewart, 1967. 87 p.

WILD GRAPE WINE. Toronto: McClelland & Stewart, 1968. 128 p.

LOVE IN A BURNING BUILDING. Toronto: McClelland & Stewart, 1970. 128 p.

With Phyllis Gotlieb et al. POEMS FOR VOICES. Toronto: CBC Publications, 1970. vii, 97 p.

Geddes, Gary, and Phyllis Bruce, eds. 15 CANADIAN POETS. Toronto: Oxford University Press, 1970. xvi, 301 p.

> Purdy's poems appear on pages 25-42.

SELECTED POEMS. Toronto: McClelland & Stewart, 1972. 127 p.

HIROSHIMA POEMS. Trumansburg, N.Y.: Crossing Press, 1972. 12 p.

Mandel, Eli, ed. POETS OF CONTEMPORARY CANADA. Toronto: McClelland & Stewart, 1972. xvi, 141 p.

> Purdy's poems appear on pages 1-22.

SEX AND DEATH. Toronto: McClelland & Stewart, 1973. 126 p.

2. Prose

"Canadian Poetry in English since 1867." JOURNAL OF COMMONWEALTH LITERATURE, 3 (July 1967), 19-33.

THE NEW ROMANS. Edmonton, Alta.: Hurtig, 1968. 172 p.

> Candid Canadian opinions of the United States.

Ed. FIFTEEN WINDS: A SELECTION OF MODERN CANADIAN POEMS. Toronto: Ryerson, 1969. 157 p.

Ed. STORM WARNING: THE NEW CANADIAN POETS. Toronto: McClelland & Stewart, 1971. 152 p. Photographs.

3. Criticism

Atwood, Margaret [Eleanor]. "Love Is Ambiguous . . . Sex is a Bully." CANADIAN LITERATURE, 49 (Summer 1971), 71-75.

Bowering, George. AL PURDY. Toronto: Copp Clark, 1970. 117 p.

_____. "Purdy: Man and Poet." CANADIAN LITERATURE, 43 (Winter 1970), 10-35.

Colombo, John Robert. "On Top of the Pyramid." CANADIAN LITERATURE, 25 (Summer 1965), 62-64.

Geddes, Gary. "A.W. Purdy, an Interview Conducted by Gary Geddes." CANADIAN LITERATURE, 41 (Summer 1969), 66-72.

Helwig, David. "The Winemaker." QUEEN'S QUARTERLY, 76 (Summer 1969), 340-44.

Jones, D.G. BUTTERFLY ON ROCK; A STUDY OF THEMES AND IMAGES IN CANADIAN LITERATURE. Toronto: University of Toronto Press, 1970. x, 197 p.

Purdy is discussed on pages 169-71 and 174-76.

Lee, David. "Running and Dwelling: Homage to Al Purdy." SATURDAY NIGHT, 87 (1972), 14-16.

Mathews, Robin. "Rejoinder." SATURDAY NIGHT, 87 (1972), 30-33.

Miller, Susan Marlis. "Al Purdy and the Unity of Man." M.A. thesis, Queen's University, Kingston, Ont., 1971.

Stevens, Peter. "The Beowulf Poet Is Alive and Well." CANADIAN LITERATURE, 55 (Winter 1973), 99-102.

_____. "In the Raw: The Poetry of A.W. Purdy." CANADIAN LITERATURE, 28 (Spring 1966), 22-30.

Webb, Phyllis. "Magnetic Field." CANADIAN LITERATURE, 15 (Winter 1963), 80-81.

Wilson, Jean. "The Sense of Place and History in the Poetry of A.W. Purdy." M.A. thesis, University of Saskatchewan, Saskatoon, 1968.

Woodcock, George. Introduction to SELECTED POEMS, by Al Purdy. Toronto: McClelland & Stewart, 1972, pp. 8-15.

REANEY, JAMES (1926-)

Born in Stratford, Ontario (a region he celebrates and satirizes in much of his work), James Reaney studied at the University of Toronto, apart from a brief spell of teaching at the University of Manitoba in Winnipeg. He is now with the English Department at the University of Western Ontario in London.

From its beginnings Reaney's work has focused on the state of innocence of childhood and the fall into experience. He first used simple forms and diction, with allusions to Biblical and mythological stories. His technique later became more sophisticated, with a reliance on literary and mythic allusion dominating. Recently, however, he has returned to the earlier simple style in his dramas, upon which he now concentrates in a nonrealistic, nonlinear kind of parade of scenes, using songs, poems, and short scenes to build composite pictures. At present he has abandoned poetry almost completely in favor of drama, though he retains in the main an interest in the same themes which dominated his poetry, themes which have been summarized by Germaine Warkentin as the contrasting worlds of innocence and experience, the evil forces that lie beneath the surface of every man, the power of love to redeem men, the process of growth from childhood through adolescence to maturity.

Reaney has also been interested in establishing the fact of Canadian poetic tradition and has written several articles pertaining to this subject; this interest is particularly apparent in his championing of the verse of Isabella Valancy Crawford. For some years he edited ALPHABET, an important literary magazine.

1. Poetry

THE RED HEART. Toronto: McClelland & Stewart, 1949. 73 p.

A SUIT OF NETTLES. Toronto: Macmillan, 1958. 54 p.

TWELVE LETTERS TO A SMALL TOWN. Toronto: Ryerson, 1962. 32 p.

THE DANCE OF DEATH AT LONDON, ONTARIO. London: Alphabet Press, 1963. 32 p.

Wilson, Milton, ed. POETRY OF MIDCENTURY 1940-1960. Toronto: McClelland & Stewart, 1964. xvi, 237 p.

Reaney's poetry appears on pages 130-63.

POEMS. Ed. with an introd. by Germaine Warkentin. Toronto: New Press, 1972. xviii, 283 p. Illustrated.

2. Prose

"The Canadian Poet's Predicament." UNIVERSITY OF TORONTO QUARTERLY, 26 (April 1957), 284-95.

"The Canadian Imagination." POETRY (Chicago), 94 (June 1959), 186-89.

"Isabella Valancy Crawford." In OUR LIVING TRADITION, 2nd and 3rd ser. Ed. Robert L. McDougall. Toronto: University of Toronto Press, 1959, pp. 268-86.

"The Bully." In CANADIAN SHORT STORIES. Ed. Robert Weaver. Toronto: Oxford University Press, 1960, pp. 370-85.

> This short story, originally published in CANADIAN SHORT STORIES (Toronto: Oxford University Press, 1952), is an example of Reaney's fiction. Excerpts from an unpublished novel were published in the short-lived magazine HERE AND NOW, and he has also written a novel for children, THE BOY WITH AN R IN HIS HAND (See below, this section).

"The Third Eye: Jay MacPherson's THE BOATMAN." CANADIAN LITERATURE, 3 (Winter 1960), pp. 23-34.

"An Evening with Babble and Doodle." CANADIAN LITERATURE, 12 (Spring 1962), 37-43.

THE BOY WITH AN R IN HIS HAND. Toronto: Macmillan, 1965. 107 p.

> A historical novel for children.

"Ten Years at Play." CANADIAN LITERATURE, 41 (Summer 1969), 53-61.

"Manitoba as a Writer's Environment." MOSAIC, 3 (Spring 1970), 95-97.

Introduction to THE COLLECTED POEMS OF ISABELLA VALANCY CRAWFORD. Toronto: University of Toronto Press, 1972, pp. vii-xxxiv.

Ed. THE COLLECTED POEMS OF ISABELLA VALANCY' CRAWFORD. Toronto: University of Toronto Press, 1972. xl, 309 p.

3. Drama

Because Reaney has been concentrating on drama for some years, the plays are listed here separately.

POET AND CITY--WINNIPEG. Toronto: Ryerson, 1961.

THE KILLDEER, AND OTHER PLAYS. Toronto: Macmillan, 1962. 224 p.

LET'S MAKE A CAROL. Waterloo, Ont.: Waterloo Music Co., 1965.

COLOURS IN THE DARK. Vancouver/Toronto: Talon Books with Macmillan, 1969. 90 p.

NAMES AND NICKNAMES. New York: New Plays for Children, 1969; Toronto: Longman's, 1969.

LISTEN TO THE WIND. Vancouver, B.C.: Talonplays, 1972. 119 p.

MASKS OF CHILDHOOD: THE EASTER EGG, THREE DESKS, THE KILLDEER. Ed. with an afterword by Brian Parker. Toronto: New Press, 1972. ix, 292 p.

> This includes a preface by Reaney giving some brief background to the plays, and a revised version of the THE KILLDEER (1962, above, this section).

APPLE BUTTER AND OTHER PLAYS FOR CHILDREN. Vancouver, B.C.: Talonbooks, 1973. 193 p. Illustrated.

4. Criticism

Atwood, Margaret [Eleanor]. "Eleven Years of ALPHABET." CANADIAN LITERATURE, 49 (Summer 1971), 60-64.

Beattie, [A.] Munro. "Poetry 1950-1960." In LITERARY HISTORY OF CANADA; CANADIAN LITERATURE IN ENGLISH. Ed. Carl F. Klinck et al. Toronto: University of Toronto Press, 1965, pp. 787-88.

Bowering, George. "Why James Reaney Is a Better Poet (1) Than Any Northrop Frye Poet (2) Than He Used to Be." CANADIAN LITERATURE, 36 (Spring 1968), 40-49.

Brown, Mary. "Experiment in Canadian Theatre." CANADIAN LITERATURE, 31 (Winter 1967), 54-58.

Frye, Northrop. "From 'Letters in Canada.'" In his THE BUSH GARDEN: ESSAYS ON THE CANADIAN IMAGINATION. Toronto: Anansi, 1971, pp. 87-91.

James, Esther. "Crime and No Punishment." CANADIAN LITERATURE, (Summer 1971), pp. 56-59.

Lee, Alvin. JAMES REANEY. New York: Twayne, 1968. 187 p.

_____. "Reaney's New Play." CANADIAN FORUM, 47 (September 1967), 34-35.

_____. "A Turn to the Stage: Reaney's Dramatic Verse (Part I)." CANA-DIAN LITERATURE, 15 (Winter 1963), 40-51; "(Part II)." CANADIAN LITERA-TURE, 16 (Spring 1963), 43-51.

Pacey, Desmond. "The Literature of the Fifties." In his CREATIVE WRITING IN CANADA; A SHORT HISTORY OF ENGLISH-CANADIAN LITERATURE. Rev. ed. Toronto: Ryerson, 1961, pp. 235-38.

Sutherland, John. "Canadian Comment." NORTHERN REVIEW, 3 (April-May 1950), 36-42.

Tait, Michael. "Drama and Theatre." In LITERARY HISTORY OF CANADA; CANADIAN LITERATURE IN ENGLISH. Ed. Carl F. Klinck et al. Toronto: University of Toronto Press, 1965, pp. 648-49.

_____. "The Limits of Innocence: James Reaney's Theatre." CANADIAN LITERATURE, 19 (Winter 1964), 43-48.

Watson, Wilfred. "An Indigenous World." CANADIAN LITERATURE, 15 (Winter 1963), 64-66.

Wilson, Milton. "On Reviewing Reaney." TAMARACK REVIEW, 26 (Winter 1963), 71-78.

Woodman, Ross G. JAMES REANEY. Toronto: McClelland & Stewart, 1971. 61 p.

SOUSTER, RAYMOND (1921-)

Raymond Souster was born in Toronto and has lived most of his life there, apart from a tour with the Royal Canadian Air Force during World War II. He has been very active in editing literary magazines and in founding the small Contact Press. He was the first chairman of the League of Canadian Poets. Souster is considered to be the most fully urban of Canadian poets, devoting his poetry to Toronto, past and present, and its people, particularly its outcasts and vic-tims. His poetry is modeled along the lines of William Carlos Williams, in a direct and often colloquial language. He has written two novels under the pseudonym of Raymond Holmes.

1. Poetry

Hambleton, Ronald, ed. UNIT OF FIVE. Toronto: Ryerson, 1944. xi, 87 p.
  Souster's poems appear on pages 55-67.

WHEN WE ARE YOUNG. Montreal: First Statement Press, 1946. 28 p.

GO TO SLEEP WORLD. Toronto: Ryerson, 1947. 59 p.

CITY HALL STREET. Toronto: Ryerson, 1951. 8 p.

CERBERUS. Toronto: Contact Press, 1952. 98 p.
  Poems by Louis Dudek, Irving Layton, and Raymond Souster.

SHAKE HANDS WITH THE HANGMAN: POEMS, 1940-1952. Toronto: Contact Press, 1953. 24 p.

A DREAM THAT IS DYING: POEMS. Toronto: Contact Press, 1954. 27 p.

WALKING DEATH: POEMS. Toronto: Contact Press, 1954. 24 p.

FOR WHAT TIME SLAYS: POEMS. Toronto: Contact Press, 1955. 24 p.

SELECTED POEMS. Chosen by Louis Dudek. Toronto: Contact Press, 1956. 135 p.

CREPE-HANGER'S CARNIVAL: SELECTED POEMS, 1955-1958. Toronto: Contact Press, 1958. 65 p.

A LOCAL PRIDE: POEMS. Toronto: Contact Press, 1962. 131 p.

PLACE OF MEETING: POEMS, 1958-1960. Toronto: Gallery Editions, 1962. 67 p.

THE COLOUR OF THE TIMES: THE COLLECTED POEMS OF SOUSTER. Toronto: Ryerson, 1964. 121 p.
  This work and TEN ELEPHANTS ON YONGE STREET (1965, below, this section) were reprinted as one volume in 1973 (Toronto: McGraw-Hill/Ryerson. 178 p.

Wilson, Milton, ed. POETRY OF MIDCENTURY 1940-1960. Toronto: Mc-

Clelland & Stewart, 1964. xvi, 237 p.

    Souster's poetry appears on pages 112-29.

TEN ELEPHANTS ON YONGE STREET. Toronto: Ryerson, 1965. 84 p.

    This work and THE COLOUR OF THE TIMES (1964, above, this section) were reprinted as one volume (Toronto: McGraw-Hill/Ryerson, 1973. 178 p.)

AS IS. Toronto: Oxford University Press, 1967. 102 p.

LOST AND FOUND, UNCOLLECTED POEMS, 1945-1965. Toronto: Oberon Press, 1968. 113 p.

SO FAR SO GOOD: POEMS, 1938-68. Ottawa: Oberon Press, 1969. 100 p.

Geddes, Gary, and Phyllis Bruce, eds. 15 CANADIAN POETS. Toronto: Oxford University Press, 1970. xvi, 301 p.

    Souster's poems appear on pages 63-76.

THE YEARS. Ottawa: Oberon Press, 1971. 164 p.

SELECTED POEMS OF RAYMOND SOUSTER. Ed. with an introd. by Michael Macklem. Ottawa: Oberon Press, 1972. 128 p.

2. Prose

Holmes, Raymond (pseud.). THE WINTER OF TIME. Toronto: Export Publishing, 1949.

Ed. POETS 56. TEN YOUNGER ENGLISH-CANADIANS. WITH AN INTRODUCTORY "LETTER" BEING A REPLY TO LOUIS DUDEK'S "OU SONT LES JEUNES?" Toronto: Contact Press, 1956. Unpaged.

Ed. NEW WAVE CANADA. Toronto: Contact Press, 1966. vii, 172 p.

Ed. with John Robert Colombo. SHAPES & SOUNDS: POEMS OF W.W.E. ROSS. Memoir by Barry Callaghan. Toronto: Longmans, 1968. 145 p.

Ed. with Douglas Lochhead. MADE IN CANADA: NEW POEMS OF THE SEVENTIES. Ottawa: Oberon Press, 1970. 192 p.

Holmes, Raymond (pseud.). ON TARGET. Toronto: Village Book Store Press,
1972. 248 p.

3. Criticism

Beattie, [A.] Munro. "Poetry 1935-1950." In LITERARY HISTORY OF CANADA;
CANADIAN LITERATURE IN ENGLISH. Ed. Carl F. Klinck et al. Toronto:
University of Toronto Press, 1965, pp. 778-81.

Carruth, Hayden. "To Souster from Vermont." TAMARACK REVIEW, 34
(Winter 1965), 81-95.

Cook, Harry Hugh. "The Poetry of Raymond Souster." M.A. thesis, Simon
Fraser University, Burnaby, B.C., 1970.

Dudek, Louis. "Groundhog among the Stars: The Poetry of Raymond Souster."
CANADIAN LITERATURE, no. 22 (Autumn 1964), pp. 34-49.

Field, Roger. "Raymond Souster." M.A. thesis, University of British Columbia,
Vancouver, 1968.

Frye, Northrop. "From 'Letters in Canada.'" In his THE BUSH GARDEN:
ESSAYS ON THE CANADIAN IMAGINATION. Toronto: Anansi, 1971, pp.
21-22, 54-55, 61-62, 97-98.

Geddes, Gary. "A Cursed and Singular Blessing." CANADIAN LITERATURE,
54 (Autumn 1972), 27-36.

Gnarowski, M[ichael]. CONTACT 1925-1954. Montreal: Delta, 1966. 37 p.
    "Being an Index to the Contents of CONTACT, a little magazine
    edited by Raymond Souster, together with notes on the history and
    the background of the periodical . . . and some afterthoughts on
    CONTACT magazine by Raymond Souster."

_____. CONTACT PRESS 1952-1967. Montreal: Delta, 1970. Unpaged.
    Contains a note on the origins of Contact Press and a checklist
    of its titles.

_____. "Raymond Souster: 'Au-dessus de la melee.'" CULTURE, 26 (March
1965), 58-63.

Pacey, Desmond. "Modern Canadian Poetry." In his CREATIVE WRITING IN
CANADA; A SHORT HISTORY OF ENGLISH-CANADIAN LITERATURE. Rev.

ed. Toronto: Ryerson, 1961, pp. 174-77.

WADDINGTON, MIRIAM [DWORKIN] (1917-)

Miriam Waddington was born in Winnipeg and studied at the University of Toronto and at the Pennsylvania School of Social Work. She returned to Canada to live in Montreal where she was a social worker. She was also one of the poets who contributed to the Montreal group in the 1940's. Later, she studied literature and is now with the Department of English at York University, Downsview, Ontario.

Waddington's early work often arose out of her experiences as a social worker. Increasingly, her poems examined states of disillusionment and loss, until she returned to an assessment of her heritage: her childhood on the prairies and her feeling for her Jewishness, which was rekindled by her visits abroad, particularly to Russia and Israel. Her language and poetic form have gradually been stripped down, shedding her early sensuous diction and traditional metrics in favor of a shorter-lined poetry which is more direct in its appeal while still retaining a sensuous quality.

1. Poetry

GREEN WORLD. Montreal: First Statement Press, 1945. 30 p.

THE SECOND SILENCE. Toronto: Ryerson, 1955. 57 p.

THE SEASON'S LOVERS. Toronto: Ryerson, 1958. 56 p.

THE GLASS TRUMPET. Toronto: Oxford, 1966. 96 p.

Monk, Lorraine, ed. CALL THEM CANADIANS: A PHOTOGRAPHIC POINT OF VIEW. Ottawa: Queen's Printer, 1968. 245 p.

    Includes poems by Waddington.

SAY YES. Toronto: Oxford, 1969. 96 p.

DREAM TELESCOPE. London: Anvil Press, 1972. 24 p.

DRIVING HOME. Toronto: Oxford, 1972. 176 p.

2. Prose

A.M. KLEIN. Toronto: Copp Clark, 1970. vi, 145 p.

Ed. ESSAYS, CONTROVERSIES AND POEMS. Toronto: McClelland & Stewart, 1972. 206 p.

3. Criticism

Frye, Northrop. "From 'Letters in Canada.'" In his THE BUSH GARDEN: ESSAYS ON THE CANADIAN IMAGINATION. Toronto: Anansi, 1971, pp. 50-52, 100-101.

Pacey, Desmond. "Modern Canadian Poetry." In his CREATIVE WRITING IN CANADA; A SHORT HISTORY OF ENGLISH-CANADIAN LITERATURE. Rev. ed. Toronto: Ryerson, 1961, pp. 167-70.

Sowton, Ian. "The Lyric Craft of Miriam Waddington." DALHOUSIE REVIEW, 39 (Summer 1959), 237-42.

Wayman, Tom. "Miriam Waddington's New Talent." CANADIAN LITERATURE, 56 (Spring 1973), 85-89.

WEBB, PHYLLIS (1927-)

Phyllis Webb was born in Victoria and attended the University of British Columbia before doing graduate work at McGill University. She worked for many years for the Canadian Broadcasting Corporation, principally as supervisor of the "Ideas" program.

In the beginning her poems were rigidly focused on the question of the self's identity, with a disciplined use of a metaphysical and dense language. Her themes are large: history and time, and public and private life. She fashions the poems around images connected with the sea and landscapes, together with figures derived from gardens and enclosed spaces. The mood of the poetry is bleak. Her work has become more and more disciplined, though there is a leavening through the play of wit and irony. Gradually, she pared her poetry to the bare essence, completely evidenced in the cycle of very spare miniatures called NAKED POEMS (1965).

1. Poetry

TRIO. Toronto: Contact Press, 1954. 89 p.

A collection of first poems by Gael Turnbull, Phyllis Webb, and Eli Mandel.

EVEN YOUR RIGHT EYE. Toronto: McClelland & Stewart, 1956. 64 p.

THE SEA IS ALSO A GARDEN. Toronto: Ryerson, 1962. Unpaged.

NAKED POEMS. Vancouver, B.C.: Periwinkle Press, 1965. Unpaged.

SELECTED POEMS: 1954-1965. Vancouver, B.C.: Talonbooks, 1971. Unpaged.

2. Criticism

Barbour, Douglas. "Review of SELECTED POEMS." QUARRY, 21 (Winter 1972), 61-63.

Beattie, [A.] Munro. "Poetry 1950-1960." In LITERARY HISTORY OF CANADA; CANADIAN LITERATURE IN ENGLISH. Ed. Carl F. Klinck et al. Toronto: University of Toronto Press, 1965, pp. 792-93.

Fox, Gail. "Review of SELECTED POEMS." CANADIAN FORUM, 52 (May 1972), 70-71.

Frye, Northrop. "From 'Letters in Canada.'" In his THE BUSH GARDEN: ESSAYS ON THE CANADIAN IMAGINATION. Toronto: Anansi, 1971, pp. 43, 64-65.

Hulcoop, J. Introduction to SELECTED POEMS 1954-1965, by Phyllis Webb. Vancouver, B.C.: Talonbooks, 1971. Unpaged.

_____. "Phyllis Webb and the Priestess of Motion." CANADIAN LITERATURE, 32 (Spring 1967), pp. 29-39.

MacFarlane, Julian. "Review of SELECTED POEMS." CAPILANO REVIEW, 1 (Spring 1972), 53-58.

Mays, John Bentley. "Phyllis Webb." OPEN LETTER, 2nd ser., 6 (Fall 1973), 8-33.

Sonthoff, H.W. "Structure of Loss: The Poetry of Phyllis Webb." CANADIAN LITERATURE, 9 (Summer 1961), 15-22.

Stainsby, Mari. "An Interview with Phyllis Webb." BRITISH COLUMBIA LI-
BRARY QUARTERLY, 36 (October 1972-January 1973), 5-8.

Stevens, Peter. "Shaking the Alphabet." CANADIAN LITERATURE, 52
(Spring 1972), 82-84.

WILKINSON, ANNE [GIBBONS] (1910-61)

Anne Wilkinson lived in Toronto and London, Ontario, as a child but was
educated in Europe and the United States. Her poetry is full of metaphysical
conceits, wit, and irony, though at times the intellectuality of the poems causes
some obscurity.

1. Poetry

COUNTERPOINT TO SLEEP. Montreal: First Statement Press, 1951. 36 p.

THE HANGMAN TIES THE HOLLY. Toronto: Macmillan, 1955. 57 p.

THE COLLECTED POEMS OF ANNE WILKINSON, AND A PROSE MEMOIR.
Ed. with an introd. A.J.M. Smith. Toronto: Macmillan, 1968. xxi, 212 p.

2. Prose

LIONS IN THE WAY: A DISCURSIVE HISTORY OF THE OSLERS. Toronto:
Macmillan, 1956. 274 p.

SWANN AND DAPHNE. Toronto: Oxford University Press, 1960. 48 p.

3. Criticism

Beattie, [A.] Munro. "Poetry 1950-1960." In LITERARY HISTORY OF CANADA;
CANADIAN LITERATURE IN ENGLISH. Ed. Carl F. Klinck et al. Toronto:
University of Toronto Press, 1965, pp. 790-91.

Frye, Northrop. "From 'Letters in Canada.'" In his THE BUSH GARDEN:
ESSAYS ON THE CANADIAN IMAGINATION. Toronto: Anansi, 1971, pp.
48-50.

Pacey, Desmond. "The Literature of the Fifties." In his CREATIVE WRITING
IN CANADA; A SHORT HISTORY OF ENGLISH-CANADIAN LITERATURE.

Rev. ed. Toronto: Ryerson, 1961, pp. 243-44.

Smith, A.J.M. "A Reading of Anne Wilkinson." CANADIAN LITERATURE, 10 (Autumn 1961), 32-39.

Chapter VIII

CONTEMPORARY POETRY: THE 1960'S AND '70'S

In this chapter the listings under each individual author are arranged in three sections. The first two sections, poetry and prose, list the primary works of the author in chronological order; the third section lists criticism about the author in alphabetical order. Collections edited by the author are included in the prose section.

ACORN, MILTON (1923-)

Born in Prince Edward Island, Milton Acorn has supported himself as a laborer and carpenter, at times devoting his energies completely to poetry. His poetry has always shown his sympathy for people--their prison of demeaning work; this feeling develops in his later work into a rather strident political tone. This tone is tempered by the gentleness of his love poems and by the reminiscent pieces about his life in Prince Edward Island and about its people.

1. Poetry

IN LOVE AND ANGER. Montreal: Author, 1956. 20 p.

THE BRAIN'S THE TARGET. Toronto: Ryerson, 1960. 16 p.

AGAINST A LEAGUE OF LIARS. Toronto: Hawkshead Press, 1961.

> A broadside of sixteen poems.

FIDDLEHEAD. Spring 1963, entire issue. 39 p.

> This issue of the magazine featured Acorn's poetry reprinted from other magazines and from Acorn's published books.

JAWBREAKERS. Toronto: Contact Press, 1963. 54 p.

I'VE TASTED MY BLOOD: POEMS 1956 to 1968. Selected with an introd. Al Purdy. Toronto: Ryerson, 1969. 136 p.

MORE POEMS FOR PEOPLE. Toronto: N.C. Press, 1972. 112 p.

Mandel, Eli, ed. POETS OF CONTEMPORARY CANADA 1960-1970. Toronto: McClelland & Stewart, 1972. xvi, 141 p.

    Acorn's poems appear on pages 23-34.

2. Prose

"I Was a Communist for My Own Damn Satisfaction." EVIDENCE, 5 (1962), 32-38.

"The Business of This Country is Selling Out." THIS MAGAZINE IS ABOUT SCHOOLS, 5 (Winter 1971), 139-58.

"Avoid the Bad Mountain." BLACKFISH, 3 (Autumn 1972), unpaged.

    See next item.

"Bowering: The Laws of Language? Or of Empire?" BLACKFISH, 4/5 (Winter/Spring 1972-73), unpaged.

    This and the preceding article by Acorn comprise his attack against the west coast poets associated with the magazine TISH. Bowering replied in BLACKFISH (below, under Criticism, section 3).

3. Criticism

Bowering, George. "Acorn Blood." CANADIAN LITERATURE, 42 (Autumn 1969), 84-86.

————. "Letter in Reply to Acorn." BLACKFISH, 4/5 (Winter/Spring 1972-73), unpaged.

Cogswell, F[red]. "Three Arc-Light Gaps." FIDDLEHEAD, 56 (Spring 1963), 57-58.

Gnarowski, M[ichael]. "Milton Acorn: A Review in Retrospect." CULTURE, 25 (June 1964), 119-29.

Livesay, Dorothy. "Search for a Style: The Poetry of Milton Acorn." CANA-

DIAN LITERATURE, 40 (Spring 1969), 33-42.

Purdy, Al. "A Man of Stances." EVIDENCE, 8 (1964), 120-24.

Wilson, Milton. "Letters in Canada: 1960." UNIVERSITY OF TORONTO QUARTERLY, 30 (July 1961), 395-96, 400.

ATWOOD, MARGARET ELEANOR (1939-)

Born in Ottawa, Margaret Atwood was educated at the University of Toronto and at Radcliffe College. She held a variety of jobs until she became a teacher and writer-in-residence at various Canadian universities.

Margaret Atwood is probably the most significant new figure in Canadian literature of the last ten years. The persona she presents in her poetry mirrors the terrors, prejudices, and instabilities of a contemporary woman. There is no certainty in Atwood's world: no reliance can be put on surfaces, and all schematic posturings merely hide the shifting ambiguities lurking beneath. Her poetry expresses these feelings in short, rather staccato lines, though paradoxically the poems seem to move at times into a plateau of accepting calmness. It is a nervy and edgy poetry admirably suited to a surface poise undercut by strange paranoias. These ideas and thematic concerns also emerge strongly in Atwood's two novels and SURVIVAL, her thematic study of Canadian literature.

1. Poetry

DOUBLE PERSEPHONE. Toronto: Hawkshead Press, 1961.

THE CIRCLE GAME. Toronto: Contact Press, 1966; rpt. Toronto: Anansi, 1967, 1968, 1969. 80 p.

THE ANIMALS IN THAT COUNTRY. Toronto: Oxford, 1968. 80 p.

THE JOURNALS OF SUSANNA MOODIE. Toronto: Oxford, 1970. 64 p.

PROCEDURES FOR UNDERGROUND. Toronto: Oxford, 1970. 80 p.

Geddes, Gary, and Phyllis Bruce, eds. 15 CANADIAN POETS. Toronto: Oxford University Press, 1970. xvi, 301 p.

    Atwood's poems appear on pages 163-80.

POWER POLITICS. Toronto: Anansi, 1971. 58 p.

Mandel, Eli, ed. POETS OF CONTEMPORARY CANADA 1960-1970. Toronto: McClelland & Stewart, 1972. xvi, 138 p.

Atwood's poems appear on pages 85-105.

2. Prose

Margaret Atwood has written many review articles on a variety of poets as well as her own answers to critics of SURVIVAL. In the following list, articles that bear some relevance to her own work are included, as well as her two novels.

"Superwoman Drawn and Quartered: the Early Forms of She." ALPHABET, 10 (July 1965), 65-82.

THE EDIBLE WOMAN. Toronto: McClelland & Stewart, 1969. 281 p.

"MacEwen's Muse." CANADIAN LITERATURE, 45 (Summer 1970), 24-32.

"Eleven Years of ALPHABET." CANADIAN LITERATURE, 49 (Summer 1971), 60-64.

"Love Is Ambiguous . . . Sex Is a Bully." CANADIAN LITERATURE, 49 (Summer 1971), 71-75.

SURFACING. Toronto: McClelland & Stewart, 1972. 192 p.

SURVIVAL: A THEMATIC GUIDE TO CANADIAN LITERATURE. Toronto: Anansi, 1972. 287 p.

"Travels Back." MACLEAN'S, 86 (January 1973), 28-31, 48.

"Surviving the Critics." THIS MAGAZINE, 8 (May-June 1973), 29-32.

"Poetry in the Buffer Zone." TIMES LITERARY SUPPLEMENT, 26 October 1973, pp. 1305-6.

3. Criticism

Ayre, John. "Margaret Atwood and the End of Colonialism." SATURDAY NIGHT, 87 (November 1972), 23-26.

Bowering, George. "Get Used to It." CANADIAN LITERATURE, 52 (Spring

1972), 91-92.

Davey, Frank. "Atwood Walking Backwards." OPEN LETTER, 2nd ser., 5 (Summer 1973), 74-84.

Jonas, George. "A Choice of Predators." TAMARACK REVIEW, 54 (Summer 1970), 75-77.

Mathews, Robin. "Survival and Struggle in Canadian Literature." THIS MAGAZINE IS ABOUT SCHOOLS, 6 (Winter 1972), 109-24.

Ondaatje, Michael. Review of THE CIRCLE GAME. CANADIAN FORUM, 47 (April 1967), 22-23.

Piercy, Marge. "Margaret Atwood: Beyond Victimhood." AMERICAN POETRY REVIEW, 2 (November/December 1973), 41-44.

Purdy, Al. "Atwood's Moodie." CANADIAN LITERATURE, 47 (Winter 1971), 80-84.

_____. "Poet Besieged." CANADIAN LITERATURE, 39 (Winter 1969), 94-96.

Stephen, Sid. "THE JOURNALS OF SUSANNA MOODIE: A Self-Portrait of Margaret Atwood." WHITE PELICAN, 2 (Spring 1972), 32-36.

Stevens, Peter. "Dark Mouth." CANADIAN LITERATURE, 50 (Autumn 1971), 91-92.

_____. "On the Edge, on the Surface." CANADIAN LITERATURE, 32 (Spring 1967), 71-72.

Webb, Phyllis. "Letters to Margaret Atwood." OPEN LETTER, 2nd ser., 5 (Summer 1973), 71-73.

Woodcock, George. "Margaret Atwood." LITERARY HALF YEARLY, 13 (July 1972), 233-42.

_____. "Surfacing to Survive: Notes of the Recent Atwood." ARIEL, 4 (July 1973), 16-28.

BISSETT, WILLIAM (1939-)

Though born in Halifax, Nova Scotia, Bill Bissett has spent most of his life in Vancouver where he has been a leading figure in the west coast poetry school, both through his own work and through his editing of the magazine BLEW OINT-MENT and its offshoot, the Blew Ointment Press. Such an idiosyncratic poet as Bissett, however, can in no way be classed as belonging to any school. In the main he produces his own mimeographed books--blurred, smudged, and often nonlinear. This typography is often deliberate, since Bissett's whole thrust is to break down the system; even his spelling distorts normal expectations. The poems are often illustrated by his own drawings or by designs made by type-writer.

Besides writing rather mystical poems about the cosmic universals he believes in, and producing simple chants, Bissett writes angry political poems attacking all political repressions and preaching the liberation of society through an openness of human sexuality, drugs, and response to a free, anarchic spirit.

It is often difficult to keep track of the innumerable pamphlets and books Bissett issues and even more difficult to enumerate them correctly--bibliography seems to be just one more scheme Bissett rejects--so that any listing of his work will always be necessarily tentative. Many of his books and pamphlets are inter-leaved with other material and are unpaged.

1. Poetry

FIRES IN TH TEMPLE OR THE JINX SHIP ND OTHR TRIPS. Vancouver, B.C.: Very Stone House, 1966. 84 p.

WE SLEEP INSIDE EACH OTHER ALL. Toronto: Ganglia Press, 1966. Un-paged.

LEBANON VOICES. Toronto: Weed/Flower Press, 1967. 28 p.

TH GOSSAMER BEDPAN. Vancouver, B.C.: Blewointment, 1967. 47 p.

WHERE IS MISS FLORENCE RIDDLE. Toronto: Fleye Press, 1967. Unpaged.

AWAKE IN TH RED DESERT! Vancouver, B.C.: Talonbooks & See/Hear Pro-ductions, 1968. 63 p.; 1 LP phonodisc.

OF TH LAND DIVINE SERVICE. Toronto: Weed/Flower Press, 1968. 36 p.

LOST ANGEL MINING COMPANY. Vancouver, B.C.: Blewointment, 1969. Unpaged.

SUNDAY WORK? Vancouver, B.C.: Blewointment, 1969. Unpaged.

LIBERATING SKIES. Vancouver, B.C.: Blewointment, 1969. 26 p.

S TH STORY I TO; TREW ADVENTURE. Vancouver, B.C.: Blewointment, 1970. Unpaged. Illustrated.

BLEW TREWZ. Vancouver, B.C.: Blewointment, 1971. Unpaged. Illustrated.

DRAGON FLY. Toronto: Weed/Flower Press, 1971. [14] p.

DRIFTING INTO WAR. Vancouver, B.C.: Talonbooks, 1971. [50] p. Illustrated.

NOBODY OWNS TH EARTH. Toronto: Anansi, 1971. 91 p. Illustrated.

AIR (Vancouver, B.C.), no. 6 (1971), entire issue.
    An issue of the magazine devoted to Bissett's poetry.

RUSH. Toronto: Gronk and Vancouver, B.C.: Blewointment Press, 1971. Unpaged.

TUFF SHIT: LOVE POEMS. Windsor, Ont.: Bandit/Black Moss Press, 1971. Unpaged. Illustrated.

WHAT FUCKAN THEORY: A STUDY UV LANGUAGE. Vancouver, B.C.: Blew Ointment Press, 1971. Unpaged.

IBM, BY BILL BISSETT. SAGE UV TH RELEES UV HUMAN SPIRIT FROM COM-PUEWTER FUNCKSHUNS. Vancouver, B.C.: Blewointment, 1972.

ICE. Vancouver, B.C.: Blewointment, 1972. 3 Books and 11 Pieces in Bag.

With Earle Birney, Judith Copithorne and Andrew Suknaski. FOUR PARTS SAND. Ottawa: Oberon Press, 1972. Unpaged.

TH HIGH GREEN HILL. Vancouver, B.C.: Blew Ointment Press, 1972. Unpaged. Illustrated.

POLAR BEAR HUNT. Vancouver, B.C.: Blew Ointment Press, 1972.

Unpaged. Illustrated.

POMES FOR YOSHI. Vancouver, B.C.: Blew Ointment Press, 1972. 58 p.

WORDS IN TH FIRE. Vancouver, B.C.: Blew Ointment Press, 1972. Unpaged.

Mandel, Eli, ed. POETS OF CONTEMPORARY CANADA 1960-1970. Toronto: McClelland & Stewart, 1972. xvi, 141 p.
Bissett's poems appear on pages 107-15.

PASS TH FOOD, RELEASE TH SPIRIT BOOK. Vancouver, B.C.: Talonbooks, 1973. Unpaged.

TH FIRST SUFI LINE. Vancouver, B.C.: Blew Ointment Press, 1973. 30 p.

AIR (Vancouver, B.C.), no. 10-1-2 (1973) entire issue.
A collection of Bissett's poetry.

2. Criticism

Davey, Frank. Review of FIRES IN TH TEMPLE. CANADIAN FORUM, 52 (July/August 1972), 44-45.

David, Jack. "Concrete Poetry." M.A. thesis, University of Windsor, Windsor, Ont., 1973.

Livesay, Dorothy. Review of FIRES IN TH TEMPLE. FIDDLEHEAD, 72 (Spring 1967), 64-66.

Scobie, Stephen. "A Dash for the Border." CANADIAN LITERATURE, 56 (Spring 1973), 89-92.

BOWERING, GEORGE HARRY (1935-)

George Bowering was born and raised in British Columbia and educated at the University of British Columbia. He was a student in the Department of Creative Writing there and was instrumental in starting the organ of the so-called west coast movement in Canadian poetry, TISH. Bowering has taught and been writer-in-residence at various Canadian universities. He is presently with the English department at Simon Fraser University, Burnaby, British Columbia.

Bowering's poetry has been influenced principally by William Carlos Williams, filtered through projective verse and the search for a spontaneously oral poetry. In this search he has offered an extensive range of poetry from short lyrics to long sequences.

Bowering has devoted his energies to writing defenses of his poetics and editing magazines, particularly IMAGO which focused on long poems, sequences, and serial poems. He has also written criticism, much of it concerned with the question of language and poetic form and their relation to content. He has also written a novel, short stories, and autobiographical pieces.

1. Poetry

STICKS AND STONES. Vancouver, B.C.: Tish Books, 1963.

POINTS ON THE GRID. Toronto: Contact Press, 1964. 67 p.

THE MAN IN YELLOW BOOTS. Mexico: El Corno Emplumado, 1965. 112 p.

THE SILVER WIRE. Kingston, Ont.: Quarry Press, 1966. 72 p.

BASEBALL; A POEM IN THE MAGIC NUMBER 9. Toronto: Coach House, 1967. 21 p.

ROCKY MOUNTAIN FOOT: A LYRIC, A MEMOIR. Toronto/Montreal: Mc-Clelland & Stewart, 1968. 127 p.

THE GANGS OF KOSMOS. Toronto: Anansi, 1969. 64 p.

"Sitting in Mexico." IMAGO, no 19. (1969), entire issue.

TWO POLICE POEMS. Vancouver, B.C.: Talonbooks, 1969. 23 p.

GEORGE VANCOUVER, A DISCOVERY POEM. Toronto: Weed/Flower Press, 1970. 39 p.

Geddes, Gary, and Phyllis Bruce, eds. 15 CANADIAN POETS. Toronto: Oxford University Press, 1970. xvi, 301 p.

Bowering's poems appear on pages 219-33.

GENEVE. Toronto: Coach House Press, 1971. Unpaged.

TOUCH: SELECTED POEMS 1960-1970. Toronto: McClelland & Stewart, 1971. 128 p.

THE SENSIBLE. Toronto: Massassauga Editions, 1972. 17 p.

Mandel, Eli, ed. POETS OF CONTEMPORARY CANADA 1960-1970. Toronto: McClelland & Stewart, 1972. xvi, 141 p.

Bowering's poems appear on pages 61-69.

CURIOUS. Toronto: Coach House Press, 1973. 68 p.

LAYERS. Toronto: Weed/Flower Press, 1973. 19 p.

2. Prose

"Poets in Their Twenties." CANADIAN LITERATURE, 20 (Spring 1962), 54-64.

"Poetry and the Language of Sound." EVIDENCE, 7 (1963), 19-26.

MIRROR ON THE FLOOR. Toronto: McClelland & Stewart, 1967. 160 p.

HOW I HEAR HOWL. Montreal: Beaver Kosmos Folios, 1969. 19 p.

"Purdy: Man and Poet." CANADIAN LITERATURE, 43 (Winter 1970), 24-35.

AL PURDY. Toronto: Copp Clark, 1970. 117 p.

Ed. THE STORY SO FAR. Toronto: Coach House Press, 1971. 112 p.

Ed. with Robert Hogg. INTERVIEW WITH ROBERT DUNCAN, APRIL 19, 1969. Toronto: Coach House Press, 1971. 32 p.

AUTOBIOLOGY. Vancouver, B.C.: Georgia Straight Writing Supplement, 1972. 103 p.

"Get Used to It." CANADIAN LITERATURE, 52 (Spring 1972), 91-92.

"Confessions of a Failed American." MACLEAN'S, 86 (November 1972), 79-81.

"Letter in Reply to Acorn." BLACKFISH, 4/5 (Winter/Spring 1972-73), unpaged.

With Irving Layton, Hugh Hood and Kerry Allard. "Conversation: Jewish Layton, Catholic Hood, Protestant Bowering." OPEN LETTER, 2nd ser., 5 (Summer 1973), 30-39.

"The Test of Real is the Language." In CONVERSATIONS WITH CANADIAN NOVELISTS. Ed. Donald Cameron. Toronto: Macmillan, 1973, pp. 3-16.

3. Criticism

Abbey, Lloyd. "The Organic Aesthetic." CANADIAN LITERATURE, 46 (Autumn 1970), 103-4.

Davey, Frank. "The Message of George Bowering." U.B.C. ALUMNI CHRONICLE, 24 (Summer 1970), 13-15.

_____. "A Note on Bowering's GENEVE." OPEN LETTER, 2nd ser., 1 (Winter 1971-72), 42-44.

Dudek, Louis. "Trouncing the Younger Poets." CANADIAN LITERATURE, 34 (Autumn 1967), 80-84.

Jones, D.G. BUTTERFLY ON ROCK; A STUDY OF THEMES AND IMAGES IN CANADIAN LITERATURE. Toronto: University of Toronto Press, 1970. x, 197 p.
  Bowering is discussed on pages 171-72, 175, and 180.

Mitchell, Beverley Jean. " A Critical Study of the Tish Group, 1961-1963." M.A. thesis, University of Calgary, Calgary, Alta., 1967.

Sowton, Ian. "Moving from Word to Word." EDGE, 3 (Autumn 1964), 119-22.

COHEN, LEONARD (1934-)

Born in Montreal, Leonard Cohen studied at McGill University and Columbia University. He embarked on his poetic career early and has pursued it rigorously, achieving popularity as a folksinger until he renounced that aspect of his life in the early 1970's.

Cohen has assumed various religious and metaphysical poses: his own Jewishness, eastern philosophy, and scientology. His poetry, with its intricate formality occasionally broken by freer forms, maps his search for a personal, meaningful response to life through ritual--transcending the ordinary levels of life through sensuality. His last book of poems is to some extent a departure from his earlier work, since it contains sparser diction and fragments of statement rather than the earlier and carefully structured poetry with its rhetorically decadent language.

Cohen's two novels also embody his concern with ritual and sensuality.

1. Poetry

LET US COMPARE MYTHOLOGIES. Montreal: McGill Poetry Series, 1956. 79; rpt. Toronto: McClelland & Stewart, 1966. 76 p.

THE SPICE BOX OF EARTH. Toronto: McClelland & Stewart, 1961. 99 p.

FLOWERS FOR HITLER. Toronto: McClelland & Stewart, 1964. 128 p.

Wilson, Milton, ed. POETRY OF MIDCENTURY 1940-1960. Toronto: McClelland & Stewart, 1964. xvi, 237 p.

Cohen's poems appear on pages 183-200.

PARASITES OF HEAVEN. Toronto: McClelland & Stewart, 1966. 80 p.

SELECTED POEMS, 1956-1968. Toronto: McClelland & Stewart, 1968. 245 p.

SONGS OF LEONARD COHEN. New York: Amsco Music Publishing Co., 1969. 96 p.

Geddes, Gary, and Phyllis Bruce, eds. 15 CANADIAN POETS. Toronto: Oxford University Press, 1970. xvi, 301 p.

Cohen's poems appear on pages 79-95.

Mandel, Eli, ed. POETS OF CONTEMPORARY CANADA 1960-1970. Toronto: McClelland & Stewart, 1972. xvi, 141 p.

Cohen's poems appear on pages 46-60.

THE ENERGY OF SLAVES. Toronto: McClelland & Stewart, 1972. 127 p.

2. Prose

THE FAVOURITE GAME. London: McClelland & Stewart, 1963. 223 p.
Rpt., New Canadian Library Series. Toronto/Montreal: McClelland & Stewart,
1970, 223 p.

BEAUTIFUL LOSERS. Toronto: McClelland & Stewart, 1966. 243 p.

3. Criticism

Batten, Jack. "Leonard Cohen: The Poet as Hero." SATURDAY NIGHT, 84
(June 1969), 23-26.

Beattie, [A.] Munro. "Poetry 1950-1960." In LITERARY HISTORY OF CANADA;
CANADIAN LITERATURE IN ENGLISH. Ed. Carl F. Klinck et al. Toronto:
University of Toronto Press, 1965, pp. 814-16.

Djwa, Sandra [Ann]. "Leonard Cohen: Black Romantic." CANADIAN LITERATURE,
34 (Autumn 1967), 32-42.

Elson, Nicholas William. "Love in the Writings of Leonard Cohen." M.A.
thesis, University of New Brunswick, Fredericton, 1969.

Frye, Northrop. "From 'Letters in Canada.'" In his THE BUSH GARDEN:
ESSAYS ON THE CANADIAN IMAGINATION. Toronto: Anansi, 1971, pp.
66-68.

Harris, Michael. "Leonard Cohen: The Poet as Hero--2." SATURDAY
NIGHT, 84 (June 1969), 26-31.

Jones, D.G. BUTTERFLY ON ROCK; A STUDY OF THEMES AND IMAGES IN
CANADIAN LITERATURE. Toronto: University of Toronto Press, 1970. x, 197 p.

    Cohen is discussed on pages 166-67, and 178-80.

Kerwin, Elizabeth Anne. "Themes of Leonard Cohen." B.A. honors thesis,
Acadia University, Wolfville, N.S., 1969.

Knelsen, Richard John. "Flesh and Spirit in the Writings of Leonard Cohen."
M.A. thesis, University of Manitoba, Winnipeg, 1969.

Lyons, Roberta. "Jewish Poets from Montreal: Concepts of History in the
Poetry of A.M. Klein, Irving Layton and Leonard Cohen." M.A. thesis, Carle-
ton University, Ottawa, 1966.

Ondaatje, Michael. LEONARD COHEN. Toronto: McClelland & Stewart, 1970. 64 p.

Owen, Don. "Leonard Cohen: The Poet as Hero--3." SATURDAY NIGHT, 84 (June 1969), 31-32.

Pacey, Desmond. "The Literature of the Fifties." In his CREATIVE WRITING IN CANADA; A SHORT HISTORY OF ENGLISH-CANADIAN LITERATURE. Rev. ed. Toronto: Ryerson, 1961, pp. 247-48.

_____. "The Phenomenon of Leonard Cohen." CANADIAN LITERATURE, 34 (Autumn 1967), 5-23.

Purdy, A.W. "Leonard Cohen: A Personal Look." CANADIAN LITERATURE, 23 (Winter 1965), 7-16.

COLOMBO, JOHN ROBERT (1936-)

Born in Kitchener, Ontario, and educated at the University of Toronto, John Robert Colombo has been an entrepreneur of poetry for many years, organizing readers and running the Hawkshead Press which published broadsheets and pamphlets of his own and others' poetry. He has worked as an editor for some publishers in Toronto and has been managing editor of TAMARACK REVIEW since 1960.

In his own poetry he has experimented with new forms, mainly "found" poetry or, as Colombo himself defines it, "redeemed prose." His poems often deal with artifacts--works of art, architecture, and fictional characters--in an attempt to present a continuing process of culture as it is constantly reassembled and reassessed in his reinterpretations.

1. Poetry

THE GREAT WALL OF CHINA. An Entertainment by Colombo. Drawing by Harold Town. Montreal: Delta, 1966. 62 p.

With William Lyon MacKenzie. THE MacKENZIE POEMS. Toronto: Swan Publishing, 1966. 94 p.

MIRACULOUS MONTAGES. Drawings by Don Jean-Louis. Don Mills, Ont.: Heinrich Heine Press, 1966. 20 sheets in portfolio.

ABRACADABRA. Toronto: McClelland & Stewart, 1967. 127 p.

JOHN TORONTO: NEW POEMS BY DR. STRACHAN FOUND BY COLOMBO. Ottawa: Oberon Press, 1969. 94 p.

NEO POEMS. Vancouver, B.C.: Sono Nis Press, 1970. 86 p.

LEONARDO'S LIST. Toronto: Weed/Flower Press, 1972.

PRAISE POEMS. Toronto: Weed/Flower Press, 1972.

THE GREAT SAN FRANCISCO EARTHQUAKE AND FIRE. Fredericton, N.B.: Fiddlehead Books, 1972.

2. Prose

Ed. with Jacques Godbout. POESIE/POETRY 64. Montreal: Editions du Jour; Toronto: Ryerson, 1963. 157 p.

"Letter from Toronto." CANADIAN LITERATURE, 23 (Winter 1965), 53-62.

Colombo, John Robert. "Inside the Trade: An Editor's Notes." CANADIAN LITERATURE, 33 (Summer 1967), 44-55.

Ed. with Raymond Souster. SHAPES & SOUNDS: POEMS OF W.W.E. ROSS. Memoir by Barry Callaghan. Toronto: Longsmans, 1968. 145 p.

Ed. HOW DO I LOVE YOU? Edmonton, Alta.: Hurtig, 1970. 184 p.

Ed. NEW DIRECTION IN CANADIAN POETRY. Toronto: Holt, Rinehart & Winston, 1971. 87 p.

Ed. RHYMES AND REASONS: NINE CANADIAN POETS DISCUSS THEIR WORK. Toronto: Holt, Rinehart & Winston, 1971. 117 p.

3. Criticism

Christy, Jim. "Ornaments and Embellishments." CANADIAN LITERATURE, 50 (Autumn 1971), 84-85.

Gustafson, Ralph. "Mighty Nothing Called a Wall." CANADIAN LITERA-TURE, 34 (Autumn 1967), 90-91.

Stevens, Peter. "The Gospel According to Pop." CANADIAN LITERATURE, 34 (Autumn 1967), 91-93.

DAVEY, FRANKLAND WILMOT (1940-)

Frank Davey was born and educated in British Columbia. At the University of British Columbia, he was editor of TISH, a magazine that represented concepts of poetry derived from such American poets as Charles Olson, Robert Duncan, and Robert Creeley. Davey has taught at various universities in Canada and is now teaching at York University, Downsview, Ontario. He is the editor of OPEN LETTER, a magazine devoted to poetry and criticism.

His poetry has been singularly consistent in its attention to the tenets of projective verse. He has attempted more and more to map through his poems the sequence of his total response of the whole self to the outer world. His later books take the form of personal narrative woven around place, historical event, or such esoteric symbolic schemes as the tarot pack.

1. Poetry

D-DAY AND AFTER. Vancouver, B.C.: Rattlesnake Press for TISHBooks, 1962. 24 p.

CITY OF THE GULLS AND SEA. Victoria, B.C.: Author, 1964. 34 p.

BRIDGE FORCE. Toronto: Contact Press, 1965. 77 p.

"The Scarred Hull, a Long Poem." IMAGO, no. 6 (1966), entire issue.

FOUR MYTHS FOR SAM PERRY. Vancouver, B.C.: Talonbooks, 1970. Unpaged.

WEEDS. Toronto: Coach House, 1970. 18 p.

L'AN TRENTIESME: SELECTED POEMS 1961-1970. Vancouver, B.C.: Vancouver Community Press, 1972. 82 p.

GRIFFON. Toronto: Massassauga Editions, 1972. 12 p.

KING OF SWORDS. Vancouver, B.C.: Talonbooks, 1972. Unpaged.

ARCANA. Toronto: Coach House Press, 1973. 77 p.

THE CLALLAM. Toronto: Talonbooks, 1973. Unpaged.

2. Prose

Much of Davey's critical prose is a reading of other poets in terms of his own ideas about projective verse and his rhetorical ruminations about the nature of poetry. As such, his criticism can often be read as critical exegesis of his own poetry.

"Bad Days on Black Mountain." TAMARACK REVIEW, 35 (Spring 1965), 62-71.

"Rime: A Scholarly Piece." EVIDENCE, 9 (Winter 1965), 98-103.

FIVE READINGS OF OLSON'S MAXIMUS. Montreal: Beaver Kosmos Folio, no. 2, 1970. 56 p.

EARLE BIRNEY. Toronto: Copp Clark, 1971. 128 p.

3. Criticism

Barbour, Douglas. "Play in the Western World." CANADIAN LITERATURE, 52 (Spring 1972), 77-81.

_____. Review of ARCANA and KING OF SWORDS. CANADIAN FORUM, 53 (September 1973), 42-43.

Bowering, George. "Poets in Their Twenties." CANADIAN LITERATURE, 20 (Spring 1964), 54-64.

Coleman, Victor. "Now We are Six." CANADIAN FORUM 45 (March 1966), 283-84.

Dudek, Louis. "Trouncing the Younger Poets." CANADIAN LITERATURE, 34 (Autumn 1967), 83-84.

Mitchell, Beverley Jean. "A Critical Study of the Tish Group, 1961-1963." M.A. thesis, University of Calgary, Calgary, Alta., 1967.

Stevens, Peter. "Facts, to Be Dealt with." CANADIAN FORUM, 47 (September 1967), 139.

Tallman, Warren. "Poet in Progress." CANADIAN LITERATURE, 24 (Spring 1965), 23-27.

GOTLIEB, PHYLLIS FAY [BLOOM] (1926-)

Born in Toronto, where she has lived for most of her life, Phyllis Gotlieb has published only sparsely. Her poetry has been consistently devoted to an examination of her own Jewishness as she sees it in her childhood and in family life. Often the poetry takes on an e.e. cummings-like exuberance, with the use of remembered names, childhood rhymes, place names, and colloquialisms. At times a surrealistic streak intrudes, giving a new and often humorous twist to her poetry. Increasingly, she has been turning to dramatic verse. She has also written novels, including science fiction.

1. Poetry

WITHIN THE ZODIAC. Toronto: McClelland & Stewart, 1964. 87 p.

ORDINARY, MOVING. Toronto: Oxford, 1969. 70 p.

With Al Purdy et al. POEMS FOR VOICES. Toronto: CBC Publications, 1970. 97 p.
    Includes her radio verse play DR. UMLAUT'S EARTHLY KINGDOM.

2. Prose

SUNBURST. Greenwich, Conn.: Fawcett, 1964. 160 p.

"Klein's Sources." CANADIAN LITERATURE, 26 (Autumn 1965), 82-84.

WHY SHOULD I HAVE ALL THE GRIEF? Toronto: Macmillan, 1969. 149 p.

3. Criticism

Cogswell, Fred. "Imprisoned Galaxies." CANADIAN LITERATURE, 23 (Winter 1965), 65-67.

Jones, D.G. "Voices in the Dark." CANADIAN LITERATURE, 45 (Summer 1970), 68-74.

HELWIG, DAVID (1938-)

David Helwig was born in Toronto, grew up in Niagara-on-the-Lake, and studied at the University of Toronto and the University of Liverpool. For some years he taught at Queen's University, Kingston, Ontario, during which time he also taught the inmates of Kingston Penitentiary. He has been an editor of WORDS FROM INSIDE, devoted to the writings of prison inmates. He is now literary adviser for TV Drama with the Canadian Broadcasting Corporation.

Helwig's early poetry derived from a quiet concentration on his personal life-- memories of childhood, his own family life, and his travels--as well as from his literary and historical reading. Increasingly, his poetry has taken a darker turn, meditating on the transience of human relationships and the gradual collapse of life. He has fashioned a quietly meditative style, drawing on traditional forms, as well as a tightly controlled free verse with subtly shifting rhythms.

He has also written drama and fiction, together with a reconstruction of the life of a prisoner, based upon taped interviews.

1. Poetry

FIGURES IN A LANDSCAPE. Ottawa: Oberon Press, 1967. 217 p.

THE SIGN OF THE GUNMAN. Ottawa: Oberon Press, 1969. 152 p.

THE BEST NAME OF SILENCE. Ottawa: Oberon Press, 1972. 138 p.

2. Prose

THE STREETS OF SUMMER. Ottawa: Oberon Press, 1969. 188 p.

THE DAY BEFORE TOMORROW. Ottawa: Oberon Press, 1971. 184 p.

Ed. with Tom Marshall. FOURTEEN STORIES HIGH: BEST CANADIAN STORIES OF 71. Ottawa: Oberon Press, 1971. 172 p.

With Billie Miller. A BOOK ABOUT BILLIE. Ottawa: Oberon Press, 1972. 168 p.

Ed. with Joan Harcourt. STORIES 73. Ottawa: Oberon Press, 1973. 175 p.

JOHNSTON, GEORGE BENSON (1913-)

George Johnston was born in Hamilton, Ontario, and was educated at the University of Toronto. He served in the Royal Canadian Air Force during World War II and has been on the faculty of Carleton University, Ottawa, since 1949.

Johnston's poetic output has been sparse, limited to three volumes spanning his writing of the past forty years. His work has been consistently within the traditional mode, although his most recent work has shown some loosening of structure. Johnston's poetry is unique in Canadian literature in that he has invented a set of characters around whose lives he erects a consistent vision of the world, by turns pessimistic and satiric, but with an expression of a stoic contentment in the later poems.

1. Poetry

THE CRUISING AUK. Toronto: Oxford University Press, 1959. 72 p.

Trans. THE SAGA OF GISLI THE OUTLAW. Toronto: University of Toronto Press, 1963. 146 p.

HOME FREE. Toronto: Oxford University Press, 1966. 64 p.

HAPPY ENOUGH: POEMS 1935-1972. Toronto: Oxford University Press, 1972. 154 p.

2. Prose

Ed. with Wolfgang Roth. THE CHURCH IN THE MODERN WORLD. Toronto: Ryerson, 1967.

3. Criticism

Beattie, [A.] Munro. "Poetry 1950-1960." In LITERARY HISTORY OF CANADA; CANADIAN LITERATURE IN ENGLISH. Ed. Carl F. Klinck et al. Toronto: University of Toronto Press, 1965, pp. 805-8.

Dobbs, Kildare. "Auks in the Belfry." TAMARACK REVIEW, 12 (Summer 1959), 96-101.

Frye, Northrop. "From 'Letters in Canada.'" In his THE BUSH GARDEN:

ESSAYS ON THE CANADIAN IMAGINATION. Toronto: Anansi, 1971, pp. 108-13.

Jones, Lawrence M. "THE CRUISING AUK and the World Below." CANA-DIAN LITERATURE, 48 (Spring 1971), 28-36.

Livesay, Dorothy. Review of HOME FREE. FIDDLEHEAD, 71 (Winter 1967), 65-69.

Pearson, Alan. Review of HOME FREE. CANADIAN FORUM, 47 (November 1967), 185-86.

Robinson, Meredith. "Deeper Water." ALPHABET, 3 (December 1961), 45-47.

Whalley, George. "George Johnston." CANADIAN LITERATURE, 35 (Winter 1968), 85-90.

Wilson, Milton. Review of THE CRUISING AUK. CANADIAN FORUM, 39 (September 1959), 136-37.

LANE, PATRICK (1939-)

Born in British Columbia, Patrick Lane has been a restless wanderer, mainly in Canada, though he lived for a time in New York state. His poetry records his experiences on the road, his encounters, his memories of his past, his responses to the jobs he occasionally takes and to the people he meets. His poetry is direct and undecorative, recording his life unflinchingly. He was associated for a time with Seymour Mayne and the small press Very Stone House Press. Lane now issues his own broadsides and books, which he mails out to a selected readership under his own imprint, Very Stone House Press In Transit. These publications are haphazard and understandably difficult to keep track of.

1. Poetry

LETTERS FROM THE SAVAGE MIND. Vancouver, B.C.: Very Stone House Press, 1966. Unpaged.

SEPARATIONS. Trumansburg, N.Y.: New/Books, 1969. Unpaged. Illustrated.

THE SUN HAS BEGUN TO EAT THE MOUNTAIN. Montreal: Ingluvin, 1969. 142 p.

MOUNTAIN OYSTERS. Vancouver, B.C.: Very Stone House Press, 1971. 28 p.

> Contains "The Outlaw," his personal manifesto in prose.

BEWARE THE MONTHS OF FIRE. Toronto: Anansi, 1973. 100 p.

PASSING INTO STORM. Vernon, B.C.: Very Stone House Press In Transit, 1973. Unpaged.

MacEWEN, GWENDOLYN (1941-)

Gwendolyn MacEwen was born in Toronto and has lived most of her life there. She began publishing in adolescence and has been one of the few writers in Canada to live principally by her writings.

The whole bent of her writing is toward the mythological. Her earliest poetry was rhetorical in its attempt to express her mythological concerns, but in her later work she has evolved a mature style which presents the mythic in close conjunction with ordinary life. Her poems find the mythic in all aspects of life and span from ancient Egyptian religious beliefs through Jungian psychology, with its archetypes and its interest in alchemy, to man's flight to the moon. Her poetry moves easily in these distances of time and thought, compounded of direct reference and a consistent metaphorical range of mythic allusion. The diction of the poems translates these seemingly recondite themes into a compelling style of easy movement and colloquialism.

MacEwen has also written fiction, dealing with the same themes as these of her poetry, and some verse plays for radio.

1. Poetry

THE DRUNKEN CLOCK. Toronto: Aleph Press, 1961. 13 p.

SELAH. Toronto: Aleph Press, 1961. 12 p.

THE RISING FIRE. Toronto: Contact Press, 1963. 82 p.

A BREAKFAST FOR BARBARIANS. Toronto: Ryerson, 1966. 53 p.

THE SHADOW-MAKER. Toronto: Macmillan, 1969. 93 p.

Geddes, Gary, and Phyllis Bruce, eds. 15 CANADIAN POETS. Toronto:

Oxford University Press, 1970. xvi, 301 p.

MacEwen's poems appear on pages 183-97.

THE ARMIES OF THE MOON. Toronto: Macmillan, 1972. 75 p.

Mandel, Eli, ed. POETS OF CONTEMPORARY CANADA 1960-1970. Toronto: McClelland & Stewart, 1972. xvi, 141 p.

MacEwen's poems appear on pages 117-24.

2. Prose

"Genesis." TEANGADOIR, 2nd ser., 1 (November 1961), 56-63.

JULIAN THE MAGICIAN. Toronto: Macmillan, 1963. 151 p.

KING OF EGYPT, KING OF DREAMS. Toronto: Macmillan, 1971. 287 p.

NOMAN. Ottawa: Oberon Press, 1972. 121 p.

3. Criticism

Atwood, Margaret [Eleanor]. "MacEwen's Muse." CANADIAN LITERATURE, 45 (Summer 1970), 23-32.

Barrett, Elizabeth. "A Tour de Force." EVIDENCE, 8 (1964), 40-43.

Davey, Frank. "Gwendolyn MacEwen: The Secret of Alchemy." OPEN LETTER, 2nd ser., 4 (Spring 1973), 5-23.

Dragland, Stan. Review of ARMIES OF THE MOON. QUARRY, 21 (Autumn 1972), 57-62.

Fox, Gail. Review of THE SHADOW-MAKER. QUARRY, 19 (Winter 1970), 57-59.

Gose, E.B. "They Shall Have Arcana." CANADIAN LITERATURE, 21 (Summer 1964), 36-45.

Jones, D.G. BUTTERFLY ON ROCK; A STUDY OF THEMES AND IMAGES IN CANADIAN LITERATURE. Toronto: University of Toronto Press, 1970. x, 197 p.

MacEwen is discussed on pages 31-32, and 180-84.

Sowton, Ian. "To Improvise An Eden." EDGE, 2 (Spring 1964), 119-24.

NEWLOVE, JOHN (1938-)

Born in Regina, Sasketchewan, John Newlove lived in a small Saskatchewan town which was a settlement for the Doukhobors, a Russian religious sect. Since then he has lived in many places and worked at a variety of jobs. Until recently he was an editor with a Canadian publisher in Toronto.

The dominant tone of Newlove's poetry is one of painful honesty, so painful that his vision of self and his world is one of hypocrisy, debilitation, and waste. The bleakness of this world view is only rarely relieved by a few lyric moments, occasional considered tributes to a few historical figures, or an off-hand humor, usually self-directed. The style of the poetry is a precise notation of these exhausted states. Almost without poetic devices, the language mirrors the dark world Newlove sees, though the forms of his poems show great variety in rhythmic movement.

1. Poetry

GRAVE SIRS. Vancouver, B.C.: Robert Reid & Takao Tanabe, 1962. Unpaged.

ELEPHANTS, MOTHERS AND OTHERS. Vancouver, B.C.: Periwinkle Press, 1963. 31 p.

MOVING IN ALONE. Toronto: Contact Press, 1965. 83 p.

WHAT THEY SAY. Kitchener, Ont.: Weed/Flower Press, 1967. 23 p.

BLACK NIGHT WINDOW. Toronto: McClelland & Stewart, 1968. 112 p.

THE CAVE. Toronto: McClelland & Stewart, 1970. 85 p.

Geddes, Gary, and Phyllis Bruce, eds. 15 CANADIAN POETS. Toronto: Oxford University Press, 1970. xvi, 301 p.

Newlove's poems appear on pages 199-216.

7 DISASTERS, 3 THESES, AND WELCOME HOME. CLICK. Vancouver, B.C.: Very Stone House Press, 1971. Unpaged.

Mandel, Eli, ed. POETS OF CONTEMPORARY CANADA 1960-1970. Toronto: McClelland & Stewart, 1972. xvi, 141 p.

> Newlove's poems appear on pages 71-84.

LIES. Toronto: McClelland & Stewart, 1973. 96 p.

2. Criticism

Atwood, Margaret [Eleanor]. "How Do I Get out of Here: the Poetry of John Newlove." OPEN LETTER, 2nd ser., 4 (Spring 1973), 59-70.

Barbour, Douglas. "The Search for Roots: a Meditative Sermon of Sorts." LITERARY HALF YEARLY, 13 (July 1972), 1-14.

Bowering, George. Review of BLACK NIGHT WINDOW. CANADIAN FORUM, 48 (November 1968), 187-88.

_____. "Where Does the Truth Lie?" OPEN LETTER, 2nd ser., 4 (Spring 1973), 71-73.

Ferns, John. "A Desolate Country." FAR POINT, 2 (Spring/Summer 1969), pp. 68-75.

Jones, D.G. BUTTERFLY ON ROCK; A STUDY OF THEMES AND IMAGES IN CANADIAN LITERATURE. Toronto: University of Toronto Press, 1970. x, 197 p.

> Newlove is discussed on pages 3-5, 167-69, 172-73, 176, and 184.

_____. "Moving in Alone: A Review Article." QUARRY, 15 (Winter 1965-66), 12-15.

Lane, Patrick. Review of LIES. CANADIAN FORUM, 50 (November-December 1970), 59-63.

New, W.H. ARTICULATING WEST: ESSAYS ON PURPOSE AND FORM IN MODERN CANADIAN LITERATURE. Toronto: New Press, 1972. xxvi, 282 p.

> Newlove is discussed on pages 154-55.

Pacey, Desmond. Review of THE CAVE. CANADIAN FORUM, 50 (November-December 1970), 309-10.

Purdy, A.W. Review of BLACK NIGHT WINDOW. QUARRY, 18 (Winter 1969), 43-45.

Stevens, Peter. "Two Kinds of Honesty." CANADIAN FORUM, 45 (September 1965), 139.

Warkentin, Germaine. "Drifting to Oblivion." CANADIAN LITERATURE, 56 (Spring 1973), 121-22.

NICHOL, BARRIE PETER [b p nichol] (1944-)

Barrie Peter Nichol, or b p nichol (as he prefers to write his name), was born in Vancouver, British Columbia, has lived in several Canadian cities, and now lives in Toronto where he works in a psychotherapy clinic.

He is the leading experimental poet now writing in Canada. His experiments have led him into the realm of concrete and sound poetry in which he has tried to fashion a pure language of ideogrammatic expression to lay bare the essential existence of words in their own uniqueness. Much of his work is graphic, fragmenting the normal associations of language. His work is contained not only in books but on cards, in visual equivalents of haiku or imagist poems. He includes a variety of designs with distorted and abnormal typography.

Besides his concrete poetry, nichol has written some volumes of lyrics. His long poem THE MARTYROLOGY embodies his most thorough expression of his belief in the release of language into its own mysteries beyond the loss and despair of the world. Nichol has also recorded some of his sound poetry and in recent years has been a member of a quartet of sound poets, the Four Horsemen.

Because of his belief in the magic otherness of language, nichol has produced an enormous amount of work in ephemeral form: mimeographed pamphlets, broadsheets, pieces in his own magazines GANGLIA and grOnk. These works are a part of the constant life of language, so that in a sense nichol sets no store by the fixing of language within the covers of a book: such fixity, he believes, makes for dead artifacts. It also makes for despair in bibliographers. The following lists, therefore, contain only some of the fuller expressions of nichol's experiments. There are dozens of ephemera that will require future notation. The fullest bibliography available at this time is the one compiled by b p nichol himself with the assistance of Jack David: "published autotopography." ESSAYS ON CANADIAN WRITING, no. 1 (Winter 1974), pp. 39-46.

1. Poetry

JOURNEYING & THE RETURNS. Toronto: Coach House Press, 1967.

> A package containing a book of poems, some cards of concrete poems, graphic designs, and a recording.

RUTH. Toronto: Fleye Press, 1967. Unpaged.

THE CAPTAIN POETRY POEMS. Vancouver, B.C.: Blew Ointment Press, 1970. Unpaged.

STILL WATER. Vancouver, B.C.: Talonbooks, 1970.
    Short poems printed on cards.

ABC: THE ALEPH BETH BOOK. Ottawa: Oberon Press, 1971. Unpaged.

MONOTONES. Vancouver, B.C.: Talonbooks, 1971. 52 p.

THE OTHER SIDE OF THE ROOM. Toronto: Weed/Flower Press, 1971. Unpaged.

THE MARTYROLOGY: BOOKS I AND II. 2 vols. Toronto: Coach House Press, 1972. Unpaged.

2. Prose

Review of THE JINX SHIP ND OTHR TRIPS. QUARRY, 16 (Summer 1967), 43-46.

Introduction to PNOMES JUKOLLAGES AND OTHER STUNZAS. By Earle Birney. grOnk, ser. 4, no. 3. Toronto: Ganglia Press, 1969. Unpaged.

NIGHTS ON PROSE MOUNTAIN. Toronto: Ganglia Press, 1969. 16 p.

THE TRUE EVENTUAL STORY OF BILLY THE KID. Toronto: Weed/Flower Press, 1970. 11 p.

Ed. the cosmic chef: an evening of concrete. Ottawa: Oberon Press, 1970. 80 p. Illustrated.
    A boxed anthology on loose leaves.

TWO NOVELS (ANDY/FOR JESUS LUNATICK). Rev. ed. Toronto: Coach House Press, 1971. Unpaged.

"Some Beginning Writings on 'Gertrude Stein's Theories of Personality.'" OPEN LETTER, 2nd ser., 2 (Summer 1972), 41-48.

Review of TYPEWRITER POEMS. OPEN LETTER, 2nd ser., 3 (Fall 1972), 78-81.

With Steve McCaffery. "TRG Report 1: Translation." OPEN LETTER, 2nd ser., 4 (Spring 1973), 75-93.

"Waiting." OPEN LETTER, 2nd ser., 5 (Summer 1973), 17-22.

"Gertrude Stein's Theories of Personality." WHITE PELICAN, 3 (Autumn 1973), 15-23.

"Interview of Raoul Duguay." OPEN LETTER, 2nd ser., 6 (Fall 1973), 65-73.

"Two Pages on the Nature of the Reality of Writing." OPEN LETTER, 2nd ser., 6 (Fall 1973), 104-5.

Ed. with Jiri Valoch. THE PIPE: RECENT CZECH CONCRETE POETRY. Toronto: Coach House Press, 1973.

A boxed anthology of poems on loose leaves.

3. Criticism

Barbour, Douglas. "Journey in a Mythic Landscape." CANADIAN LITERATURE, 56 (Spring 1973), 93-97.

_____. Review of several b p nichol works. QUARRY, 20 (Year End 1971), 61-63.

Bowering, George. "Cutting Them All up: Interview with b p nichol." ALPHABET, 18-19 (June 1971), 18-21.

_____. Review of MONOTONES. OPEN LETTER, 2nd ser., 2, 82-84.

Colombo, John Robert. "New Wave Nichol." TAMARACK REVIEW, 44 (Summer 1967), 100-104.

David, Jack. "Concrete Poetry." M.A. thesis, University of Windsor, Windsor, Ont., 1973.

Doyle, Mike. "Made in Canada." POETRY (Chicago), 119 (March 1972), 356-62.

_____. "Notes on Concrete Poetry." CANADIAN LITERATURE, 46 (Autumn 1970), 91-95.

McKay, Don. Review of JOURNEYINGS AND THE RETURN. ALPHABET, 14 (December 1967), 82-83.

Reaney, James. Review of JOURNEYING & THE RETURNS. QUARRY, 16 (Summer 1967), 46-47.

Scobie, Stephen. "A Dash for the Border." CANADIAN LITERATURE, 56 (Spring 1973), 89-92.

_____. "Two Authors in Search of a Character." CANADIAN LITERATURE, 54 (Autumn 1972), 37-55.

Stevens, Peter. "Canadian Writers as Artists." CANADIAN LITERATURE, 46 (Autumn 1970), 19-34.

Sullivan, D.H. "A Review of Concrete Poetry." WEST COAST REVIEW, 5 (October 1970), 69-72.

Warsh, Lewis. "Poetry Chronicle." POETRY (Chicago), 112 (July 1968), 276-82.

Woods, Elizabeth. "Out of Context." TAMARACK REVIEW, 55 (Spring 1970), 80-83.

NOWLAN, ALDEN (1933-)

Alden Nowlan, born in Windsor, Nova Scotia, left school at age fifteen and worked at various jobs until he became editor of the Hartland OBSERVER in New Brunswick. For several years he was writer-in-residence at the University of New Brunswick in Fredericton.

Nowlan's poetry has consistently focused on the life and people, including himself, of the Canadian Maritimes. He views his subject compassionately and generally prevents lapses into sentimentality by his direct and sometimes brutal recording of realistic detail. He began by using traditional modes of stanza and rhyme, but his more recent work shows a loosening of structure.

Nowlan has also written a novel and a volume of short stories.

1. Poetry

THE ROSE AND THE PURITAN. Federicton, N.B.: Fiddlehead Poetry Books, 1958. 16 p.

A DARKNESS IN THE EARTH. Eureka, Calif: Hearse Press, 1959. 14 p.

UNDER THE ICE. Toronto: Ryerson, 1960. 44 p.

WIND IN A ROCKY COUNTRY. Toronto: Emblem Books, 1960. 16 p.

FIVE NEW BRUNSWICK POETS: ELIZABETH BREWSTER, FRED COGSWELL, ROBERT GIBBS, ALDEN NOWLAN, KAY SMITH. Frederiction, N.B.: Fiddlehead Press, 1962. 64 p.

> Nowlan's poems appear on pages 41-52.

THE THINGS WHICH ARE. Toronto: Contact Press, 1962. 71 p.

Wilson, Milton, ed. POETRY OF MIDCENTURY 1940-1960. Toronto: McClelland & Stewart, 1964. xvi, 237 p.

> Nowlan's poetry appears on pages 214-24.

BREAD, WINE AND SALT. Toronto: Clarke Irwin, 1967. 74 p.

THE MYSTERIOUS NAKED MAN. Toronto: Clarke Irwin, 1969. 93 p.

PLAYING THE JESUS GAME: SELECTED POEMS. Trumansburg, N.Y.: New/ Books, 1970. 105 p.

Geddes, Gary, and Phyllis Bruce, eds. 15 CANADIAN POETS. Toronto: Oxford University Press, 1970. xvi, 301 p.

> Nowlan's poetry appears on pages 115-27.

BETWEEN TEARS AND LAUGHTER. Toronto: Clarke Irwin, 1971. 119 p.

2. Prose

MIRACLE AT INDIAN RIVER. Toronto: Clarke Irwin, 1968. 132 p.

VARIOUS PERSONS NAMED KEVIN O'BRIEN. Toronto: Clarke Irwin, 1973. 143 p.

3. Criticism

Barrett, Elizabeth. "A Kind of Truth." EVIDENCE, 7 (1963), 105-7.

Beattie, [A.] Munro. "Poetry 1950-1960." In LITERARY HISTORY OF CANADA; CANADIAN LITERATURE IN ENGLISH. Ed. Carl F. Klinck et al. Toronto: University of Toronto Press, 1965, pp. 802-3.

Bly, Robert. "For Alden Nowlan with Admiration." TAMARACK REVIEW, 54 (Winter 1970), 32-38.

Cameron, Donald. "Alden Nowlan, an 18th Century Tory in a 20th Century Fredericton Is an Expatriate Who Never Left Home." SATURDAY NIGHT, 88 (May 1973), 29-32.

Cockburn, Robert. Review of BREAD, WINE AND SALT. FIDDLEHEAD, 76 (Spring 1968), 74-76.

FIDDLEHEAD, 81 (August-October 1969), entire issue.

> This was a special issue devoted to the career and work of Nowlan. It includes an interview with Nowlan, some personal reminiscences of him by other writers, and critical essays by G.M. Cook, Louis Dudek, and others.

Fraser, Keath. "Notes on Alden Nowlan." CANADIAN LITERATURE, 45 (Summer 1970), 41-51.

Lucas, Alec. Review of UNDER THE ICE. FIDDLEHEAD, 51 (Winter 1962), 59-62.

ONDAATJE, MICHAEL (1943-)

Michael Ondaatje was born in Ceylon and educated in England before emigrating to Canada in 1962. He was educated at and has taught at several Canadian universities. He is now teaching at Glendon College, York University, Downsview, Ontario.

Ondaatje's poems grow in a Gothic atmosphere, in an ambiance of violence and the macabre. Even the ordinary and the domestic take on overtones of garish melodrama and exotic extravagance. He has elaborated his ideas in narrative, two of which are book length. His poetry offers sharply delineated pictures with dramatic flair, giving a cinematic flavor to much of his work. He has made two movies of interest to students of Canadian literature: SON

OF CAPTAIN POETRY, which is about Canadian poet b p nichol, and THE CLINTON SPECIAL, a documentary about the Canadian theatre group, Passe Muraille.

1. Poetry

THE DAINTY MONSTERS. Toronto: Coach House Press, 1967. 77 p.

THE MAN WITH SEVEN TOES. Toronto: Coach House Press, 1969. Unpaged.

THE COLLECTED WORKS OF BILLY THE KID. Toronto: Anansi, 1970. 105 p.

Geddes, Gary, and Phyllis Bruce, eds. 15 CANADIAN POETS. Toronto: Oxford University Press, 1970. xvi, 301 p.

    Ondaatje's poems appear on pages 251-63.

Mandel, Eli, ed. POETS OF CONTEMPORARY CANADA 1960-1970. Toronto: McClelland & Stewart, 1972.

    Ondaatje's poems appear on pages 125-35.

RAT JELLY. Toronto: Coach House Press, 1973. 71 p.

2. Prose

LEONARD COHEN. Toronto: McClelland & Stewart, 1970. 64 p.

Ed. THE BROKEN ARK: A BOOK OF BEASTS. Ottawa: Oberon Press, 1971. Unpaged.

3. Criticism

Barbour, Douglas. "Controlling the Jungle." CANADIAN LITERATURE, 36 (Spring 1968), 86-88.

Davis, Marilyn. Review of THE COLLECTED WORKS OF BILLY THE KID. CANADIAN FORUM, 51 (July-August 1971), 34-35.

Lane, M. Travis. "Dream as History." FIDDLEHEAD, 86 (August-October 1970), 158-62.

Schroeder, Andreas. "The Poet as Gunman." CANADIAN LITERATURE, 51 (Winter 1972), 80-82.

Scobie, Stephen. "Two Authors in Search of a Character." CANADIAN LITERATURE, 54 (Autumn 1972), 37-55.

Stevens, Peter. Review of THE COLLECTED WORKS OF BILLY THE KID. QUEEN'S QUARTERLY, 78 (Summer 1971), 326-27.

_____. Review of RAT JELLY. QUEEN'S QUARTERLY, 80 (Winter 1973), 656-58.

Watson, Sheila. "Michael Ondaatje: The Mechanization of Death." WHITE PELICAN, 2 (1972), 56-64.

AUTHOR INDEX

This index is alphabetized letter by letter. In addition to authors, it includes all editors, compilers, translators, and illustrators cited in this text.

Author Index

Author Index

TITLE INDEX

This index is alphabetized letter by letter. It includes all titles of books. Journals and titles of articles are not included.

SUBJECT INDEX

This index is alphabetized letter by letter.   Underlined page numbers refer to main entries in the subject.